Black Freemasonry

"Eminently qualified to write about black Freemasonry, Cécile Révauger depicts with great accuracy how the split of American Freemasonry along racial lines arose and how it still persists, despite some progress within contemporary society. She also perfectly analyzes why it still remains difficult today to overcome prejudices, which are part of a legacy from the Founding Fathers. Her remarkable impartiality provides a balanced analysis of the present situation. Cécile's work is an important addition to the world of scholarship as well as part of an effort to continue to build bridges in Freemasonry. I warmly recommend this book to every Mason wishing to better understand what kind of challenges remain today."

ALAIN DE KEGHEL, LIFE MEMBER OF THE SCOTTISH RITE
RESEARCH SOCIETY, SOUTHERN JURISDICTION

"In her timely new book, Cécile Révauger offers a fresh examination of race, class, and social interaction in North America and the Caribbean, through the lens of three hundred years of Masonic history. What makes the study most remarkable is the unique perspective Révauger brings to the discussion of race relations in the Americas, giving readers the advantage of her scholarly expertise, as well as her privileged status within Masonry, to help us see into the sanctuary of an organization based on the equality of brothers, but which of necessity exists and works in a world rife with inequalities. The Masonic brethren she describes are men of their time and milieu, adapting in new ways the timeless ancient landmarks of Freemasonry to fit the needs and aspirations of their lodges and communities."

SUSAN MITCHELL SOMMERS, PH.D., PROFESSOR OF HISTORY,
SAINT VINCENT COLLEGE, AND AUTHOR OF
THOMAS DUNCKERLEY AND ENGLISH FREEMASONRY

"Cécile Révauger has done a commendable job documenting the struggles and triumphs of black Freemasonry in the United States. Her book should be required reading for all members of the Craft, regardless of their race or ethnicity. It is my sincere hope that the lessons learned from this scholarly study of the history of the Prince Hall Rite will establish, among all Freemasons, a new standard by which their capacity for brotherhood will be measured."

ANTHONY T. BROWDER, FOUNDER AND DIRECTOR OF
THE INSTITUTE OF KARMIC GUIDANCE AND AUTHOR OF
FROM THE BROWDER FILE: 22 ESSAYS ON THE
AFRICAN AMERICAN EXPERIENCE

"Masonic paradoxes embodied in a book! *Black Freemasonry* is not just about African American citizens joining a traditionally white fraternity. Cécile Révauger shows how this institution can be a place to seek freedom, create identity, or be enlightened but also can intensify divisions or encourage discrimination. A must-read for people interested in Masonic history, but also for anyone who wonders what equality, brotherhood, and inclusiveness mean."

MARÍA EUGENIA VÁZQUEZ-SEMADENI, PH.D.,
ASSISTANT ADJUNCT PROFESSOR OF HISTORY AT UCLA

"Among the fascinating social and cultural insights offered by the history of Freemasonry and fraternal organizations, one of the most remarkable and most compelling stories is that of the role of African Americans in Freemasonry, particularly Prince Hall Freemasonry, established in Boston. In this engaging and accessible study, Professor Cécile Révauger provides an introduction to the history of blacks within Freemasonry, analyzing the racism and other obstacles they confronted. The story told by Professor Révauger is by turns heroic, unsettling, and thought provoking."

ANDREW PRESCOTT, PROFESSOR OF ENGLISH LANGUAGE,
UNIVERSITY OF GLASGOW

Black Freemasonry

From Prince Hall to the Giants of Jazz

Cécile Révauger

Translated by Jon E. Graham

Inner Traditions

Rochester, Vermont • Toronto, Canada

Inner Traditions
One Park Street
Rochester, Vermont 05767
www.InnerTraditions.com

Text stock is SFI certified

Originally published in French under the title *Noirs et Francs-Maçons: Comment la ségrégation raciale s'est installée chez les frères américains* by Éditions Dervy in the collection directed by René LeMoal.
First U.S. edition published in 2016 by Inner Traditions

Library of Congress Cataloging-in-Publication Data

Révauger, Cécile.
   [Noirs et francs-maçons. English]
   Black freemasonry : from Prince Hall to the giants of jazz / Cécile Révauger ; translated by Jon E. Graham.
      pages cm
   Includes bibliographical references and index.
   ISBN 978-1-62055-487-6 (hardcover) — ISBN 978-1-62055-488-3 (e-book)
   1. African American freemasonry—History. 2. African Americans—Politics and government. 3. Freemasonry—United States—History. 4. United States—Race relations—History. I. Graham, Jon E., translator. II. Title.
   HS883.R4813 2014
   366'.108996073—dc23

                                                                          2015015840

Printed and bound in the United States by Lake Book Manufacturing, Inc.
The text stock is SFI certified. The Sustainable Forestry Initiative® program promotes sustainable forest management.

10 9 8 7 6 5 4 3 2 1

Text design and layout by Priscilla Baker
This book was typeset in Garamond Premier Pro with Helvetica Neue and 1676 Morden Map used as display typefaces

Inner Traditions wishes to express its appreciation for assistance given by the government of France through the National Book Office of the Ministère de la Culture in the preparation of this translation.

Nous tenons à exprimer nos plus vifs remerciements au gouvernment de la France et au ministère de la Culture, Centre National du Livre, pour leur concours dans la préparation de la traduction de cet ouvrage.

To send correspondence to the author of this book, mail a first-class letter to the author c/o Inner Traditions • Bear & Company, One Park Street, Rochester, VT 05767, and we will forward the communication, or contact the author directly at **http://revaugercecile.over-blog.com/#fromadmin**.

Contents

Part One
The Genesis of Black Freemasonry

Part Two
A Militant Tradition

Appendices

Foreword

By Margaret C. Jacob, Ph.D.

When the first lodges opened their doors in Paris, in the first decade of their existence, the 1740s, there were in attendance merchants, army officers, women, a priest or two, and, not least, a black musketeer from the King's Guard. Reading that evidence for the first time in the 1980s and knowing the tortured history of race relations in American Freemasonry, the historian could only be amazed and heartened. It did not, however, augur the future for lodges in the colonies of the European powers. Anyone who has ever lectured to an audience of Freemasons in the contemporary American South would notice immediately the sea of white, male faces cordially greeting the speaker. The segregation of Freemasonry in the Americas, but particularly in the United States, is as old as the American republic. That is why the story that Cécile Révauger tells in this fascinating book about black Freemasonry is so important.

Prince Hall must have been a remarkable man who possessed a deep understanding of the evils of slavery and worked to do something about them. As this book tells us, we know so little about his life that conjecture must replace hard facts. What is clear is that he took the message about all men meeting upon the level and brought Freemasonry into the lives of free blacks living in the North. He spoke eloquently about the horrors of slavery that he knew personally. Did he think that a full integration would someday be possible?

We will never know. What we do know is that all the idealism inherent within Freemasonry could not match the virulence of American racial hatred and suspicion.

Perhaps black Freemasons were right to keep themselves apart from mainstream white Freemasonry. Certainly its structure of having a grand lodge for every state and no national umbrella grand lodge worked until very recently in favor of the segregationists and white supremacists. Lodges for blacks may have helped build community among men whose masculinity had been denied or derided. We can only hope that the separatism is no longer necessary, because it is a black mark on American Masonic history. Books like this one show us how the mark was made and bring to the subject a refreshing look by a master historian, woman, and French Freemason. We are all in her debt.

MARGARET C. JACOB, PH.D., is a professor of history at the University of California, Los Angeles. One of the world's foremost Masonic scholars, she is considered a pioneer in the field of the history of civil society with emphasis on Masonic history. Her work in the early development of Freemasonry documents connections between early European Freemasons and the Craft as we know it today. She is the author of *The Radical Enlightenment: Pantheists, Freemasons and Republicans; Living the Enlightenment: Freemasonry and Politics in Eighteenth-Century Europe;* and *The Origins of Freemasonry: Facts and Fictions.*

Foreword

By Peter P. Hinks, Ph.D.

*Freemasonry is universal, of course, but the American
Freemason is first or foremost a white or a black man.
. . . American Freemasonry, like a fine kaleidoscope,
prefers the juxtaposition to the merger of colors.*

CÉCILE RÉVAUGER

In a brilliant and provocative new study of black Freemasonry in the
United States, Cécile Révauger, professor of history of the anglophone
world at the University of Bordeaux, has executed a remarkable balancing act—holding before the reader the history of the troubled machina-
tions separating black from white Masons in the United States while
simultaneously delineating the surprising ways in which they actually
bonded with each other. In so doing, she argues, they formed a com-
posite American Freemasonry where race—a physiognomic distinction
among humans dismissed by Freemasonry as irrelevant to the universal
fellowship it extols—has played a foundational role. Unlike its role in
Freemasonry anywhere else in the world, race uniquely distinguished
the organization of American Freemasonry as it confounded and troubled it.

Professor Révauger recognizes that American Freemasonry was
born amid a slavery and brutal racial hierarchy that almost necessarily

xi

mandated the separation of black Masons from white. While Prince Hall and his small coterie did initially seek certification from white Masons in Boston, their failure to secure a lodge charter led them by the 1780s to seek a charter from the then most powerful grand lodge in the world—the Grand Lodge of England. In 1784 it duly chartered them as African Lodge #459, readily affirming that they understood they were chartering men of African descent. With that charter in hand, the band of black Masons then knew they did not have to seek validation from white American Masons who themselves were in disarray for many years after the American Revolution. On the bedrock of that charter Prince Hall and his descendants would anchor an African American Freemasonry that grew and prospered dramatically over the following decades.

However, the growth of black Freemasonry in the nineteenth and twentieth centuries brought more aggressive challenges to their legitimacy from white Masons, aspersions to which black Masons responded. Professor Révauger's volume affirms the centrality of black Freemasons' quest for recognition from the white American Masons whom they never ceased identifying as their brethren. But the author recognizes the complexities of this quest, that black Masons eschewed approaching white Masons with "cap in hand" (p. 200), and instead pursued a sort of "entente cordiale . . . a kind of establishing of diplomatic relations between equals" (p. 201). As she explains, black Masons remained throughout "sticklers" to a fault for Masonic regularity. Yet this fidelity was not followed simply out of slavish mimicry of white Masons in order to solicit their regard. While, on the one hand, it evinced that their Masonry was in no way illegitimate—or "clandestine"—as white Masons contended, this fidelity on the other hand avowed the Masonic integrity of the Prince Hall Masons *by themselves*. Indeed, their unflagging commitment to ultimate fellowship with their white brethren promoted—more quietly, yet crucially—that they were the better Masons, the ones more faithful to its most precious Universalist tenets.

Yet Professor Révauger's study probes even more deeply. Amid this history of organizational conflict, she discerns that black and white Masons actually shared a commonality grounded in black Masons' continued adherence to what she calls "the white American model" of Freemasonry. In three crucial categories—belief in God, preferably Christian and Protestant; the inadmissibility of women; and the necessity for loyalty and patriotism to the state—black and white Masons found a surprising but enduring concordance. It is important to note that black Masons did not display a Christian faith to placate white Masons. Since the founding era of Prince Hall, black Masons were deeply embedded in a Christian faith and fervency that they and numerous other African Americans had crafted in the context of their singular oppression in America. Indeed, black Masons used their Christianity precisely to witness against white Masons—and white Americans as a whole—for failing to live the fellowship to which Jesus Christ called all humans. They understood themselves as prophets, those imbued much more fully with the Holy Spirit (and thus the better Christians) than those white Masons and Americans who hypocritically upheld the wilderness of slavery and brutal racial injustice. Nevertheless, both white and black Masons heartily agreed that belief in God was fundamental to being a Mason. Moreover they both decisively excluded women from induction into the mysteries and craft of Freemasonry. Although both enthusiastically supported the Order of the Eastern Star—a female auxiliary for the wives of Masons—they concurred that induction for men only was a landmark, or cornerstone, of Freemasonry. As Professor Révauger observes, both "give their female companions a completely subaltern role . . . where they can run receptions, charity bazaars, and other good works" (p. 91, 223). Finally she emphasizes that both agreed that Masons should submit faithfully to the duly appointed authorities in their jurisdiction and not use lodges as a base for opposing them. Masonry was not about politics but rather the enlightenment and moral improvement of its individual members. "Prince Hall Masons are constantly striving to show proof of their patriotism," she has written. While the Prince Hall Masons certainly fought against slavery and racial inequality in the political sphere, they also understood that opposition as fundamental to their enlightenment and benevolence as Masons. When the governor of Massachusetts sought troops to suppress an insurgency of aggrieved and impoverished farmers in western Massachusetts in the 1780s, Hall and his brothers were among the first to offer to enlist (see pp. 192–93). Patriotism and service to defend a state that actually oppressed them also curiously bound black Masons to white (p. 222).

Yet this very commonality—the supposed foundation of an enduring identity shared by black and white Masons—in fact created problems, Professor Révauger observes, for forwarding the very objectives, recognition and fellowship, black Masons hoped commonality would. On the one hand it actually helped to nurture a stasis in the extant organizational order, because, despite fissures over race, broad agreement over other fundamentals tended to bind them together. Moreover, Professor Révauger illuminates how this bond of commonality actually worked to isolate African American Freemasons from other Masons who condemned American white supremacy and sought to ally with their black brethren against it. Perhaps only a scholar such as Cécile Révauger, who is herself a dedicated Mason from the Grand Orient of France—which readily embraces women as Masons and does not require that its members profess a belief in God—could perceive this complicated balancing of paradox that she argues is American Freemasonry. From her French perch she illustrates how despite the longstanding opposition of the Grand Orient to white American Masons' exclusion of blacks from their lodges—and indeed to the whole of American white supremacy—Prince Hall Masons rejected, especially in the twentieth century, the benevolent overtures of Grand Orient Masons to collaborate with them. With white Masons, they refused to recognize as legitimate the Masonry of the Grand Orient because of its supposed "atheism," its position on women, and even for what associations it had with opposition to established civil authority since the eighteenth century. Thus, black Masons living amid the historic racial oppression of the United States rejected a fraternal—and sororal—alliance to extend Masonic Universalism in order to sustain, Professor Révauger argues, their understanding of what constitutes a true Mason in common with the very white Masons whose embrace of racial exclusion and injustice they had contested since their inception with Prince Hall. As more American historians now study the ways in which African American activists after 1945—some of whom were Prince Hall Masons—summoned the international forum to aid them in their struggle against racial injustice in America, Professor Révauger calls us to recognize this—and other—lost opportunities to forge such alliances and how they point to a conservatism among African American Freemasons that conflicted with what was also evidently progressive and even radical about them.

Such is the strange and convoluted history Professor Révauger traces as she carefully follows the contest between white and black Masons over Masonic regularity, jurisdiction, and recognition. Certainly she recognizes that America is where African American Freemasons found themselves, and it was within that troubling context that they also had of necessity to navigate and negotiate their way as faithful Masons. In an environment where they could wield so little social leverage, they did the best they could. Thus the importance of this commonality she so astutely characterizes cannot be fully appreciated and analyzed outside of the separation it also nurtured, a separation that in American Masonry simultaneously testifies to the grossest hypocrisy and the most estimable integrity and perseverance.

Cécile Révauger has graced us with an elegant and erudite volume that *every* person intent on understanding American Freemasonry—not just that of black Freemasons—must read.

Peter P. Hinks, Ph.D., is the author of the award-winning book *To Awaken My Afflicted Brethren: David Walker and the Problem of Antebellum Slave Resistance* (1997). He has worked extensively in public history and served as the senior research historian for several major exhibitions at the New York Historical Society, including "Slavery in New York" (2005), "New York Divided" (2006), and "Revolutions!" (2011). With the late Professor John Blassingame and Professor John McKivigan, he coedited Frederick Douglass's three autobiographies, *Narrative of the Life of Frederick Douglass, My Bondage and My Freedom,* and *The Life and Times of Frederick Douglass,* for Yale University Press. With Professor McKivigan, he was the editor of the *Encyclopedia of Antislavery and Abolition* (2006). He has recently coauthored with Stephen Kantrowitz *All Men Free and Brethren: Essays on the History of African American Freemasonry* (2013).

Acknowledgments

To the Franco-American Commission for Educational Exchange for awarding me a Fulbright grant;

to the Schomburg Center for Research in Black Culture, New York;

to the library of the Grand Lodge of New York, the Chancellor Robert R. Livingston Masonic Library, and most particularly to its director, Tom Savini, and archivist, Catherine Walker;

to the Masonic library of London, the Library and Museum of Freemasonry, and most particularly to the director, Diane Clements, archivist, Susan Snell, and librarian, Martin Cherry;

to the library of the Grand Orient of France and to the Museum of Freemasonry in Paris, and most particularly to their directors, Pierre Mollier and Ludovic Marcos;

to Paul M. Bessel, an expert in the history of American Freemasonry and officer of the Grand Lodge of Washington, D.C.;

to Joseph Cox, author of *Great Black Men of Freemasonry,* who graciously welcomed me to his home in the Bronx, New York;

to Michael A. Delgado, secretary of the Scottish Rite Research Institute of Prince Hall;

to the Prince Hall Grand Lodge of New York and its past grand master, Thomas Jessamy, who invited me to the Harlem Temple;

to the Prince Hall Grand Lodge of the Caribbean and most particularly to the past grand master Hermon A. Gaskin;

to the Lodge Fraternité de la Caraïbe n° 10 and most particularly to one if its members, Roland Nestoret;

to René Le Moal, the director of the L'Univers Maçonnique collection of Dervy Éditions, for his support since the publication of the first edition of this book and his participation in making it better;

to Alain de Keghel, life member of the Scottish Rite Research Society and author of *Le défi maçonnique américain* (Paris, Dervy, 2014), who was instrumental in bringing about the Italian and American editions of this book.

Interpreting the Black Experience

Writing a book on black American Freemasons when one is white, female, and French can seem like an insurmountable challenge. How dare I disdain in this way the following remarks made by Joseph Walkes, a highly respected historian in the mid-twentieth century, regarding the Prince Hall Grand Lodges?

1. The history of the black man in America is the history of Prince Hall Freemasonry.
2. The history of Prince Hall Freemasonry must be written by the black Prince Hall Freemason, for only he can understand and interpret the black experience.[1]

This fairly haughty statement reduces the history of American blacks to that of the so-called Prince Hall Grand Lodges, named after their founder, a black freeman who lived in Boston during the second half of the eighteenth century. The first quality required for a historian of black Freemasonry would therefore be, according to Walkes, his "negritude."

A high officer of the Prince Hall Grand Lodge also stated during a personal interview that a female historian was an impossibility.[2]

What can I say about the alleged necessity of being black in order to speak about blacks, a woman to speak about women, or a Freemason to speak about Freemasons? It is equal to loudly proclaiming that only cobblers would have a right to write a history of shoes! It is equivalent to denying any scientific approach and abandoning once and for all the notion of critical distance. No one can claim ownership of history, no matter who they are.

In fact, black Freemasonry has been the object of precious little study, and often in the beginning only by its own members. It is a grand officer of the Prince Hall Grand Lodge of New York to whom we owe the existence of the major Masonic collection available today at the Schomburg Center for Research in Black Culture.*

Walkes is the author of two books, *Black Square and Compass* and *A Prince Hall Masonic Quiz Book*. Despite his racial biases, his skill as an expert researcher must be recognized. He refused to be satisfied with the compilation of a "house" history and took to heart the need to verify all his sources and to disentangle the skein of facts and legends.

The Phylaxis Society, an offshoot of the research lodge created by Harry A. Williamson in 1942, expanded rapidly in the 1970s thanks to Walkes. The first issue of *Phylaxis* magazine was published in January 1974, and it still appears today.[3]

Several white American Freemasons took an early interest in the black obedience, most often with an idea in mind of rehabilitating it in the eyes of their compatriots. Two such authors are William H. Upton and Harold Van Buren Voorhis, to mention only the two primary examples.[4] Two academic authors, William Muraskin and Loretta Williams, wrote the first sociological studies on the Prince Hall Grand Lodges; both studies appeared in the 1980s.[5]

More recently, Jessica Harland-Jacobs has devoted several pages to the Prince Hall Freemasons in her history of the British Empire and Freemasonry.[6] Alton Roundtree and Paul Bessel published a book that offers extremely helpful extracts from source documents and focuses on the official relations between the Prince Hall and the white grand

---

*These are the Harry A. Williamson Papers preserved at the Schomburg Center for Research in Black Culture of New York. Harry A. Williamson himself was the author of a number of particularly laudatory books on black Freemasonry, as well as monographs and instruction manuals for black Freemasons.

lodges.[7] Mark Tabbert makes many references to Prince Hall Masonry in his illustrated history of American Freemasonry.[8] We are currently seeing a renewed interest for black American Freemasonry among researchers.[9] Furthermore, an archival collection of Prince Hall's correspondence has just been created in the Library and Museum of Freemasonry in London.[10] Recently, Martin Cherry has retrieved and analyzed the correspondence between Harry Sadler, historian for the United Grand Lodge of England, who provided the first scientific explanation for the creation of the Ancient Grand Lodge in England,[*11] and a master of the Prince Hall Grand Lodge of Massachusetts in the beginning of the twentieth century.[†12]

It should be noted, however, that proportionally speaking, of all the books devoted to Freemasonry, those that deal specifically with the American black grand lodges are quite few. There are several possible reasons for these gaps. First, we should recognize that this is a very sensitive subject. Black Freemasons were long the target of the racism of a large part of American society, including that of their white "brothers," and are still quite touchy in this regard.

On the other hand, the Prince Hall Grand Lodges are reluctant to make their archives available to researchers. The Harry A. Williamson Papers collection of the Schomburg Center, mentioned earlier, is one of a kind. Several American libraries placed under the authority of the white grand lodges hold archives. Among these, I would like to first mention the Chancellor Robert R. Livingston Masonic Library of New York. This library, as well as the Schomburg Center and the Washington Memorial Library in Alexandria, Virginia, provided the core of the documentation used for the completion of this book. Bessel's Internet site, especially dedicated to the Prince Hall Grand Lodges and the

---

*Henry Sadler shows in *Masonic Facts and Figures* (originally published in 1887) that the long-advanced theory of a schism to explain the creation of the Ancient Grand Lodge in England was in error. He shows that the Ancient Grand Lodge appeared when a large number of Irish Masons, often Catholic and of very humble social status, had been rejected when they sought to join the English lodges on their arrival in London.

†Cherry also gave a talk titled "Grand Lodges and Official History? An Early Twentieth-Century Tale" at the International Conference on the History of Freemasonry symposium in Edinburgh, May 2013.

development of diplomatic relations between the various obediences, played a pioneering role and was extremely helpful.

Another difficulty lies in the fragmentary nature of the sources. Some grand lodges have preserved their archives and have made them available to researchers, but this is not true for all. From 1784, the date the first black lodge was created, to the present, some periods can be studied with greater precision than others.

Instead of a chronological approach, which would have been highly flawed, I preferred to make a thematic study, which does not claim to cover everything but instead focuses on those areas that were particularly conclusive, both for the history of Freemasonry and for that of black Americans. Also, geographical areas were not covered exhaustively because of the impossibility of gaining access to certain sources.

Finally, the choice of terminology needs to be explained. At the risk of being "politically incorrect," to adapt the accepted American expression, this book has deliberately refrained from using the expression "Afro-Americans." The fact is, resorting to this circumlocution implies adherence to the communitarian—or multiculturalist—philosophy found in Anglo-Saxon countries, according to which individuals are classified based on their ethnic origins or sex into various communities. These communities, which make claims based on their differences, maintain they have specific rights.

Because it reduces men and women to an identity defined a priori, this essentialist definition conflicts with the French approach, which places individuals on an equal plane as citizens of one nation and considers any kind of classification based on ethnicity as discriminatory. This theory dates from the French Revolution and proclaims that all citizens had equal rights and duties and eliminates all the intermediary bodies.

So, where the communitarian or multiculturalist approach exalts group identity, the Jacobin approach claims the rights of citizens with no thought as to their origins. Although no value judgment is intended here about multiculturalism, it is the citizenship approach adopted by the French that guided my choice of terminology. Although it is not an entirely satisfactory solution, for it too refers to a community, it does so without encaging people within a category based on a portrait type, like the term "Afro-American." The phenotype is an element that is as objective and mundane as eye color, whereas the communitarian choice is the product of very recent history, whether imposed by the weight of circumstance or the result of an intentional choice.

But as black Freemasonry has a specific history that is completely distinct from white Freemasonry, we really must use a specific expression like "American blacks," without adopting the communitarian approach implied by such an expression. The black Freemason will therefore be studied as an American citizen just like any other inhabitant of the United States. Naturally, this does not mean we need to ignore the role played by the Freemasons in the promotion of black Americans in particular.

The election of the first black president of the United States, something unthinkable even a dozen years ago, seems to lend support to this approach. Blacks, at least those of the middle class, are less and less inclined to consider themselves as a separate community and more and more as citizens who recognize themselves in the values—sometimes the most conservative ones—of the American nation. Just like the Prince Hall Freemasons, President Obama, who to my knowledge is not a member of the Order, pays allegiance to Christian morality like any other self-respecting American and emphasizes his family on multiple occasions as if to exorcise the long-standing stigmatization of black family behavior in the United States.

The social role played by black Freemasonry is at the heart of this study. The chief question is clearly the evaluation of the role played by Freemasonry for the integration of blacks into American society, although the term *integration* itself remains the subject of debate. Freemasonry was the first institution created by blacks in a large number of states, and on a colony-wide scale outside the United States, even before black churches. This shows that it played a specific role in both North American society and in the English-speaking regions of the Caribbean.

It is generally accepted today that Freemasonry had a relatively minor influence on the French Revolution despite certain trends of ideas and the survival of some lodges. On the other hand, it was a major presence in the American Revolution and was later persecuted by fascist regimes, particularly that of the Nazis. How great an influence was it on black Americans? What role did Freemasonry play in the fight to abolish slavery and bring about emancipation? Was Freemasonry purely honorific, rewarding to individuals for its wealth of rites and symbols, or did it really help them fight against discrimination and improve their social status? These questions will not all be answered with equal success. Nevertheless, they are worth raising.

Black Americans have adopted different tactics in the fight against slavery and the battle for civil rights, and they are still struggling today against the remaining forms of discrimination. Some have opted for separatism, others for integration. Nor has black Freemasonry spoken with one unanimous voice. Men, like the institutions to which they belong, have wavered between the desire for full recognition in American society and that of proclaiming their difference and stressing what sets them apart and separates them. Freemasonry is not an institution that stands outside of time. Like all associations, it is shaped by history. Rites and symbols give it a certain equanimity, sometimes even a healthy step backward, but they never remove it from public affairs.

PART ONE

The Genesis of
Black Freemasonry

ONE

Prince Hall Legend and History

Too much ink has already been spilled; too many polemics have already erupted around the subject of Prince Hall's specific origins, particularly the time and place of his birth. Even though there are some today who maintain that no room for doubt remains, other historians still have reservations. It is not a question of offering a new theory here but of providing some clarity.

First of all, we need to distinguish between what is essential and what it not. The "Caucasian" Masons (as Joseph Walkes calls them), whom I will simply refer to as "whites" (if it is absolutely necessary to attach labels), and the black American Freemasons seem to confuse the history of Prince Hall's birth with that of the genesis of black Freemasonry. Now, inasmuch as it seems of vital importance to dispel all the historical ambiguity surrounding the first lodge, it seems proportionately less important to desperately hunt for every little detail of Prince Hall's biography. This interest in the person of Prince Hall is justified from an emotional and symbolic point of view, but it is hardly essential for establishing the history of Prince Hall Freemasonry.

But let's try to calmly examine Prince Hall's life and separate the facts from the legend. How proudly the Barbados lodges, in the presence of Henrick Ellis, grand master of the Prince Hall Grand Lodge of the Caribbean, and that of Jean-Claude Bousquet, grand master of the Grand Lodge of France, inaugurated a monument to the glory of Prince Hall. These simple words were carved on its stone:

> This building was erected to the memory of Prince Hall who was born in Barbados on the 12th September 1748 and died in Boston USA on the 18th December 1807.

However, these dates and place of birth are far from receiving unanimous assent. In his 1992 book on the life of Prince Hall, Arthur Diamond drew up the following chronology.

1735: Birth of Prince Hall, probably in Western Africa.

1749: Prince Hall became the slave of William Hall, in Boston.

1756: He married a slave named Delia. Birth of their son: Primus Hall.

1763: Hall wed Sara Ritchie. He joined the Congregational Church of Reverend Andrew Croswell.

1770: He was freed by William Hall; he wed Flora Gibbs; birth of their son, Prince Africanus.

1775: Hall joined the fraternal order of Freemasons; he founded the African Lodge in Boston.

1776: He enlisted in the Continental Army.[1]

Fig. 1.1. Prince Hall (courtesy of the Chancellor Robert R. Livingston Masonic Library)

Diamond, who remains cautious, thinks that Prince Hall was born in Africa, like the majority of slaves brought into the United States during this time, but that he may have spent several years in the Antilles before coming to Boston, where he was sold to William Hall, an Irishman known for his philanthropy and who presided over the Charitable Irish Society of Boston.[2] The master, William Hall, was also said to be a Quaker. This is an entirely plausible scenario. Given the antislavery notions of the Quakers, this would explain why Hall freed his slave fairly quickly. However, proofs are lacking here too.

Joseph Walkes, meanwhile, refutes the hypothesis of Prince Hall's birth in Barbados—mainly because it is historian William H. Grimshaw's contention. If there is any consensus among the historians of black Freemasonry, it clearly seems to be criticism of the unfortunate Grimshaw, whose work does actually contain some errors.[3] However, as Walkes acknowledges, there is no certainty with regard to Prince Hall's birthplace, and nothing exists that would tilt the decision in favor of any one place over another. The mystery remains complete, and it seems equally possible to claim that he was born in Barbados, Africa, or the United States. Walkes refers to an article by John M. Sherman, published in issue 92 of *Ars Quatuor Coronatorum,* the magazine of the research lodge of the United Grand Lodge of England. Sherman writes:

> I had the good fortune of finding in the Athenaeum Library of Boston, a copy of the manumission document that proves Prince Hall was originally a slave in the family of the tanner William Hall, who freed him in 1770.[4]

Walkes believes this copy is of dubious authenticity. That may be so, but it is just as difficult to prove that it is not authentic. It does clearly seem that Prince Hall was freed in 1770. Harry A. Williamson certainly gives a completely different interpretation in his *Prince Hall Primer.*

> Who was Prince Hall? He was the son of Thomas Hall, an Englishman, a leather merchant, whose wife was a free Negro woman of French descent. He came to New England during the middle of the

eighteenth century, settling in the city of Boston, in the Massachusetts Colony.[5]

No one believes this version today, despite the Masonic renown of its author. Williamson did in fact put together an impressive collection of papers on the history of the Prince Hall lodges, which is housed today at the Schomburg Center in New York. It is likely that if several Masonic historians attempted to completely refute that Prince Hall was a slave, it was not to discredit the obedience he created. In fact, the ban formulated by James Anderson in his famous *Constitutions* concerning the initiation of slaves was still a concern in people's minds at that time. The United Grand Lodge of England certainly replaced the phrase "born free" with "free" in its 1847 Constitution in order to authorize the entry of recently emancipated men into Freemasonry. The expression "born free" had excluded until this time all slaves or former slaves. On the other hand, the Landmarks of Albert Mackey, which comprised the authoritative guide in the United States, still clearly stated at the beginning of the twentieth century that is was impossible to initiate any man who had been born a slave.

> That is to say a woman, a cripple or a slave, or one born in slavery, is disqualified for initiation into the rites of Freemasonry.[6]

Walkes made the reasonable assertion that there were likely several Prince Halls in Boston at this time, which therefore makes it quite difficult to establish a connection between Prince Hall and Primus Hall.[7] We know that Primus Hall definitely existed, as he signed, by Prince Hall's side, a petition against slavery addressed to the House of Representatives and Senate of Massachusetts on February 27, 1788.[8] There is

Fig. 1.2. Signature of Prince Hall from the Edward R. Cusick Collection (courtesy of the Chancellor Robert R. Livingston Masonic Library)

no proof from this to support the claim that Primus Hall was the son of Prince Hall. We do know, though, that Prince Hall married Sarah Ritchie in 1763, and she died three years later. We know that he married again to Flora Gibbs in 1770.[9] His enlistment in the Continental Army has not been proved, but this may be a case of too much evidence. In fact, Walkes found three different Prince Halls who were all soldiers in the Continental Army![10]

A Mason longing to be a poet, a certain D. T. V. Huntoon, gave credence to the legend of the watch chain, a most splendid legend no doubt, which he told to Grand Master Lewis Hayden, who took it as the gospel truth. He had the story entered into the archives of the lodge during the centennial celebrating the granting of a charter to African Lodge n° 459. According to the story, a Reverend Bowman married Elizabeth Hancock, the daughter of a Reverend Hancock. Six children were born of their union; the youngest was named Lydia in honor of her Uncle Thomas Hancock's wife. This Lydia married James Baker and received as a wedding gift a young slave named Phoebe. Shortly thereafter, Lydia and James Baker hired a servant, a freeman of color named Prince Hall. Phoebe continued to take care of the Baker children: Edmund and another Lydia. It was to this Lydia she gave a gold bead necklace that she had worn on her wedding day. Lydia altered this necklace, probably a gift from Prince Hall, to be a watch chain. Lydia married the Reverend Benjamin Huntoon. On his death, his son, D. T. V. Huntoon, inherited the chain, which he gave to the African Lodge.[11]

While the story appears fundamentally banal, it enchanted several generations of Masons, which was a source of extreme annoyance to Walkes. It is easy to understand the irritation of a man who took the trouble to go over all the archives with a fine-tooth comb. However, the very fact that the Masons felt the need to invent a legend like this and, more importantly, to believe it, is significant. We know so little about the lives of slaves and their ancestors. Biographies are quite often invented and traced over those of former masters. Under these conditions, why not seek to embellish the facts? Prince Hall would be no exception. We have to accept the evidence; no one knows very much, actually, about any part of his life. This did not prevent some Masons from delivering judgment on his moral and intellectual qualities. For example, on behalf of the white Masons of Alaska, Thomas Harkins, a 33rd-degree Mason of the Scottish Rite, wrote a particularly hostile essay on black Freemasonry in which he described Prince Hall as "cunning, intelligent but illiterate."[12]

Returning to Walkes, we see that he stigmatized the errors committed by Grimshaw and several other fine storytellers of Freemasonry. Of course it is always annoying to find fable and reality commingled. The truly obscure points concern Prince Hall's date and place of birth, his liaison with a certain Phoebe, and his relation to Primus Hall— who may have been his son or just simply a friend. The least that can be said is that none of these points seem truly decisive with respect to the history of the Prince Hall Grand Lodges. However, Walkes is right to note the lack of details concerning Prince Hall's initiation into Freemasonry. We think this took place on March 6, 1775, in a military lodge attached to General Thomas Gage's regiment. This lodge operated under the authority of the Grand Lodge of Ireland, a lodge that accepted a certain number of blacks. Sherman contests this hypothesis and shows that the regiment in question had left Boston by this date. He believes that it was actually a member of the military lodge, a certain John Batt, who took it upon himself to initiate some blacks irregularly but without the support of the Irish Grand Lodge. This would have been right after he deserted, as he remained in Boston rather than following his regiment.[13] Naturally this version cannot help but offend current members of the Prince Hall Grand Lodges, because it supplies additional reinforcement to the hypothesis of the "Masonic irregularity" of the founding fathers. This interpretation totally contradicts the report drawn up by a committee of former grand masters and unanimously adopted by the Grand Lodge of Massachusetts in 1946 that established the perfect regularity of the initiation of Prince Hall and his friends.*[14]

Whatever the case may be, the fact remains that Prince Hall

---

*I will examine this report in detail in chapter 14, which deals with relations between the white and black grand lodges in the United States.

founded a lodge a very short time later, probably in 1775,[15] with several other black brothers.

Knowing whether Prince Hall was initiated regularly may not be essential. We have to establish an understanding about just what regularity meant in the historical context of his time. How could the white grand lodges have lightheartedly accepted the advent of a black Masonry in the segregationist context of that time period? It is extremely likely that Prince Hall and his companions sought to create a lodge by whatever means necessary. Furthermore, as underscored by the report adopted by the Grand Lodge of Massachusetts (Prince Hall) in 1946, it is absurd to examine the regularity question by putting on contemporary eyeglasses, without keeping the criteria of the era concerned in mind.[16] The main thing is that Prince Hall created the first black lodge, the African Lodge, in Boston around 1775, and a charter was granted him by the Grand Lodge of England in 1787.*[17] Furthermore, subject to future discoveries, this charter is probably the only English charter granted to an eighteenth-century American lodge that has been preserved to this day.†

---

*The charter was most likely granted on 1784 but did not reach the lodge until 1787.
†Several such lodges existed, naturally, during the eighteenth century, such as the Saint John Grand Lodge of Massachusetts, but they did not take as much care of their original charter, because the stakes were not as high as they were for the African Lodge.

TWO

The Birth of Black Freemasonry

African Lodge n° 459

The lack of archives has long provided a convenient excuse to the white American grand lodges for not extending recognition to their black brothers. This is most likely the reason that several historians of the Prince Hall Grand Lodges, with the exception of Walkes, have tried to be so positive concerning their origins and remain steadfast in this pursuit come hell or high water. For example, Harry A. Williamson stated in his 1956 book, *The Prince Hall Primer,* a kind of catechism for black Masons, that Prince Hall was initiated on March 6, 1775, by Lodge 441.

This lodge, which held its charter from the Grand Lodge of Ireland and was attached to the regiment of General Gage, left Boston for the state of New York. It then granted Prince Hall and his black brothers a "dispensation" authorizing them to meet as Masons. "It gave those Freemasons the right to assemble in such capacity for the purpose of attending church and burying their dead."[1]

The committee of former grand masters of the Grand Lodge of Massachusetts confirms the existence of this dispensation, which was granted by Grand Master John Rowe of the Saint John Grand Lodge of Boston. This lodge consisted primarily of loyalists, in other words, men who remained faithful to the English crown.[2] This dispensation, however, did not authorize these black Masons to initiate new members.

In a letter to the editor of a Boston newspaper, Prince Hall corrected the name this paper had saddled his lodge with. It was not Saint Black's Lodge but the African Lodge! All the scorn the Boston elite felt toward Prince Hall and his friends is perceptible in this ironic turn of phrase.[3] While they continued to meet, it seems that the lodge initiated no new members, thus respecting the dispensation granted them by Rowe.

In any case, Prince Hall and his friends were not satisfied with this dispensation granted by the Saint John Lodge, which followed the "modern rite," and apparently asked to join the rival grand lodge, the Grand Lodge of Massachusetts. This lodge followed the "ancient rite," and its members included a large number of patriots who were supporters of the American Revolution.* The provincial grand master at that time and a Revolutionary War hero, Joseph Warren was said to have promised them a warrant, but he never fulfilled his plan† as he was killed in the Battle of Bunker Hill.[4]

Subsequently, in the name of the principle of territorial exclusivity American Masons had always maintained that only one grand lodge per state could exist, and this would naturally be a white grand lodge, while still asserting the absolute sovereignty of each grand lodge. Yet, paradoxically, in this same state of Massachusetts there were two white grand lodges, the provincial Grand Lodge of Massachusetts and the provincial Saint John Grand Lodge, which had coexisted since 1769. Confronted by the hypocrisy of the Massachusetts Masons, Prince Hall made the decision to address the Grand Lodge of England.

Eleven of the original letters signed by Prince Hall have recently been discovered and can be consulted at the library of the United Grand Lodge of England.[5] Written in phonetic English that transposes

---

*The distinction between "modern rite" and "ancient rite" reflects the quarrels separating the Modern Grand Lodge (from 1717) and the Ancient Grand Lodge (from 1751) in Great Britain.

†According to Martin Robison Delany, Warren even had enough time to draft the warrant intended for the African Lodge, but this document went astray.

the popular tongue of the era, they can be somewhat off-putting to the modern reader. They have the merit of authenticity, however, and shed a valuable light on the first steps of the African Lodge.

Some of these letters appeared earlier in the correspondence of Prince Hall from 1782 to 1806 that was reproduced with commentary by Carter G. Woodson in an issue of *The Journal of Negro History,* which has unfortunately not been available for researchers.[6] Woodson was able to clearly establish that the Grand Lodge of England had sent Prince Hall and his friends a charter dated September 29, 1784, which unfortunately did not reach its destination until 1787 because of delays in payment. The fact is that William Gregory, a member of the African Lodge, and then a certain Hartfield, a sailor by profession, successively misappropriated the money entrusted to them by Prince Hall. The Grand Lodge of England, which did not grant charters just for the sake of it, held on to the valuable document.

It was necessary to wait until 1787 for the misunderstanding to be cleared up, when Captain Scott turned over the requested sum, which was five pounds, fifteen shillings, six pence, to Grand Secretary White and finally took possession of the charter. Prince Hall acknowledged receipt of it May 2, 1787.*

Once these little logistical problems had been regulated, the Grand Lodge of England, who in the context of the war for independence was probably not at all vexed at the prospect of annoying the Grand Lodges of Boston, granted the black Masons a document that the American institutions refused them. The English warrant has survived to the present day, having escaped a conflagration almost miraculously.†

Among the originals preserved in London can be found the general rules of the lodge as well as Prince Hall's correspondence from the years following the acquisition of the warrant. These regulations paraphrase the main principles of Anderson's *Constitutions:* the Mason should not be an "atheist" or an "irreligious libertine" and should be

---

*A copy of this charter is in the library of the United Grand Lodge of England on Great Queen Street in London.

†The original Prince Hall Charter is in appendix 1.

an honorable man and "freeborn" (thus the black Masons ironically reemployed on their own behalf the ban on men born as slaves). In the case of a rule violation, penalties were foreseen for the guilty Masons: a fine of ten shillings and the risk of being expelled from the lodge for those who used coarse language, or a fine of three shillings for lack of diligence. The brothers were under an obligation to behave properly both inside and outside the lodge.* Prince Hall kept an eye on the lodge members' attendance and made sure the lodge functioned properly, both locally and in its relations with the English Modern Grand Lodge.

There can be no doubt that transport to the metropolis of accounts and monies due posed a real problem. For example, Prince Hall wrote Grand Secretary White on November 9, 1789, then on November 10, 1791, worried that White had not acknowledged receipt of ten dollars donated to the Charity Committee.[7] In another letter, dated May 24, 1789, Prince Hall explains to the grand secretary that the brother Newport Davies, charged with delivery of a contribution from the African Lodge to the charity collection of the Grand Lodge of England, as well as a number of speeches given on the occasion of Saint John's Day at midsummer, had perished during the crossing.[8]

By all evidence the United Grand Lodge of England had no desire to hear Prince Hall's explanations, as the African Lodge vanished from its registry in 1813 on the pretext that it was not in compliance with their treasury and had not made contributions to its charity funds since 1791.[9] For close to two centuries white American Freemasons have held up this voiding of the African Lodge's charter as a reason for not recognizing the Prince Hall Grand Lodges. This is an unfair attitude, as shown by both the letters of Prince Hall and the fact that the grand lodge annulled a considerable number of lodge charters in 1813 for nonpayment. The white Saint John Grand Lodge, created in Boston in 1773, also found itself in this same situation as it vanished from the United Grand Lodge of England registry in 1813.

One hundred years later the Prince Hall Grand Lodge of Massa-

---

*See "The General Regulations of the African Lodge" in appendix 1.

chusetts denied that its past members were in the wrong concerning lack of payment to the Modern Grand Lodge treasury.

In fact, the Prince Hall Grand Lodge of Massachusetts wrote on August 25, 1870:

> It has been charged that there was a difficulty between the Grand Lodge of England and the Lodge n° 459 relative to dues; but the reading of the charter refuted all such groundless statements. The charter makes provisions for dues but only requires the remittance of just such sums of money as would suit the circumstances of the Lodge, and be reasonably expected toward the Grand Charity. The following statement of remittances for the African Lodge forwarded by the Deputy Prince Hall to the Grand Lodge of England proves that they conform to the requirements of the charter; Nov. 25th, 1789: $2; April 18th, 1792: $2.20; Nov. 27th, 1792: $1.56; Nov. 22nd, 1797: $1.50.[10]

This could mean that the Grand Lodge of England had displayed great flexibility with regard to the African Lodge by granting it favor and then later sought to go back on its decision. This hypothesis would furthermore confirm a change of policy on the part of the Grand Lodge of England with respect to the African Lodge.

Reading Prince Hall's letters tends to show that the African Lodge had its share of mishaps, and the English refused to give them any credence. It can be asked if the English desire to include a black lodge in their number may have weakened as there was no longer any need to rile the Americans once the war for independence was over.

Nonetheless, the African Lodge remained quite active in Boston, as shown by the lodge minutes. Those for the period of 1779 to 1846 are available for consultation at the Grand Lodge of Massachusetts library.[11] Other sources confirm the activities of Prince Hall and his colleagues. Joseph Walkes has established the list of the lodge's first members. For example, we can mention the lodge chaplain, John Marrant, who moved to London before returning to the United States, becoming a wandering preacher who sought to convert the Native Americans to Christianity. He fought against the American patriots on the side of the British. Another member of the lodge, Prince Saunders, enjoyed special relations with the English and in 1809 became a teacher in a school for Boston's black children. He founded the Belles Lettres Society of Boston before meeting William Wilberforce, the abolitionist champion, in London. This latter charged him with the mission of creating schools in Haiti. Richard Allen, another member of Lodge n° 459, was the first black bishop and founder of the African Episcopalian Methodist Church, the AME. We should note that another black Mason held similar duties; this would be Absalom Jones, worshipful master of the first black lodge in Philadelphia and the first black reverend of the African Methodist Episcopal Church.[12]

It was in Boston and Philadelphia that black Masons began working in specific lodges. The birth of the first black grand lodges inspired as many polemics as did the African Lodge, from both the English and Americans.

The First Black Grand Lodges

The first black grand lodge could be dated from 1797. But here too the terms need to be specified. What do we mean by "grand lodge"? If it was a structure that had long united several lodges, this was most likely the case. On the other hand, it is very probable that the Prince Hall Lodge chose to call itself a grand lodge, just like the Saint Andrew's Lodge decided to transform itself into the Grand Lodge of Massachusetts in order to have the power to grant charters to new lodges.

What failed to shock Massachusetts Freemasons was condemned, however, when it involved black Freemasonry. It is not impossible that to get around the absence of ties with the Grand Lodge of England from approximately 1797, and because they were loath to ruffle that organization's feathers, the members of the African Lodge proclaimed themselves to be a grand lodge starting in either 1797 or 1808. Harry A. Williamson states in *The Prince Hall Primer* that a black grand lodge was already in existence in 1808 and at that time simply changed its name.

> What transpired at the General Assembly of the craft in 1801? The title of the Negro organization for the State of Massachusetts was changed from "African Grand Lodge of North America" to its present title of "Prince Hall Grand Lodge, F. & A. M. of Massachusetts."[13]

Upton repeated this version in 1900.[14] On the other hand, Sherman states that the first Prince Hall Grand Lodge was not created until 1848, which seems highly debatable.[15] Williamson wrote that the first Prince Hall Grand Lodge dates from 1791, for, according to him, Prince Hall would have assumed the title of grand master at this date and this lodge at that time was proclaimed African Grand Lodge of North America before adopting the title of Prince Hall Grand Lodge, F. & A. M. of Massachusetts in 1808.[16] What is certain is that the African Lodge was the only black Masonic organization in the United States when it was formed and could therefore claim the title of Grand Lodge of North America, which it could no longer do in 1801 as another similar body existed in Pennsylvania. Walkes uses the date of 1791 advanced by Williamson but specifies that the first black grand lodge only claimed this title in 1827.[17]

Given the fact that the title of grand lodge could not have been granted by the United Grand Lodge of England, it is somewhat futile to hunt for legal documentation. It does actually seem clear that the African Lodge did one day proclaim itself a grand lodge. It is doubtful that this was a premature decision directly following their receipt of their charter, which would have needlessly annoyed the English Modern Grand Lodge. If we take a look at it from a practical perspective we can reasonably maintain that the African Lodge conducted itself as a grand lodge from the time it took under consideration a demand for a charter from another lodge. This was the case when the first Philadelphia lodge made this request on March 2, 1797.

The First Lodge in Philadelphia
Philadelphia, March 2, 1797
To the Right Worshipful Prince Hall of the African Lodge n° 459,
of Boston.

Worshipful Sir and Brother,
We congratulate you for having been invested with the high and holy trust
conferred upon you by the authorities in England, together with your
success in obtaining the warrant constituting African Lodge n° 459.

In the name of the most holy Trinity, Father, Son and Holy Ghost, we
most respectfully solicit you, Right Worshipful Sir, for a Dispensation for an
African lodge. We are all ready to go to work, having all but a Dispensation.

We have been tried by five Royal Arch Masons. The white Masons
have refused to grant us a Dispensation, fearing that black men living in
Virginia, would get to be Masons, too.

We would rather be under you, and associated with our Brethren
in Boston, than to be under those of the Pennsylvania Lodge; for, if we
are under you, we shall always be ready to assist in the furtherance of
Masonry among us.[18]

Prince Hall granted a favorable outcome to this request in his letter of
March 22, 1797, to the author of the previous letter.

Mr. Peter Mantore,
Sir: I received your letter of the 2 which informed me that there are a
number of blacks in your city who have received the light of Masonry
and I hope they got it in a just and lawful manner. If so, dear brother, we
are willing to set you at work under our charter and Lodge n° 459, from
London; under that authority and by the name of the African Lodge, we
hereby and herein give you the license to assemble and work as aforesaid,
under that denomination as in the sight and fear of God. I would advise
you not to take any in at present till your officers and your Master be
installed in the Grand Lodge, which we are willing to do, when he thinks
convenient, and he may receive a full warrant instead of a permit.

Prince Hall[19]

This correspondence shows beyond any possibility of doubt that a Philadelphia lodge had run up against the refusal of a white American grand lodge to grant it a warrant. It naturally then turned to the black lodge of a nearby state, which de facto conducted itself as a grand lodge by acceding to its request. This is how the transformation of the African Lodge into a grand lodge took place in a completely natural fashion without great concern shown by Prince Hall and his friends for formal procedures. These are the circumstances that activated that process.

Other Prince Hall Grand Lodges came into existence subsequently without giving rise to such controversies, at least concerning their dates of creation. Walkes considers the Philadelphia Lodge, constituted in 1797, to be a grand lodge. He then proposes the following ranking.

n° 3: Boyer Grand Lodge, New York, March 12, 1845

n° 4: African Grand Lodge of Baltimore, Maryland, 1845

n° 5: Union Grand Lodge or Prince Hall Grand Lodge District of Columbia, March 27, 1848

n° 6: Prince Hall Grand Lodge of New Jersey, June 24, 1848

n° 7: Prince Hall Grand Lodge of Ohio, May 3, 1849

n° 8: Prince Hall Grand Lodge of Delaware, June 9, 1849

n° 9: Grand Lodge of the Free, Ancient, and Accepted Masons of York, San Francisco, June 19, 1855, predecessor of the current Prince Hall Grand Lodge of California

n° 10: Prince Hall Grand Lodge of Indiana, September 13, 1856

n° 11: Harmony Grand Lodge of the Rhode Island and Providence Plantations, October 7, 1858, which is today the Prince Hall Grand Lodge of Rhode Island

n° 12: Eureka Grand Lodge, January 5, 1863, in New Orleans; today it is the Prince Hall Grand Lodge of Louisiana.[20]

As a general rule, the grand lodges carry the appellation "Prince Hall" and use the expression "Free and Accepted Masons" instead of "Ancient, Free, and Accepted Masons." Williamson explains that the term *ancient* could have been taken to refer to the *Ancient* Grand Lodge of England and thus sow confusion as the Freemasons of Prince Hall owed their gratitude to the *Modern* Grand Lodge of England for being the first to have granted them a charter.[*][21]

Like so many other grand lodges, those of Prince Hall could not avoid finding themselves in troubled waters. For example, a dissident grand lodge appeared in Philadelphia in 1832. This Hiram Grand Lodge of the State of Pennsylvania would vanish in 1847.[22] However, it was the creation of the National Grand Lodge in 1847 that stirred up the greatest controversy and most significantly left its mark on the history of black Freemasonry. This National Grand Lodge, also known as the Compact Grand Lodge, took as its purpose the task of giving black Freemasons a national federal structure that would thereby strengthen their power and allow them to confront the attacks of the white grand lodges and, more broadly, defend themselves in the society of their time. This organization would more or less prosper for thirty years, from 1847 to 1877.

It was naturally a target of fierce criticism, particularly by the Masons of New York, who refused to join the new organization. This led to the scission of the black Grand Lodge of New York in 1847: the Boyer Grand Lodge brought together the supporters of the new grand lodge, while the United Grand Lodge welcomed the Masons who were hostile to a federal organization and therefore refused to give their allegiance to the National Grand Lodge. One nationalist, Martin Robison Delany, was highly enthusiastic about the creation of this National Grand Lodge, which he described in the most glowing terms as a means of putting an end to the divisions between the black grand lodges and allowing them to form an enduring union.

> In December 1847 by a Grand Communication of a representative body of all the colored lodges in the United States, held in the city of New York, the differences and wounds, which long existed, were all settled and healed, a complete union formed, and a National Grand

---

*The Virginia Grand Lodge, however, used the appellation "Ancient Free and Accepted Masons."

Lodge established, by the choice and election, in due Masonic form, of Past Master, John T. Hilton of Boston, Massachusetts, Most Worshipful Grand Master of the National Grand Lodge, and William E. Ambush, Most Worshipful National Grand Secretary. This, perhaps, was the most important period in the history of colored Masons in the United States; and had I the power to do so, I would raise my voice in tones of thunder, but with the pathetic affections of a brother, and thrill the cord of every true Masonic heart throughout the country and the world, especially of colored men, in exhortation to stability and to Union. Without it, satisfied I am, that all our efforts, whether as men or Masons must fail—utterly fail. [23]

Carried away by his eloquence, Delany failed to mention the new rifts created by the constitution of this national authority, particularly in the black Grand Lodge of New York. Walkes explains that this initiative was fueled by the desire of the Masons of that time to feel stronger, thanks to a national organization, in their fight against the surrounding racism. For example, he recalls that during the very year of its creation, the black children of Boston were denied access to the city's white schools, despite a petition sent by members of the black and white communities to the School Committee of Boston. A black man had even sued the municipality of Boston because his five-year-old daughter had not been accepted into a white school, and he lost his suit. In the name of each lodge's sovereignty, Walkes condemns the idea of a federal Masonic structure and believes this to be a veritable anomaly. [24] However, even though he did not approve a posteriori of the creation of the National Grand Lodge, he does explain that such an organization could never have come into existence were it not for the discrimination blacks then suffered from.

Starting in 1873 the grand lodges withdrew, one by one, from the National Grand Lodge until 1877, the year of its dissolution. The Grand Lodge of Massachusetts, which had taken the initiative of creating it, was the first to leave. [25] Criticisms had arisen from inside the National Grand Lodge itself starting in 1865. Walkes cites a harsh report that recommends a union of the grand lodges on a different basis.

Your committee is of the opinion that an honorable union, without compromising any cardinal principle of the ancient usages and customs of the fraternity, ought to be formed. They think, that should the system of government known as the National Grand Lodge be abandoned by the body, the Grand Lodges in the several states could immediately take measures to unite upon the basis of common Masonic usage, for the government of the Craft.[26]

The existence of a federal Masonic organization posed a real problem for the Prince Hall Masons. These Prince Hall Masons were not particularly inclined to respect the white Masonic jurisprudence, which only recognized one single grand lodge per state, and also opposed any federal Masonic structure at the same time.

In the eighteenth century white American Freemasonry held firm against the sirens of megalomania by refusing to create a federal grand lodge, even under the direction of a grand Mason as prestigious as General George Washington. A large number of Prince Hall Freemasons, therefore, had no hesitation about taking the plunge and giving themselves a federal grand lodge when they deemed it good. However, Masonic historians like Walkes, anxious to show that traditionally black Freemasonry was just as respectful of Masonic jurisprudence as any white obedience, disapproved of this initiative, even though there were mitigating circumstances because of its historical context.

This episode left its mark on the history of Prince Hall Freemasonry, but the attempt to endow itself with a federal organization was never repeated. Today the Prince Hall Grand Lodges proclaim their autonomy loud and clear and remain satisfied with the existence of a federal headquarters, which is also the local of the New York Grand Lodge. It is located in the heart of Harlem, next door to the retirement home built by and for the Masons of Prince Hall.

THREE

The Major Principles

An Oral Culture

It is common knowledge that writing confers greater power to people than the oral tradition. From the ancient Egyptians to the present day, the great civilizations have always asserted themselves thanks to their written culture, whereas peoples attached to oral expression have remained, for the most part, little known. It so happens that the black American culture is essentially oral.

In his book that has now become one of the great classics, *The Signifying Monkey,* Henry Louis Gates has clearly shown the predominance of oral culture in African American literature. On the one hand, the speaker is inspired by conventional Western narratives and repeats them in his own way, thereby producing a text in two voices—the Western voice and the African American voice. On the other hand, when the written output is original, it most often echoes a collective oral tradition. This is true for countless slave narratives.

The authenticity of these stories has often been contested. Some people have suggested that slaves did not write them but that authors claiming to speak in their name did so after the fact. It is likely that this was sometimes the case, actually. Gates explains that even narratives whose authors are incontestable, like those by Frederick Douglass or Mary Prince, were written in the name of all other slaves by a spokesperson. Other less well-known slave narratives were put down in writing by abolitionist organizations on the basis of oral accounts of authors who were often illiterate.

The famous appeal flung out in 1829 by David Walker, *An Appeal to the Colored Citizens of the World,* also sits at a crossroads between oral and written traditions, according to Peter Hinks.[1] In fact, its very form is borrowed from the oral tradition of Protestant sermons that Walker might have heard among the Methodists. Furthermore, Hinks shows that the final work, if it was truly the work of Walker, was enriched by various suggestions and observations from those around him.

One of the major problems encountered by the historians of the black movement is the complete absence of any civil documentation for former slaves. The majority of slaves lost not only their freedom but also their identity during the "middle crossing." It was customary for slave owners to rebaptize the slaves when they took possession of them, and they found it amusing to rig the slaves with Roman names when they did not bestow them with their own names. Several black individuals could carry the same pseudo-patronymic for this reason, as shown, for example, by the difficulties Walkes encountered when trying to identify Prince Hall. The parties concerned generally did not know their own birth dates, hence the uncertainty concerning Prince Hall's date and place of birth. Hinks stumbled into the same difficulty concerning Walker, who was also a member of the African Lodge.[2]

Under these conditions it is easy to grasp why African American culture gave primacy to the oral tradition over the written, which was conspicuous in its absence.

It so happens that Freemasonry is one of the rare institutions to have always proclaimed the superiority of the oral tradition over texts. This explains why the marriage between Masonic culture and black American culture has been so successful. Similarly, the British Masons always assumed as their duty to learn the rituals by heart and refused to consign anything to paper. The first revelations of rituals were due to the works of the Englishman Samuel Pritchard and certain other authors animated by the desire for financial gain.

With respect to Masonic jurisprudence, we must look instead toward the American Masons of the nineteenth century to find actual legislation. The most famous of these writers was Albert Mackey, who thought it wise to write down the Landmarks and thereby codify for future generations certain Masonic principles that he felt were sacrosanct, such as the ban on initiating women or the obligation of believing in God. Traditionally, while English Freemasonry favored these values, it had always refused to imprison them in the straitjacket of writing. Now we know that Prince Hall turned to the Grand Lodge of England in search of official recognition. He was therefore able to appreciate the preference shown by the English Masons for the oral tradition.

Paradoxically though, oral transmission was not enough to legitimize the existence of a lodge, which had to be able to show a written document, a warrant that vouched for its official creation. We know the importance granted this document by Prince Hall and his heirs concerning the very first black lodge, African Lodge n° 459. Excepting this restriction, however, oral tradition is sovereign.

By all evidence, Prince Hall knew eighteenth-century England and, more specifically, the Masonic context. Anderson's *Constitutions* probably served the works of the African Lodge as a reference. However, if we apply the theory of Gates to the first members of the African Lodge, it is likely that the first black American Masons did indeed rely on Anderson's *Constitutions,* a foundational Western text, but by appropriating it and adding distinguishing references to it. In the same way Delany, in the following century, was inspired by the history written about Anderson, a history that exhibited many scientific errors but was enlivened by personal touches. Delany explains that Moses was the descendant of slaves and was himself an African slave when he was brought before the pharaoh.

> Are we not as Masons, and the world of mankind, to him the Egyptian slave—may I not add, the fugitive slave—indebted for a transmission to us of the Masonic Records, the Holy Bible, the Word of God?[3]

This line of thinking allowed Delany to introduce a distinction between slaves. According to him there are two categories of slaves. The first unites all the men reduced to slavery against their will, the second those who have renounced their freedom for some financial compensation. Only the second category is targeted by article II of Anderson's *Constitutions,* and Moses, according to Delany, is naturally part of the first category. God appearing to Moses in Ethiopia and Africa is therefore part of Masonic tradition.

> Truly, if the African race have no legitimate claims to Masonry, then it is illegitimate to all the rest of mankind.[4]

Delany gets carried away and admits to revealing the Masonic secret by claiming to tell the origin of the word *Eureka*.

> Must I hesitate to tell the world that, as applied to Masonry, the word *Eureka* was first exclaimed in Africa? But, there I have revealed the Masonic secret, and must stop.[5]

John Jones maintains in his essay "An Argument in Relation to Free Masonry among Colored Men" that Pythagoras was raised to the grade of master in Africa! About forty years later, in a speech to the Craftsmen's Club, one of those mutual-aid societies grafted to a Masonic lodge, another Mason, Edward Bruce, claimed the existence of a black operative tradition. He had the audacity to evaluate in full fantasy the precise cost of the construction of Solomon's Temple to demonstrate its magnificence. He even went so far as to convert pounds sterling into dollars, which is rather mind-boggling, to say the least, with regard to King Solomon's era. The author also gets in a few digs at white society, as these few lines show:

> The cost of this magnificent structure was 6,904,822,500 pounds sterling, or in our money $33,143,148,000. The gold vessels used cost 542,296,203 pounds, four shillings, or in round American money $2,617,421,775. The silver vessels cost $2,108,851,200. This will give you some idea of the magnificence and splendor of this great Temple dedicated to Almighty God and reared by the hands of black men. . . . It ought to be gratifying to the Negroes who know their history to reflect upon the fact that this, the greatest architectural triumph of mankind, was the work of black men, and that they were Masons, skilled artisans, and mechanics of the highest order. The Carnegies, Clarks, Rockefellers, Vanderbilts, and others who

boast of their great riches are clearly not in the class with these black Croesuses of the days of Solomon and Herod.[7]

The author casually blends places and eras. It is true that the Scotsman Anderson also took some liberties with history in his introduction. The Craftsmen's Club orator was not only seeking to legitimize black Freemasonry but also to show that the blacks were at the origin of Freemasonry inasmuch as they were the master builders of Solomon's Temple. He concluded his speech by encouraging the Masons of his time to fight back against the injustices to which they were subject.

This approach is typical of black Freemasonry. As a general rule the Prince Hall Freemasons are more oriented outward, more sensible to the society that surrounds them than to introspection. Although any generalization is risky, black Freemasonry overall seems to be more militant than esoteric in its essence. Even if it draws its references from a symbology that blends European religious traditions, it gives these traditions an African coloring and, by so doing, encourages a militant attitude among its adepts. It encourages their involvement in the society of their time and thereby promotes their social ascent. Gradually a black Masonic identity was crafted that was based on an oral discourse, on speeches given in lodges, like those of Prince Hall, Martin Robison Delany, and later by less famous Masons like John Jones or Edward Bruce. This oral discourse allowed these Masons to appropriate the European Masonic discourse as we know it, that of Anderson's *Constitutions* and that of the "Masonic sermons" given in the English lodges of the eighteenth century. When Anderson wrote his introduction he was putting a polish on facts and legends. The English Masonic tradition is above all an oral tradition to which black Freemasons could add their heritage, fed on Ethiopian tales. This is why this graft was so particularly successful.

The Promotion of Work

The success of the lodges in the American black milieu was also certainly due to the promotion of work in Masonic philosophy. In the same way African American oral tradition and Masonic oral culture found perfect agreement, the work ethic encouraged by Freemasonry found a favorable echo in the black population, where slavery had even depreciated its value. Paradoxically, the notion of work was rehabilitated this way in the context of postslavery America.

Anglo-Saxon Freemasonry is often designated with the term *the Craft,* a term that is peculiarly English in this context. In fact, people in other countries where Masonry had established a presence, particularly the French, found it easier to speak of a Masonic order. It so happens that the concept of the Craft brings to mind an art, know-how, a skilled trade, and thereby implicitly reflects the notion of work. Furthermore, British Freemasons aligned themselves with the "operative" tradition.

While the English had difficulty establishing a line of descent between the modern-type lodges created after 1717 and the trade lodges of earlier centuries, the Scottish lodges could legitimately claim a continuity between operative Freemasonry and speculative Freemasonry, between the lodges of the seventeenth century and those that appeared after 1736. In fact, the Grand Lodge of Scotland united around a hundred existing lodges, a large number of which were essentially operative in nature, which is to say their members were drawn together on a professional basis. Throughout its history, the Grand Lodge of Scotland has encouraged its members to build the "City." In a very concrete way it gave its sanction to the main buildings of Edinburgh by presiding over the official ceremonies of laying the first stones. In the eighteenth century several lord provosts of Edinburgh, who performed to some extent the same duties as mayors, were grand masters at the same time to ensure an easy transition. Even today the Lodge of Journeymen Masons n° 8 of Edinburgh proudly proclaims its operative origins.

The Protestant work ethic, which expanded rapidly at the time of the Industrial Revolution and throughout the nineteenth century, was an easy addition to this operative tradition of British and particularly Scottish Freemasonry during the ascent of the British middle class. Of course the American context was not the same. However, it is thinkable that the Protestant work ethic, which profoundly stamped British Freemasonry, also had an influence on the Prince Hall Masons. This would be of particular significance during the postslavery period. Thus, at the very time when labor had lost all credibility to the recently emancipated slaves, black Freemasonry offered an alternative to its members by rehabilitating a value that had been brought into disrepute by recent history.

Until the end of the Civil War, American blacks had not been spontaneously inclined to attribute any value to something that essentially belonged to the ideology of the former slaveholders. Now, given the fact that Prince Hall had obtained recognition for the first African lodge from an English and not an American grand lodge, it was easier for black American Freemasons to refer to British texts, in which work was a constant theme, rather than to white American ideology. They could find a justification for work in another tradition, that of Scotland and England, without having the humiliation of adopting the values of their former masters. This artifice permitted them to rid themselves of the weight of white American ideology and not be considered "Uncle Toms" (a reference to Harriet Beecher Stowe's famous novel *Uncle Tom's Cabin,* published in 1852), as blacks who adopted white values would later be called. The expression "Uncle Tom" later became a pejorative expression to describe blacks who were overly concerned about making compromises with white people.

In the name of Freemasonry, in the name of the battle waged by Prince Hall in his time to earn recognition for his lodge, black Masons encouraged their brothers to work together, to educate themselves, and to take their place in complete dignity in the society from which they

Fig. 3.1. Harriet Beecher Stowe, circa 1852

had been absolutely excluded. At the end of the Civil War, once slavery had been abolished in the United States of America, the rejection of work inevitably meant social exclusion. It was therefore imperative to reject the culture of slavery, which had until then encouraged passivity and opposed all notions of progress with great inertia. This was something the educator Booker T. Washington quickly realized when he undertook the task of restoring the value of work to his students.* Work should no longer be regarded as a form of debasement but as a factor for elevation. Thanks to work, every individual could restore his or her self-confidence.

> In our industrial teaching we kept three things in mind: first, that the student shall be so educated that he shall be enabled to meet conditions as they exist now, in the part of the South where he lives—in a word, to be able to do the things which the world wants done; second, that every student who graduates from the school shall have enough skill coupled with intelligence and moral character to enable him to make a living for himself and others; third, to send every graduate out feeling and knowing that labor is dignified and beautiful—to make each one labor instead of trying to escape it.[7]

Booker T. Washington was able to present this program with all the more authority as he was himself a former slave, as he was fighting to improve the lot of blacks in the Southern United States, and as he belonged to Freemasonry. Washington stated that work needed to be restored to honor not only among the black population but the white population of the South as well, as they had attempted to shirk labor during the time of slavery.[8]

By rehabilitating work and focusing on the oral tradition, Freemasonry allowed blacks to recover the dignity needed to realize their desire to become part of American society. Freemasonry was all the more apt at fulfilling this role as it had prompted many of its members to take part in the abolitionist struggle.

---

*For more on Booker T. Washington, see chapter 5, "Education."

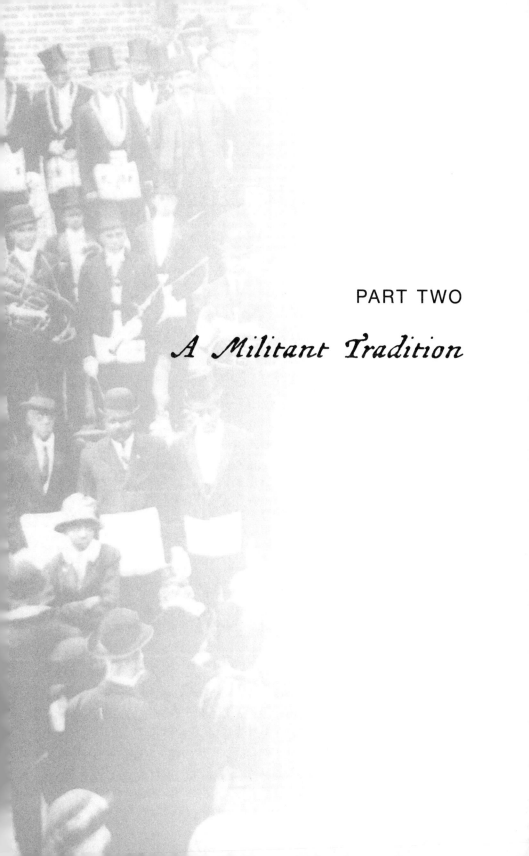

PART TWO

A Militant Tradition

FOUR

Abolitionism

Prince Hall, Abolitionist

Studying the history of abolitionism in the United States amounts to giving priority to study of the Northern states. In fact, even while some exceptions prove this rule, it was in the North of the United States where abolitionists could express themselves most freely. It was also in the North where the first black lodges were created.

In 1790 the number of slaves in the entire United States was 697,900; in 1800 the figure had climbed to 893,600; in 1810 the number was 1,191,300; in 1820 it was 1,538,000; and in 1860, 3,953,700.[1] The slave population therefore grew explosively over the nineteenth century, which is explained by the growing need in the South for manual labor, essentially to pick cotton. The division of slaves in the North and South is quite clear. According to Claude Fohlen, slaves represented 2.1 percent of the American population in the North and 33.5 percent in the South. In 1840 it was 0.83 percent in the North and 37.9 percent in the South. By 1860 it was 0 percent in the North and 38 percent in the South.[2] The evolution and proportion of free blacks with respect to the number of slaves in the United States is equally striking: in 1820 there were 1,538,000 slaves and 230,000 free blacks in the entire territory; in 1840 the respective numbers were 2,248,700 and 386,000; and in 1860, 3,953,700 slaves and 488,000 free blacks.[3]

Let's now take a look at the states that were the cradle of black Freemasonry: Massachusetts followed by Pennsylvania. In 1790 there were no slaves in Massachusetts and 3,707 in Pennsylvania. At this same time there were 5,369 free blacks living in Massachusetts and 6,531 in Pennsylvania.[4]

It was naturally free blacks who founded the first black lodge, African Lodge n° 459. While Massachusetts no longer had any slaves in its territory in 1790 that does not mean that all its inhabitants were abolitionists—far from it. There is no reason to believe that Freemasonry was synonymous with antislavery beliefs. The grand master of the white Grand Lodge of Massachusetts, Joseph Warren, who died in the Battle of Bunker Hill in 1775, advertised the sale of slaves in the *Boston Press,* as Grand Master Emmanuel Sullavou recalled somewhat bitterly in 1884 during the centennial celebration of the delivery of the African Lodge charter.[5] Sullavou contrasted Prince Hall with Joseph Warren: while the first fought for the betterment of his compatriots, the second "was cursing the race by enslaving it."[6] Sullavou's judgment is a bit harsh, though, knowing that Warren had promised Prince Hall a warrant to create the African Lodge, a promise he could not keep because of his death at Bunker Hill and one that his brothers of the Grand Lodge of Massachusetts were in a hurry to forget.

Starting in 1773, Prince Hall and his friends sent multiple petitions, which can now be found in the archives of the Massachusetts Historical Collection.[7] All requested the Massachusetts House of Representatives and the Senate to end the slave trade and slavery.[8] On the occasion of the centenary of the African Lodge, Grand Master Sullavou read the text of the 1777 petition in extenso, a text that was also cited by Donn A. Cass.[9] Prince Hall and seven other signatories, probably all members of the African Lodge, demanded that the House of Representatives put to a vote legislation putting an end to slavery in Massachusetts and stipulating that the children of slaves born on American soil, "in this land of liberty," must be automatically emancipated at the age of twenty-one.[10]

According to Joseph Cox, Paul Cuffee—who signed one of these petitions—was also a Freemason, thus certainly a member of the Prince Hall Lodge.[11] The son of a slave, a shipowner, and a sea captain, he later demanded voting rights for the free blacks of Massachusetts, and in 1810, he left Massachusetts in the company of thirty-eight other blacks for Sierra Leone, a colony created in 1787 by the English to inspire emancipated slaves to flock to an African land for the purpose of installing a new kind of plantation society.*[12]

Prince Hall involved his entire lodge in the fight against slavery, as shown by an incident that took place in 1788. As was then a common occurrence, free blacks had been pressed into service by force by a ship captain and enslaved anew.[13] It was common for captains to trick free blacks aboard their vessels, whom they would then imprison and sell as slaves, thereby realizing a fruitful commercial venture. It so happens that on this occasion one of the kidnapped blacks was a member of the African Lodge. On February 27, Prince Hall sent a petition to the Senate and House of Representatives of Massachusetts, which opened as follows:

> To the Honourable Senate and House of Representatives of the Commonwealth of Massachusetts Bay, in General Court assembled, on the 27th of February 1788.
>
> The Petition of a great number of BLACKS, Freemen of this Commonwealth, humbly sheweth,
>
> That your petitioners are fully alarmed at the inhuman and cruel treatment that three of our Brethren, free citizens of the town of Boston lately received. The Captain under pretense that his vessel was in distress on an Island in this harbour, having got them on board, put them in irons, and carried them off from their wives and children to be sold for slaves; this being the unhappy state of these poor men, what can your petitioners expect but to be treated in the same manner by the same sort of men? What then are our lives and our liberties worth, if they may be taken away in such a cruel and unjust manner as this? May it please your Honor's, we are not insensible, that the good laws of this state, forbid all such bad actions; notwithstanding we can assure your Honors, that many of our Free Blacks, that have entered on board of vessels as seamen, have been sold for slaves; and some of them we have heard from,

---

*The experiment was an outright failure, and would soon make itself evident.

but know not who carried them away. Hence it is that many of us, who are good seamen, are obliged to stay at home through fear, and the one half our time loiter through the streets, for want of employ; whereas if they were protected in that lawful calling, they might get a livelihood for themselves and theirs, which in the situation they are now in, they cannot. One more thing we would beg your leave to hint—that is that your petitioners have for some time past beheld with great grief ships cleared out from this harbor for Africa and there they either steal or cause others to steal our brothers & sisters, fill their ships holds full of unhappy men and women crowded together, then set out to find the best market, sell them there like sheep for the slaughter and then return here like honest men; after having sported with the lives and liberties of their fellow men and at the same time call themselves Christians. Blush, o Heavens! At this, these our weighty grievances! We cheerfully submit to your Honors, without dictating in the least, knowing by experience that your Honors have, and we trust will in your wisdom for us that justice that our present condition requires, as God and the good laws of this commonwealth shall dictate you. And as in duty bound, your petitoners shall ever pray. PRINCE HALL.[14]

According to Carter G. Woodson, the twenty-three signers of this petition were all members of the African Lodge. By comparing Woodson's list with Prince Hall's correspondence, I have found at least three: Matthew Cox, Joseph Hicks, and James Hicks (or Hicke).

Between July 6, 1787, and today, we have initiated four members into our lodge, Matthew Cox a mulatto aged 22 years on December 11, George Meller, 24 years, and Joseph Hicks, 23 years, on December 24, and James Hicke, 25 years, all black men of good morality, and who we hope shall be good men. . . .[15]

Woodson, the editor of *The Journal of Negro History*, also mentions a letter coming from a white Mason who was a member of the Portland n° 1 Lodge in Maine. This letter explains how the three men were put on sale as slaves on the island of Saint Bartholomew, but, miraculously, the merchant who bought them was also a Freemason, who freed them and returned them to Boston. Unfortunately Woodson does not provide any references for this letter.[16] The facts are therefore hard to verify, but it must be acknowledged that while it does not have what historians require in the way of solid proof, it is a good story.

In the speech he gave to his lodge brothers on June 24, 1797, Prince Hall referred to slavery and the slave trade. However, he believed that the situation for free blacks in Boston was preferable to that of slaves in the Antilles.

> My brethren, let us remember what a dark day it was with our African brethren six years ago, in the French West Indies. Nothing but the snap of the whip was heard from morning to evening; hanging, broken on the wheel, burning, and all manner of torture afflicted on these unhappy people, for nothing else but to gratify their master's pride, wantonness, and cruelty.[17]

It is true that Robespierre had just freed the slaves three years before in Santo Domingo and the French Antilles. However, Prince Hall was unaware that Napoleon would restore slavery in 1802 and that it would be necessary to wait until 1833 in the British Empire, and 1848 in France, for the definitive abolition of slavery. Prince Hall is looking at the situation in the Antilles with great optimism, even if he does not explicitly acknowledge the benefits of the French Revolution in this regard. This only leads him to condemn all the more the discriminations to which the free blacks of Boston were still victims. He was probably also influenced by the speeches and writings of the Englishmen William Wilberforce and Thomas Clarkson, or those of his neighbor Anthony Benezet of New England, all of whom were demanding an end to the slave trade at this time. However, Prince Hall was not calling on his brothers to rebel but to remain vigilant. Masons were expected to show respect for the social hierarchy while making sure that their dignity was not besmirched.

My brethren, let us pay all due respect to all whom God hath put in places of honor before us: do just and be faithful to them that hire you, and treat them with the respect they deserve but worship no man. Worship God; this is your duty as Christians and Masons.[18]

Prince Hall's main concern was the integration of his black brothers into Boston society. His reference to Christianity is no cause for surprise. It obviously represents a guarantee of respectability and reflects the desire of the Prince Hall Freemasons to obtain full freedom of worship for the black community. Quakers, Baptists, and Methodists had all come out in favor of religious education for the blacks in several states. However, the white Methodists of Boston had physically driven out their black members in 1787 by refusing them the best places and ordering them all to squeeze into the hall. Following this incident, Boston blacks created the Free African Society and established an independent Methodist church: the Independent Bethel Church. The founder and first bishop of this black church, Richard Allen, was a member of the African Lodge.[19] The African Methodist Episcopal Church was created in 1816 with the aid of several Freemasons.[20] Since 1789 the lodge had enjoyed the services of a chaplain, John Marrant, who gave his first sermon to the brothers on June 24, 1789. John Marrant seems to have obtained a good deal of personal assistance from Prince Hall, who gave him lodging in his home. Walkes quotes a letter that Prince Hall wrote to Lady Huntingdon, a Calvinist who assisted and backed Prince Hall.

We, the members of the African Lodge, had received him as a member of our honorable organization and named him chaplain of the lodge, which will greatly aid him in his missions, and can do much good for our organization.[21]

Recognition of Boston blacks would necessarily have to go through their recognition on the religious plane. Under these conditions, it is easy to see why Prince Hall and his friends gave such importance to Christian discourse. It was essential to publicize the sermons preached in the lodge. Marrant's preaching was published as the lodge grasped the necessity of consigning the word to paper to expand its prestige. This is yet another example of the decisive role played by Freemasonry to facilitate the transition of black Americans from an oral to a written tradition.

The career of Absalom Jones in Philadelphia provides another example of a rise in social status that clearly illustrates the symbiosis between Freemasonry, churches, and the black elite. In a fairly extraordinary manner, he managed to educate himself while still a slave. He learned to read thanks to an employee in his master's shop, then took night courses and purchased his freedom in 1784. He continued to work for his master, but as a salaried employee and not a slave, was able to buy property, and gradually made himself into an influential figure in the black community.[22] He served simultaneously as the first black reverend of the African Methodist Episcopal Church and as first worshipful master of the African Lodge of Philadelphia. He then became the lodge's first grand master when it constituted itself into a grand lodge. Prince Hall and Absalom Jones conceived of Masonic lodges as places of heightened awareness in the fight against slavery, if not as militant structures. A letter written by Prince Hall to Absalom Jones confirms this hypothesis.

> May God prosper you in . . . all your undertakings for the good of your African brethren. We here are not idle, but are doing what we can to promote the interest and good of our dear brethren that stand in such need at such a time as this.[23]

According to Peter Hinks, Prince Hall and his friends contributed to the abolition of the slave trade in Massachusetts by rising up in 1788 against the sale of those three black men discussed earlier (see pp. 38–39).[24] Jones and his friends could only have acted similarly in Pennsylvania.

Black Mason Abolitionism between 1800 and 1860

An Appeal to the Colored Citizens of the World appeared in 1829. This was a veritable call to revolt launched by Freemason David Walker, a free black and a native of Wilmington, North Carolina, who had moved to Boston around 1822, probably right after having taken part in the insurrection organized by Denmark Vesey. Walker, a close friend of Vesey's, ran the risk of being arrested and even executed if he had stayed.

Denmark Vesey had purchased his freedom in 1800 and would most likely have ended up as a peaceful carpenter in Charleston, South Carolina, if he had not decided to organize a slave revolt. For several years, in the company of several friends but also, without knowing it, surrounded by spies, Vesey had been collecting weapons of all kinds, from simple pickax handles to daggers. He had requested aid from Haiti in the preparation of this revolt and had even set a first date: the second Sunday of July 1822. He vainly tried to postpone it for a month when he got wind of a betrayal, but his collaborators, scattered over a wide region, were not all informed of the change and were thereby caught in the trap. At least 139 blacks were arrested and 37 executed.[25] Walker, Vesey, and several other organizers of this rebellion were deeply involved in the African Methodist Episcopal Church, created in 1816. By persecuting the organizers of the movement, the authorities seized an opportunity to remove the most active members from a church they deemed subversive.

In his *Appeal,* Walker addressed black slaves although most were illiterate. Like Vesey, he incited them to rebel and justified resorting to violence against their white masters when they deemed it necessary.

Fig. 4.1. Denmark Vesey (1767–1822)

Fig. 4.2. The home of Denmark Vesey in Charleston, South Carolina

Hinks, who devoted a book to the life and work of David Walker, believes that Walker not only knew Vesey but most likely took part in his plan to foment insurrection. The fact remains that after this episode Walker found refuge in Boston, where he met blacks who had managed to carve a path into the white society of Massachusetts. Hinks underscores the role played by the Freemasonry of Prince Hall in their integration and awakened awareness. According to him the lodges of Prince Hall were even the sole black organizations to have worked in this direction until the creation of the African Methodist Episcopal Church. The black lodges stood out completely from the traditional American lodges.

> The African lodges were much more than simple replicas of white institutions . . . they were black institutions primarily created to serve a black cause. Contrary to white Masonry, African Masonry takes root in its fight against slavery and racial discrimination.[26]

Even if Hinks tends to overestimate the role played by black Freemasonry (by drawing inspiration from the since severely criticized book by Grimshaw), it is certain that black lodges played a much more socially significant role than that of white lodges. It can be seen that the major players of the black community of this era were Freemasons.

This was clearly the case for Walker, initiated on July 28, 1826, in the African Lodge of Boston, thus three years before the publication of his *Appeal to the Colored Citizens of the World.* He was raised to the grade of master that same year.[27] The *Appeal* was distributed in Georgia, Virginia, South Carolina, and Louisiana. In 1830 four blacks were arrested in New Orleans and accused of distributing the *Appeal.* Repressive laws against free blacks were passed during this period, probably partially in response to Walker's pamphlet, which was most definitely not advocating nonviolence.

David Walker was part of the same lodge as John Hilton, grand master of the Grand African Lodge n° 459 of Massachusetts from 1836 to 1847.[28] A barber by trade, Hilton was a diehard abolitionist and a member of the Anti-Slavery Society. Also members at that time were the Reverend Thomas Paul, minister of the first African Baptist church, as well as Walker Lewis and James Barbados, also both barbers—all three sharing the same fierce abolitionist sentiments as Hilton. This gives us reason to think that there is something about the barbering trade that predisposes its practitioners to Freemasonry and the fight against slavery; truly the ways of Freemasonry are sometimes inscrutable.

Walker, in the company of a large number of the brothers of this lodge, was an activist in the Massachusetts General Colored Association (MGCA), an organization created in 1828 for the purpose of fighting for improved living conditions for the blacks of Massachusetts. This association considered itself to be a branch of a New England abolitionist organization, the New England Anti-Slavery Society. A lodge member, Thomas Dalton, presided over this association. In 1828, Walker gave a speech before an MGCA assembly calling for the organization of a black-directed movement to fight against slavery. The members of the Prince Hall Lodge actively contributed to the writing of *Freedom's Journal,* a black abolitionist newspaper published in Boston. Furthermore, the Prince Hall Lodge participated annually in the parade celebrating the end of the slave trade in 1807.

It is therefore legitimate to speak, with Hinks, of this "unprecedented institutional interconnectedness among black communities in the Northeast" established by the lodges of Prince Hall.[29] Not only did the lodges serve to tighten the bonds between the primary players of Boston's black community, they also created links with other states, including Pennsylvania, soon followed by New York. For example, James Bias, a member of the Prince Hall Lodge of Philadelphia, was active in the Philadelphia Anti-Slavery Society and founded the Committee of Vigilance of Philadelphia in 1838.[30] The Prince Hall Lodges formed a veritable network that encouraged not only the circulation of ideas but also that of people, both fugitive slaves and free blacks. Several lodges served as stations on the famous Underground Railroad, the clandestine network that organized the flight of slaves from the Southern states to the North. Lewis Hayden, the Prince Hall grand master, was responsible for this network in the Boston region.[31]

As a general rule the Prince Hall Masons gave primacy to the integration of blacks into the society of their time by devoting themselves to the most pressing issue—which is to say the fight against slavery—and by encouraging the entrance of free blacks into workplaces and churches, in other words into the society of the Northern states. However, it is clear that the grouping of black Masons into specific lodges could also predispose them to separatism in the society of their era. The Prince Hall Freemasons fraternized more with the non-Masonic members of the black community than with white Freemasons, who haughtily ignored them, with but a few rare exceptions, as in New Jersey (see chapter 12).* Just as did other members of the black community, the Freemasons of Prince Hall also indulged in the separatist temptation and at several times nourished the dream of founding an ideal colony far from American shores.

Prince Hall personally signed the petition of January 14, 1787, addressed to the Massachusetts House of Representatives, soliciting financial assistance for the establishment of an African colony in Sierra Leone.[32] At this same time, according to Cox, the sea captain, shipowner/builder, and Freemason Paul Cuffee was also in favor of African colonization as he believed the lot of free blacks would improve if they left the United States.[33] The Prince Hall Masons were soon

---

*According to Voorhis, *Negro Masonry in the United States,* 77, several white abolitionist Freemasons looked favorably on the admission of blacks into their lodges.

seduced by the idea of emigration in their haste to flee a racist America.

The history of the creation of the National Grand Lodge or Compact Grand Lodge in 1847 forms the best example of the separatist mentality of the years preceding the Civil War. In fact, the creation of a federal type of obedience was not as harmless as it appeared. The creation of a transversal structure meant that the grand lodges of each state would lose some of their autonomy. However, if the sole problem had been of an organizational nature, it would not have taken such amplitude; Walkes correctly explained the appearance of the National or Compact Grand Lodge by the racist context of the era.

It would be helpful to push this analysis further. When we closely examine the situation in New York it is easy to understand that the quarrel was not solely founded on form, even if Masons have a habit of doing so. One year after the creation of the National Grand Lodge, therefore in 1848, the Grand Lodge of New York split in two, or to be more precise, lodges left the Boyer Grand Lodge, criticizing it for its support of the National Grand Lodge. The dissident lodges called themselves the Grand Lodge of New York (National Union). The Boyer Grand Lodge then adopted the name of United Grand Lodge.[34] Now the original title of the first New York Grand Lodge is not meaningless. It was no accident that the members opted to take the name of the president of the Republic of Haiti, Jean-Pierre Boyer, for their lodge. The independence of Haiti, which had caused such alarm among the countries of Europe because it had crowned a slave revolt, by all evidence was a source of rejoicing for a large number of Prince Hall Masons.

The flight to Haiti was a myth, if we can rely on the figures. In 1826, according to Hinks, six thousand African Americans moved to Haiti, but one-third of this number returned to the United States.[35] Several Prince Hall Freemasons, such as James Forten and Richard Allen, led the Haitian Emigration Society. It was the Bostonian John Hilton, grand master of the African Grand Lodge of Massachusetts, who took the initiative to create the National Grand Lodge, probably to supply Masons with a stronger and therefore more effective tool, but also most likely to facilitate exchanges between black Americans wishing to relocate to Haiti. This is probably what the black Freemasons who chose to secede from the Boyer Grand Lodge found so objectionable. The reasons for their departure were never explained, or at least never consigned to writing where historians could benefit from them.

We can assume, however, that these Masons were not only sensitive to the vice of form, which is to say the unwarranted creation of a federal type of structure, but also were guided by ideological considerations. Not all were supporters of emigration to Haiti or of separatism; some preferred to play the integration card and even more specifically favored a merger with the white grand lodges. The creation of the National Grand Lodge widened the divide between white Masons and black Masons, because it was in contradiction with the customary mode of organization of the grand lodges and because it boosted the separatist option by giving black Freemasons a stronger organization.

The National Grand Lodge ceased activities in 1877 when a convention of fifteen Prince Hall Grand Lodges decided to dissolve it and proclaim the absolute sovereignty of each grand lodge. It is hardly likely that the schism between Latin Freemasonry and Anglo-Saxon Freemasonry that arose when the Grand Orient of France removed from its constitutions the obligation to believe "in the immortality of the soul" had any real bearing on this decision. However, it is possible that the Prince Hall Masons had tried this way to come together with the white American grand lodges, who, with the United Grand Lodges of England, were holding up the supporters of freedom of conscience for public ridicule. In fact, in May 1878, all the black grand lodges met in convention for the purpose "of putting an end to all the differences that can exist in our Order and to form, if possible, a more satisfactory union for all."[36] The Prince Hall Masons were content with proclaiming their solidarity but without feeling any need to establish anew any federal grand lodge that could frighten white Freemasons.

The creation of the National Grand Lodge had triggered sharp reactions at the time. In 1870 the grand master of Pennsylvania deplored the fact that it was the youngest Masons who were most suspicious of "a union of all the colored Masons of the United States," and thus the most distrustful of the National Grand Lodge.[37] The debate continues even today among the historians of Prince Hall. It is significant that

Walkes, while condemning the existence of the National Grand Lodge, found mitigating circumstances for its founders and that Grand Master Sullavou, in his commemoration address, preferred to connect it with the figure of John Hilton rather than mention the very history of the National Grand Lodge. Mindful of Masonic legitimacy, Grand Master Sullavou, just like Walkes later, was at pains to avoid recalling a somewhat turbulent past. However, he had no hesitation about singing the praises of the National Grand Lodge's founder, a dyed-in-the-wool antislavery proponent and enthusiastic supporter of Haitian president Boyer.

> He led an upright and blameless life as a man and a Mason thus being a shining example to all in every good cause, an honored member and worker identified as a member to the day of his death with the original anti-slavery society, where were wont to assemble Garrison, Loring, Jackson, Phillips, and other philanthropists who were engaged in the war against slavery.[38]

I mentioned in chapter 3 another Mason who displayed separatist tendencies, Martin Robison Delany, who proclaimed Freemasonry's black origins.

> I believe it is a settled and acknowledged fact; conceded by all intelligent writers and speakers, that to Africa is the world indebted for its knowledge of the mysteries of Ancient Freemasonry.[39]

Delany was made a major in the 104th South Carolina Regiment during the Civil War, then a lieutenant colonel. Born in 1812, in Charleston, Virginia (now West Virginia), he boasted that he descended from a lineage of African kings and chiefs. Whatever his lineage may have been, he was the first black American to obtain a diploma from the medical school of Harvard University. He spent time in England, where he was accepted into the prestigious Royal Society.

Delany was supportive of the emigration of American blacks. He believed that instead of imitating whites they should cultivate their differences and be proud of their race, a word he used without any restraint.

> We have then inherent traits, attributes—so to speak—and native characteristics, peculiar to our race—whether pure or mixed blood—and all that is required of us is to cultivate these and develop them in their purity, to make them desirable and emulated by the rest of the world.[40]

Delany's remarks fall fully into a separatist philosophy. He exalts the black race and asserts its superiority, thereby making himself guilty of racism in turn. Delany does not demand equality for blacks and whites for he has no interest in this equality. In 1860 he was the coauthor of a book titled *Search for a Place, Black Separatism and Africa*. However, he later abandoned his dreams of emigration to Africa and at that point was not entirely insensitive to the virtues of integration. He founded an organization in Pittsburgh for the furtherance of the education of black children, the Pittsburgh, Pennsylvania, African Education Society,[41] and wrote numerous letters to the governors of the Southern states seeking to bring their attention to the plight of the blacks.

The Civil War

In 1865, Delany gave a speech before a gathering of around five hundred people in a non-Masonic setting. He called on the black slaves to rebel and criticized them for accepting their lot toiling for white masters. He said that if he were a slave like them he would make it a duty to sow disorder on the plantations and that no fear of punishment would restrain him.[42] At this time Delany was not prepared to make any compromises with whites. However, he did accept fighting for President Lincoln against the Confederates. It is not known if Lincoln was aware of Delany's Masonic ties. Lincoln was not wild about enlisting blacks into his armies. Although Lincoln was not a Freemason, he was friends with a certain number of them, quite certainly all of whom were white. Paul Bessel recalls that he gave the funeral oration for Bowling Green, a worshipful master of the New Salem Lodge in Kentucky in 1842.[43]

Of course not all the Prince Hall Masons played a decisive role during the Civil War, but this was indeed the case for some individuals like Martin Robison Delany and the Massachusetts grand master Lewis Hayden. As this latter was a personal friend of Massachusetts governor John Albion Andrew, a confirmed abolitionist, his activity had considerable scope. Hayden ran the Committee of Vigilance in Boston and provided a relay for the Underground Railroad. When Governor Andrew called for black volunteers to enlist in the 54th Massachusetts Volunteer Infantry Regiment, he quite naturally turned to Grand Master Hayden. The 54th Regiment was the first to be composed entirely of black soldiers. It was this regiment to which was attached the first military lodge of Prince Hall in 1863. According to Walkes, this lodge, which followed the regiment on its maneuvers, was the origin for the South Carolina Grand Lodge.[44]

Williamson cites another military lodge, Phoenix Lodge n° 1, attached to the 29th Regiment of black volunteers in 1864.[45] Walkes confirms the existence of the lodge and reproduced the text of the charter granted in 1864 to postulants belonging to the 29th Regiment by the famous Compact Grand Lodge of New York, in other words the National Grand Lodge.[46] The worshipful master of this lodge was Alexander Newton, the child of a slave father and a free mother, pastor of the African Methodist Episcopal Church, the same church that played such a major role for men like David Walker. These two lodges are the only ones whose existence has been established for certain. Others may have existed in ephemeral fashion, but there is nothing to prove it.

It is certain that the Prince Hall lodges multiplied to a good extent during the three years following the end of the Civil War. At the time of emancipation Prince Hall lodges existed in fourteen states. Loretta Williams shows, with supporting figures, that the Reconstruction period was an extremely prosperous one for black Freemasonry. The Prince Hall Grand Lodge of Illinois, founded in 1867, included fifteen lodges in the city of Chicago alone in 1885.[47] This can be explained by the desire of African Americans to break out of their stalemate and improve their social situation.

It so happens that Freemasonry offered them an exceptionally welcoming structure in the society of that era. Few organizations allowed them to take the floor to practice democracy in a convivial setting. The Independent Order of Odd Fellows, a mutual-aid society also known as just the Odd Fellows, worked the same way, although it wasn't, strictly speaking, a Masonic organization. All the same it was entirely inspired by the operational system of the lodges and included numerous Freemasons among its members. On the other hand, white American Freemasonry kept its distance from the Prince Hall lodges, and its distrust of them was only doubled.

While the lodges allowed men from all walks of life to spend time together, they rarely brought men of opposing political sensibilities together. Just like the patriots and loyalists of the American Revolutions the pro- and antislavery supporters carefully kept their distance before, during, and after the Civil War. When author Allen Roberts expresses amazement at the Masonic miracle by showing how Northern Masons came to the aid of their Southern brethren to assist them in dealing with the heavy financial losses they incurred from the war and the abolition of slavery, he is speaking of the help given by white Masons to other white Masons![48]

Harold Van Buren Voorhis, however, cites the example of the white abolitionists of New Jersey who were in favor of accepting blacks into their lodges. It seems, though, that this is just another instance of the exception confirming the rule.[49] Moreover, when, after much difficulty, a lodge that accepted blacks was created in the white Grand Lodge of New Jersey, only black Masons remained as members of this lodge.

The Freemasons of Prince Hall were therefore involved to varying degrees and more or less effectively in the Civil War. However, it is certain that their essential role was the work of educating former slaves and even free blacks over a period of years to realize their new status and permit them to find their place in an American society that was enmeshed in the throes of change.

The Memory of Slavery

In 1847 the United Grand Lodge of England made a gesture aimed at former slaves: they replaced in their constitutions the expression "free-born man" with "free man." It would be a mistake to underestimate the importance of this nuance. Great Britain had abolished the slave trade in 1807 and slavery in 1833, some fifteen years before France, and had begun hunting the ships that still plied the waves with their slave cargoes. British Freemasonry could not maintain its decency by remaining the sole institution in the kingdom by continuing to treat former slaves like inferior beings, unworthy of initiation. However, the United Grand Lodge of England could not encroach any further than that on the ancient *Landmark,* meaning one of its fundamental principles, according to which only freemen could become Freemasons. It therefore found a subtle compromise: the ban still blocked slaves but not emancipated slaves. Moreover, it was a lodge of Barbados planters that encouraged the United Grand Lodge of England to take this step.

One would think that American Freemasons would have followed in the footsteps of the United Grand Lodge of England. Officially, at least, they did nothing of the kind. Quite the contrary; when Albert Mackey in 1857 drew up the list of Landmarks that all proper American Freemasons would be expected to respect, he reinforced the ban raised by James Anderson on the initiation of slaves.

Landmark n° 18. Certain qualifications of candidates for initiation are derived from a Landmark of the Order. These qualifications are that he shall be a man, unmutilated, free-born and of mature age. That is to say, a woman, a cripple, or a slave or one born in slavery, is disqualified for the initiation into the Rites of Freemasonry.[50]

These words carry a heavy weight in the context of America just before the Civil War. There was no question of white lodges accepting blacks as members, no matter who they were. This ban must have served generations of white Masons as a pretext for shutting their doors to black Freemasons. This also serves to explain why the Prince Hall Freemasons were at such pains to find the Ethiopian roots of Freemasonry and to discourse on the various kinds of slaves, as Delany did. Visibly irked by the foundational text of Anderson's *Constitutions,* the black Grand Lodge of New York found a replacement for the word *slave: eunuch!* In fact, in the list of Landmarks it added to its constitutions and statutes, it adopted the following wording.

> Landmark n° 9. That men made Masons must at least be twenty-one years of age, free-born, of good report, hale and sound, not deformed or dismembered, and no woman, no eunuch.

On December 3, 1879, the grand master also commented in his speech to the officers of the Grand Lodge of New York on the Masonic ban that affected slaves. However, with the change of context there was no longer any need to speak of eunuchs instead of slaves, several years after slavery had been abolished in the United States. The grand master indulged in a metaphysical reflection on the very notions of slavery and freedom.

> We of this country claim to believe that "all men are created equal and are endowed by their creator with certain inalienable rights, among which are life, liberty, and the pursuit of happiness." Or, in other words, we believe that liberty is a birthright: that as such it is inalienable; that is, we cannot give it up; it may be taken from us, but it was ours at the first. The Great Creator of the Universe never made a slave. God made man free, man made man slave.[51]

The New York grand master repeated the argument advanced by Delany a few years earlier: only those who voluntarily renounced their freedom, which is not the case with American blacks, are unworthy of becoming Masons. Black Masons could not be held responsible for the violence committed against them—it is tempting to add, whether by African rulers or white slavers. In the essay he published shortly after the Civil War ended, John Jones, without mincing any words, rehabilitated black Freemasonry, which had been treated with scorn by the white grand lodges. He even described the white Masons as "poor prejudiced simpletons!"[52] He even borders on anti-Semitism and racism in general when he states that an educated black is better than an ignorant Jew or Indian. However, with great optimism he observes the social rise of the former slaves and salutes their determination and courage.

> We have advanced from actual slavery and barbarism to a high state of civilization. . . . Everywhere the black man has sprung of his own free will and determination, in spite of Church and State (for both were against him), from the position of slavery and its consequences of every description, to the bar, the pulpit, the lecture-room, the professorship, the degrees of M.D. and D.D., and to the bar of the Supreme Court of the United States.[53]

Black American Masons honored the former slaves and commemorated abolition. Among many other examples, the Celestial Lodge n° 3 placed a spray of flowers on the grave of Frederick Douglass, slave and author of a renowned autobiography.[54]

Most fortunately, a large number of black Masons did not satisfy themselves with fine words and pious, nostalgic commemorations, even those intended to preserve the memory of slavery, but undertook the task of educating their brothers and, on a wider scale, all black children.

FIVE

Education

Prince Hall and His Colleagues

The Masons of Prince Hall granted a place of top importance to education. Prince Hall introduced the topic in two speeches he gave as the worshipful master of the African Lodge in 1792 and 1797. It is the Mason's duty to educate himself and to educate others. Prince Hall observed that blacks in Massachusetts and the other states were denied access to education. To begin, he advised his lodge brothers to consider this point:

> Although you are deprived of the means of education, yet you are not deprived of the means of meditation.[1]

He added that Masons had a duty to ensure their children received the education that they had not received themselves and to encourage the creation of schools for blacks. He cited the example of Philadelphia, Pennsylvania, where a specific school had been created, paying homage to that "friendly city," undoubtedly alluding to the Society of Friends, as the Quakers are known. The most famous Quaker, William Penn, had even given his name to that colony.

> But in the meantime, let us lay by our recreations, and all superfluities, so that we may have that to educate our rising generation, which was spent in those follies. Make you this beginning, and who

knows but God may raise up some friend or body of friends, as he did in Philadelphia, to open a school for the blacks here, as that friendly city has done there.[2]

Prince Hall was not satisfied with fine words. On October 4, 1796, he sent a letter to the Boston selectmen demanding the creation of a school for black children.[3] Under his impetus, that school was actually created in 1800.

The Boston Prince Hall Freemasons in the Nineteenth Century

In Prince Hall's footsteps, several Freemasons played a major role in the field of education. In chapter 2, I cited the case of Prince Saunders, another member of the African Lodge, who founded the Belles Lettres Society and, after meeting the famous English abolitionist William Wilberforce, contributed to the implementation of an educational system in Haiti. I should also mention Don Carlos Bassett, who headed the Institute for Colored Youth in Philadelphia in 1869 and then performed the duties of consul for Haiti, not to overlook educators in the Southern states like Grand Master Norris Wright Cuney of Texas.[4] Bassett's example corroborates the involvement of the Prince Hall Masons in Haiti, regarded as almost the Promised Land.

There is then John Peterson, who was both a man of the cloth and a teacher. He was the first black educator appointed in New York. He taught in the school for black children created in that city between 1855 and 1858. At the same time he held positions of responsibility in the Grand Lodge of New York, where he served as grand chaplain from 1855 to 1858, grand secretary in 1859, and grand treasurer from 1860 to 1869, before, during, and after the Civil War.[5]

On December 20, 1883, the grand master of the Prince Hall Grand Lodge of Boston, Thomas Thomas, focused his speech on the importance of education for the Prince Hall Masons.

We must remember that our institution, philosophical in character, cannot safely exist without the extension of education to a still
higher and higher position. It is consequently clear that it is our
duty to encourage and advance education.[6]

He proceeded to provide a detailed list: according to him, 4,239
schools had been created between 1865 and 1870, thereby permitting
the schooling of 247,333 black children. Out of these 4,239 establishments, 1,324 had been funded by the black community. Also, according
to him, in 1870 there were 74 establishments of higher learning with
8,147 students, and 91 trade schools containing 1,750 students. The
black population would have paid $200,000 of the $1,002,896 necessary for the funding of these institutions.

The very fact he provides such precise figures shows that Masons
took a very close interest in the education of all black children, not only
the children of Masons, and this was on a very practical level. However,
no report was made of any precise financial contributions to the educational field on the part of the Prince Hall Masons, who most likely did
not have the means.[7]

Two Pioneers in the Field of Education

Booker T. Washington and
William Edward Burghardt "W. E. B." Du Bois

The two most famous Prince Hall Masons in the field of education are
undoubtedly Booker T. Washington and William Edward Burghardt
Du Bois, whose views in this regard were not always in accord. Both
men were "made Freemasons on sight" because of their social activities,
a very significant event. The Prince Hall Freemasons were quite sensitive to the two men's actions in society and thereby granted them spontaneous acknowledgment. They begged both men to join their ranks,
somewhat in the same way—in a different time and place—that the
famous Lodge of the Nine Sisters had asked Voltaire to honor them
with his presence, by reason of his philosophical writings. The fact that
Washington and Du Bois were solicited by the grand lodges is particu-

larly significant. It demonstrates the importance given to education by the Masons of Prince Hall.

Washington's career deserves a brief detour, for it is revealing of the notions of these educational pioneers as well as those of the Prince Hall Masons who wished to recognize their merits by enlisting them into their obedience. We have a better knowledge of Washington thanks to his autobiography, *Up from Slavery,* which was published in 1901 and recounts his career as a teacher and educator.

Washington was born a slave on a Virginia plantation and freed in 1865 at the end of the Civil War, when he was nine years old. He explained how the children of his age were suddenly capable of "getting into paradise," to quote his expression, and receiving some schooling, at least in theory. The education of black children was all the more vital as

Fig. 5.1. Booker T. Washington (1856–1915)

very few of the parents of that generation could read or write and were therefore in no position to help them. The motivation for education was so strong among the black population that the inhabitants of the village took up a collection to create the first school for black children and hire a teacher, and they took turns giving him lodging. Washington tells how in order to gain admission to the Hampton Normal and Agricultural Institute in Virginia—an institution created to serve the poorest black citizens—he agreed to sweep the building and work as a janitor to cover the costs of his room and board.

While Washington undoubtedly cut an exceptional figure in his thirst for learning, the role in which he truly excelled was that of an educator. He decided to devote his life to the education of his fellow blacks. To do this he had the ambition to create an establishment of such renown that the president of the United States would visit it personally to pay homage. This is what did indeed happen in 1898 when President William McKinley, who was also a Freemason, paid a visit to the Tuskegee Institute, the establishment that Washington had founded some seventeen years earlier.

A year later McKinley gave a speech before an assembly of white Masons to celebrate the centenary of another Freemason president, one who had employed a large number of slaves on his plantation, George Washington. It should be noted, though, that McKinley took pains to acknowledge the work of his black brother Booker T. Washington and encouraged him on several occasions to speak before meetings of white businessmen.

If we realize what great importance Prince Hall gave to the education of black children it is easy to grasp the mission with which Washington felt himself invested. Whether Freemasonry influenced his educational concepts or whether these concepts had delighted Masons so greatly that they sought to display their gratitude by conferring Washington with the title of Mason is of no import in the long run. What matters is the point where the notions of the militant pedagogue and those of the Prince Hall Freemasons converge. Education should not confine itself to teaching from books; it must be complete. In the context of the postslavery period, it was necessary to take in hand not only the intellectual education of children but also their knowledge of the basics of hygiene. On several occasions the director of the Tuskegee Institute made it a point of honor to teach children how to use a toothbrush!

The institute was coeducational and, something quite noteworthy for the time, did not seem to offer different lessons to boys and girls. Education had to be complete: "education of the hand, head and heart."[8] Intellectual and manual education went hand in hand. Every student of the Tuskegee Institute had to receive professional training in tandem with a traditional education.[9] It was particularly important to provide students with certification so they could find employment. In this way Washington, like the Prince Hall Masons, helped blacks to gain entry into the professional fields and advance on the road to emancipation. To do this it was necessary to meet one particular challenge: rehabilitate the notion of work.

Paradoxically, it was another Prince Hall Freemason, W. E. B. Du Bois, who voiced the sharpest criticisms of Washington's notions on education. Born a freeman in the state of Massachusetts, Du Bois,

Fig. 5.2. W. E. B. Du Bois (1868–1963)

contrary to Washington, was able to benefit from a public education followed by studies in a university. With a degree from Harvard University,* Du Bois became a professor of history, economics, and sociology at Atlanta University, where he said he became fully acquainted with the South.

Contrary to Washington, who dedicated his entire life to education, Du Bois was also a political activist. Founder of the National Association for the Advancement of Colored People (NAACP), he criticized Washington for not sufficiently politicizing the education debate, for making too many concessions to Southern businessmen, and for not connecting the struggle for the education of blacks to the campaign for civil rights. He was especially critical of the Atlanta Compromise, in which Washington accepted the relinquishing of certain civil rights, particularly the right to vote, in exchange for economic guarantees that the Southern businessmen would grant, according to the following famous but fairly ambiguous expression.

> In all things purely social, we can be as separate as the five fingers, and yet one as the hand in all things essential to mutual progress.[10]

On the other hand, while recognizing the merits of the Tuskegee Institute, Du Bois refused to restrict the education of blacks to learning a trade. As a product of higher education himself, he wanted young blacks to enjoy access to the same level of education. He rejected the acquisition of know-how instead of knowledge as a third-rate education. With a very modern outlook, he insisted on the necessity of educating teachers, including the teachers of trade schools like the Tuskegee Institute, by suggesting they learn the fundamentals. To him knowledge was truly perceived as liberating, because it is stripped of any aspect of race a priori. With humor, Du Bois stated, "I sit with Shakespeare, and he winces not."[11]

Frederic Monroe, the secretary in charge of external affairs for the

---

*Washington asserted that he too received a degree from Harvard in recognition of his professional experience.

Prince Hall Grand Lodge of Massachusetts before becoming grand master in 1903, shared Du Bois' views on the matter and like him was a member of his Niagara Movement.[12] Monroe did not hold back in his criticisms of Washington, condemning him for not working hard enough to have the education of blacks be made a responsibility of the public.[13]

However, even while their tools were different, Washington and Du Bois often carved the same stone. Du Bois condemned the crimes of slavery without inciting the blacks to seek revenge. While he believed in the duty of memory, he recommended to the black men and women of his time to avoid becoming mired in their complaints about the past and instead to turn their eyes toward the future. Like Washington, he thought that education should play a major role in the fight against racial prejudices.

> When truth shall have come into her own, through the media of education, the color line will be swept into oblivion of a dark and disgraceful past.[14]

Du Bois desired for all Americans to collaborate with no thought as to the differences of skin color on the construction of a republic that gave everyone an even chance. "With these duties in mind and with a spirit of self-help, mutual aid, and cooperation, the two races should strive side by side to realize the ideals of the republic and make this truly a land of equal opportunity for all men."[15] He preached tolerance and hoped that the spirit of fraternity would eventually prevail over that of racism.

> Catholicity and tolerance, reason and forbearance can today make the world-old dream of human brotherhood approach realization.[16]

"I have a dream," as someone who attained an even greater renown would say later, yet both Washington and Du Bois subscribed to the three values that were equally dear to Freemasons: liberty, equality, and fraternity. It is for the reason that they shared the same humanist values that the Prince Hall Masons made the two men honorary Masons, ignoring those things on which they did not agree.

From the Beginning of the Twentieth Century
to the Present

Later the Prince Hall Lodges would encourage their members to learn trades that would facilitate their entry into the work world, using specific actions in favor of Masons, as was the case with the Celestial Lodge n° 3 of New York. This lodge founded a school for its members, the Craftsmen School, which remained active from 1905 to 1947. This school provided a set of disciplines that were taught every Sunday for forty-two years until the "officers of the Grand Lodge lost all interest in the splendid work they had achieved during all those years," as Harry A. Williamson, grand historian of the Prince Hall Grand Lodge of New York, notes with some bitterness.[17]

The speech given in 1910 by Edward Bruce to the Craftsmen's Club in the Masonic Temple of New York (a speech whose somewhat exacerbated nationalism bordered at times on racism with respect to white Masons, as noted in chapter 3) inspired the Prince Hall Masons to promote education—not only trade schools but scientific studies at a high level as well—in a way that was more in Du Bois' footsteps than those of Booker T. Washington.[18]

Among the Masonic papers he collected throughout his life,* Williamson included press clippings of articles concerning the various public activities of Prince Hall Masons. The collection holds, for example, an article from the *Chronicle* dated March 22, 1947, reporting on the aid given by Prince Hall Masons in southern California to young graduates. The grand master of the Prince Hall Lodge of California, George R. Vaughns, announced to an assembly of worshipful masters meeting at the Los Angeles temple that a collection would be raised, fully legal, that would put in place a system of loans over periods of six months, a year, or longer, for young students. The grand master paid homage on this occasion to the Broadway Federal Savings and Loan Association.

---

*As the grand historian of the New York Grand Lodge, Williamson was the author of several books on Prince Hall Freemasonry. His private archives were donated, as the Harry A. Williamson Papers, to the Schomburg Center for Research in Black Culture, which is part of the New York Public Library.

This aid would not only be awarded to the children of Masons, but to all California youth.[19]

Prince Hall Masons also gave support to Texas teachers who were on strike demanding the same pay for the same work as was given to white teachers. In 1939 a committee of the Texas Grand Lodge cited as example the strike of black teachers in Louisville, Kentucky, as well as teacher strikes in Alabama, Tennessee, and Louisiana, and concluded their meeting with the hope that this movement would be followed throughout the entire Southern United States. The committee reminded the Prince Hall members that "the only way to obtain justice in any field of work is to fight, organize, and pay the price."[20] As can be seen, the Prince Hall Masons did not content themselves with mutual-aid activities alone but also appealed to their members' activist inclinations.

The Prince Hall Grand Lodges gave financial support to the educational field. Walkes points out that, in the year 1982 alone, the United Supreme Council of the 33rd Degree of the Southern Jurisdiction of Prince Hall gave grants totaling one hundred thousand dollars to black institutions of higher learning. Furthermore, Walkes provides a list of the lodges connected to an institute of higher learning.

Are any Lodges attached to Colleges and Universities?

There are a few:

The Jon G. Lewis Jr. Lodge, Southern University in Baton Rouge, Louisiana; "Cap" Johnson Lodge at Alcorn State University; Wayne Williams Lodge at Southern University and a Lodge at Mississippi Valley State University, all three under the jurisdiction of Stringer Grand Lodge, Prince Hall Affiliation (PHA) in Mississippi.[21]

Today there are several Prince Hall Lodges offering education grants to the children of their members and sometimes to other students to pursue university studies. Let's mention at least two specific cases, that of the Brooklyn lodge, which officially bestows a check annually to a student during the opening ceremony of the chosen college, and that of the Barbados lodges. The Austin Belle Junior Memorial Scholarship

Fund is an association that has been in existence in Barbados since 1993 and regularly grants three-year scholarships to the children of Masons. As of today, four have already been awarded. This initiative was undertaken by Austin Belle and his wife, following the accidental death of their son. All the Barbados lodges today contribute to this fund, although it is the specific responsibility of Lodge n° 1.* These are but two examples among many. Many United States lodges finance similar operations.

We have traveled a long road from Prince Hall's first speeches in which he encouraged his brothers to examine themselves, educate themselves, and promote the education of black children not only in the North where the free blacks lived but also in the slaveholding society of the South. After the Civil War professional educators like Booker T. Washington and W. E. B. Du Bois inspired a profound debate on the question of trade-school education versus scientific training, while the Masonic lodges made a concerted effort to promote establishments whose doors were open to black students. In the twentieth century the fight for education was followed on its heels by the battle for civil rights. Prince Hall Masons provided financial support to young blacks, regardless of whether they were the sons and daughters of Masons, while encouraging their members to fight for this essential right: the right to education.

---

*I had the pleasure of meeting the worshipful master of the Brooklyn Lodge, the Prince Hall Grand Lodge of New York, as well as a Mason from the Grand Lodge of Barbados whose son had been awarded a grant from the Austin Belle Junior Memorial Scholarship Fund.

SIX

The Fight for Civil Rights

The abolition of slavery in no way signified the end of racial discrimination in the South. Of course the thirteenth and fourteenth amendments, which had freed the blacks, could not be opposed directly. However, over the course of the last decade of the nineteenth century some states, like Virginia and South Carolina, stripped blacks of the right to vote by complicating procedures, practicing gerrymandering, which means they carved up voting districts in a way to systematically undercut the black vote, or even by demanding that voters pay specific local taxes.[1]

Some Southerners, Masons or not, felt a resentment that soon transformed into racial hatred. The worst example is probably that of Nathan Bedford Forrest, a former lieutenant general of the Confederate Army who joined the Ku Klux Klan immediately after it was founded in 1870. It was in full knowledge and without the slightest bit of scruples with respect to the great Masonic principles of justice and brotherhood that the Angerona n° 168 Lodge of Memphis, Tennessee, initiated him into Masonry seven years later, on October 27, 1877.[2] This was such a source of shame for William R. Denslow, the famous historian of American Freemasonry who showed greater support for the recognition of Prince Hall than the majority of his brothers, that in his book *10,000 Famous Freemasons* he mentioned Forrest's racist notions and provided his Masonic references, but without

Fig. 6.1. Nathan Bedford Forrest (1821–1877), one of the first members of the Ku Klux Klan

daring to say that he was "grand wizard" of the Ku Klux Klan.*[3]

In this context the remarks of Prince Hall Mason John Jones in 1866 appear almost moderate. Although, as noted in chapter 4, he described white Masons as "poor prejudiced simpletons," the arguments he puts forth make perfect sense. He deplored the fact that white Masons helped spread the notion that blacks were born slaves and therefore incapable of voting, in utter derision of the principles of the Declaration of Independence.

> It is a fact to be regretted, that the white Masonic Fraternity has caught up this false teaching, and has adopted it as one of the keys to lock up the beauties of Masonry and its excellent teaching, against us, contrary to the doctrines of the Declaration of Independence, in which we are taught that all men are born free and equal.[4]

It is no accident that Jones refers to the Declaration of Independence. Beyond the fact that it is a foundational document for all Americans, a large number of Masons—white, of course—had contributed to its writing. Loyal to James Anderson's tradition, the Prince Hall Masons had some scruples about talking politics in the lodge. The most traditionalist members gave their brothers' political commitment a wary glance.

However, a large number of Masons asserted the necessity of taking

---

*There can be no doubt that Forrest either founded the Ku Klux Klan, or was an early member, as it has been mentioned by several historians.

part in the fight for civil rights. In 1907, Grand Master Tinsley of the Prince Hall Grand Lodge of California lamented the fact that whites were still lynching blacks.[5] That same year W. E. B. Du Bois founded the Niagara Movement, which met at Faneuil Hall in Boston, a major shrine of the American Revolution. This movement, in fact, resumed the abolitionist fight, which was ended with a flawed victory, and appealed to blacks to fight for their civil rights instead of seeking to gain the goodwill of whites, an attitude that Du Bois notably criticized in his brother Booker T. Washington. The Niagara Movement soon disappeared to make way for the NAACP, the organization that was also created by the Mason Du Bois in 1909 and included both blacks and whites. It is most likely that Edward Bruce, in his speech delivered to the Craftsmen's Club at the Masonic Temple of New York on March 6, 1910, was thinking of the NAACP when saying this about black Freemasonry:

> As a race organization then we should extend the boundaries of our influence into other spheres of usefulness and activity for the common good, and this we can do without committing ourselves to any religious or political creed.
>
> At this crucial point in the social and political evolution of the black race in this country organized wrong must be met with intelligent organized resistance.[6]

This speech, which centered on race, perhaps reflects a certain distrust of the NAACP, which included whites among its members. Not all the Prince Hall Masons shared the political vision of Du Bois, and some preferred to exacerbate racial differences, thereby intentionally rejecting the support of whites, who were excluded on principle. Nor does it seem that a majority of the whites involved in the battle for black civil rights were Masons. Quite the contrary, in fact, as white lodges systematically practiced racial discrimination among their ranks. Harold Van Buren Voorhis, a white Mason who battled against his colleagues' racism, made it a point to unearth the exceptions that proved the rule. There were several extremely rare white lodges that initiated blacks, like the Alpha Lodge of New Jersey.

On the other hand, George D. Stevens, director of a company in Fort Wayne, Indiana, and a philanthropist and militant activist in the civil rights struggle, was a member of the Blackford Lodge nº 106 in Hartford City. He had been initiated into the high degrees of the Scottish Rite in Fort Wayne in 1925. However, Voorhis notes, "It was not known that Brother Stevens was a Negro until after his death."[7]

This laconic commentary says much about the mentality of the Masonic brothers: in short, only white Negroes could be initiated into the white lodges!

Paradoxically, the United States' entry into the First World War inspired a wave of hope among black Americans who believed their integration into society would be accelerated by obtaining the stripes of officers. Naturally, their hopes were dashed. William Muraskin is likely the one to have best studied the speeches of the Prince Hall leaders against racism.[8] He cites the Texas grand master who in 1918 stated:

> We believe that our second emancipation will be the outcome of this war. If the world is to be made safe for democracy, that means us also.[9]

In 1920, Arthur Schomburg, grand secretary of the New York Grand Lodge, whose collection of black literature is now part of the New York Public Library, initiated a correspondence with the Department of Justice concerning the violence directed against blacks. Several black Masonic temples had been burned down in the Southern United States, and lynching was a common occurrence. Schomburg put the federal government on notice that black riots were an all too real possibility if no measures were taken to bring an end to these acts of violence. The Department of Justice's response appears to have been that lynching was a local problem that needed to be handled locally and that the federal government was powerless to do anything about it.[10]

Muraskin also points out that Grand Master H. R. Butler of the Grand Lodge of Georgia gave a vehement speech against racism that same year. In it he also denounced the imprisonment of progressive leader Eugene V. Debs, segregation, lynching, biased justice, and the completely failed educational system of his state, all phenomena that explain the emigration of blacks to the North. The grand master of the Alabama Grand Lodge, Charles Hendley, also denounced the racism raging in his state and demanded for blacks the right to vote. Similarly, Muraskin adds, in 1928, William McDonald, Prince Hall Mason and influential member of the Republican Party of Texas, protested against the activities of the Ku Klux Klan, criticized the Republican party for not mobilizing against racial segregation in the South, and warned them that they were in danger of losing the black electorate.

Of course, there were other Masons who reacted negatively to these positions and stated that Freemasons should not intervene in affairs concerning governance. However, it clearly seems that they were a minority in the obedience and that the Prince Hall Freemasons played a major role in the awakened awareness in their community, in particular that of the intellectual elite and the black middle class. They were most involved—on an individual and organizational basis—in the NAACP as the black grand lodges in several states gave official support to the movement launched by Du Bois. Deemed moderate because it fought for the integration of blacks and rejected separatism, and also declared itself against the reverse racism of excluding whites from its membership, the NAACP was sometimes accused of being an Uncle Tom organization.[11]

This accusation seems all the more unfair as it was Du Bois who took a personal stand against Booker T. Washington, criticizing him for being passive and inclined to resignation and for systematically looking for compromise to gain the goodwill of white business leaders. At the University of Atlanta, where he was a professor, Du Bois led an "Annual Congress of Black Problems." From 1896 to 1914, he published a series of reports that constituted a modern encyclopedia on the problems encountered by American blacks. Du Bois oversaw scientific research on subjects such as the "efforts made to improve the living conditions for Blacks," "Blacks and Business," and "Blacks and School."[12] This academic approach was probably not to the taste of all civil rights activists. It is significant, however, that the Prince Hall Lodges gave increasingly active support to the approach taken by Du Bois and his friends at the NAACP.

In 1947, Du Bois wrote *An Appeal to the World* on behalf of the

NAACP and submitted it to the United Nations, requesting that the black community be placed under international protection. However, he broke with the NAACP in 1948 on the subject of the cold war. Several NAACP directors, in fact, seem to have succumbed to the sirens of anti-communism and given their approval to witch-hunts for communists. It so happens that Du Bois was an open critic of the criminal acts of capitalism. In 1959 he was welcomed by first Nikita Khrushchev and then Mao Tse Tung, and in 1960 he gave a lecture at the University of Wisconsin titled "Socialism and the American Negro." In this lecture he described his visits to the socialist countries, saying, "There is no doubt that the world of the twenty-first century will be overwhelmingly communistic."[13]

Obviously an error of judgment. He was ninety-three years old when he decided to join the Communist Party, before going into exile in Ghana in 1963, several months before his death. It is easy to see that the career of Du Bois was not to everyone's liking, neither his companions in the NAACP nor his Prince Hall brothers.

Without exhibiting the same degree of political commitment of Du Bois, it appears that some Prince Hall Masons had internal conflicts with other members of the NAACP for a variety of reasons. For example, in his archives Williamson included a passage from the *Pittsburgh Courier* of April 12, 1947, that mentions a quarrel between a Mr. Dobbs and his group and the NAACP chapter of Atlanta, Georgia. This is what the journalist wrote for the *Courier:*

> A group headed by John Wesley Dobbs, Dr. Brewer of Columbus, and a small group of preachers were there trying to break up a meeting of the State Chapter of the NAACP. . . . Dobbs and his group lashed out at the NAACP because he thought there were too many white people connected with it, and because its president was white.*[14]

It so happens that John Wesley Dobbs was also grand master of Georgia and director of the Georgia Voters' League, which campaigned

---

*This occurred during the primary elections of 1947.

to turn out the black vote for this state. Despite the incident reported in the *Pittsburgh Courier,* Dobbs was an active member of the NAACP and had toiled to establish official ties between this movement and the Prince Hall Grand Lodge of his state. The Prince Hall Grand Lodge of Georgia did not adopt the anti-Communist stance of other Prince Hall Lodges, who were anxious to show proof of their patriotism and to not remain idle against the "red peril." In contrast, the Georgia Grand Lodge proclaimed that the overall political instability was due less to the communist threat than to American anti-Sovietism![15] The grand master of Louisiana, John Lewis, had given active support to Dobbs to prompt blacks to go to the voter booths despite racist intimidation, and like Dobbs, he too, was one of the directors of the NAACP.

Muraskin cites two other Prince Hall grand masters who were actively involved in the civil rights struggle. In New York State, Louis Fair was fighting against segregation in the New York Militia, which was part of the National Guard. In 1948 the official organ of the black Grand Lodge of New York, the *Sentinel,* echoed Grand Master Fair's demands.[16] Then we have Ashby Carter, Illinois grand master and also an active member of the NAACP. He was best known for the legislative battle he vainly waged against the Illinois state government to establish a committee to fight against discrimination in the job field (the Fair Employment Practices Committee).[17] He created the Civil Rights Fund in 1947, thereby anticipating the massive financial support of Prince Hall Masons for the NAACP.

The year 1951 marks a vital turning point, with the official establishment of ties between the Prince Hall Grand lodges and the NAACP. The Assembly of the Prince Hall grand masters managed to reach this accord with the help of an influential leader of the organization who also was a Mason and a member of the U.S. Supreme Court: Thurgood Marshall. The Prince Hall Masons Legal Research Fund was thus established and placed under the control of the NAACP. According to Marshall, this made Prince Hall the second largest donor to the NAACP, right after the unions represented by the Congress of Industrial Organizations (CIO).[18] This confirms the status of black Freemasonry as one of the most powerful organizations inside the black American community.

Joseph Walkes mentions this intimate intertwining of the Prince Hall Grand Lodges with the NAACP. By way of example he offers the amount of the financial contribution made by the Prince Hall Masons to just the NAACP post called Legal Defense: $949,038 for legal aid to blacks. The Masons of Prince Hall donated to other parts of the NAACP, but these figures are not available. Walkes also points out the aid given by black Masons to other civil rights organizations like the Urban League and the United Negro Fund.[19]

The battle waged by black Masons for civil rights naturally inspired much commentary on the part of both Masons and the "profanes" (non-Masons), both blacks and whites. The book titled *Christianity and American Freemasonry,* by William J. Whalen, has the merit of supplying information about the engagement of some Prince Hall Masons in recent political life. This list includes Marshall; Los Angeles mayor Tom Bradley; Benjamin Hooks, director of the NAACP; Atlanta mayor Andrew Young; and Detroit mayor Coleman Young. The book's author, a die-hard Catholic and thus violently opposed to white Freemasonry, took pleasure in critiquing its racism and in noting that in the 1960s a fair number of illustrious Masons, like George Wallace, Orval Faubus, and Ross Barnett, the governors of Alabama, Arkansas, and Mississippi, respectively, were shamefully compromised in the segregationist movement.

It is not forbidden to question Whalen's motives: Was he truly indignant about the racism of white Masons, which simply reflects, in my opinion, the dominant mentality of the American South, or did he see this as an opportunity to get back at the white Masons whose battle for public schooling was causing harm to American Catholic schools? One does not cancel out the other . . .

Muraskin, who created a very complete history of Prince Hall Freemasonry, on the other hand, seems outraged by the support of several white Masons for a movement that, by all evidence, he saw as exclusively black with a separatist perspective. Now, when one is aware of the racism of the white American lodges, one cannot help but salute the courage of William H. Upton, Washington grand master, who tried to make his white "brothers" see reason and drew down on his head all the thunder of the other white grand lodges. Muraskin's commentary is not absent of some bitterness.

> These white Masons, like liberal whites generally, have been unable to fulfill that Masonic (and American) promise of brotherhood or equality since they have not represented a wide sector of their communities. All they have been able to do is keep the hope of racial unity alive—an achievement that has often had more negative than positive consequences for the black population.[20]

Whatever the case, the involvement of Prince Hall Freemasons in the fight for civil rights was real. Not only as individuals, like Du Bois, but also as institutions with the grand lodges acting in their official capacity, black Masons gave very concrete support to the movement for civil emancipation. It is significant that the Prince Hall Freemasons gave their full support to the NAACP, an organization that certainly received its full share of criticism from separatist blacks but which never petered out, in contrast to others, as it still exists today.

PART THREE

*A Community
Takes Control of
Its Own Destiny*

SEVEN

The Cooperative Ideal

Beneficence, mutual aid, and charity are at the heart of the Masonic traditions, in all forms of the Masonic obedience and nations. These values assume a particular acuteness in the black community, however, throughout the time spanning the creation of the Prince Hall Lodges, then with even greater intensity after the Civil War, and throughout the twentieth century. At the end of the Civil War everything needed to be constructed with respect to social protections. The Prince Hall Masons were savvy enough to then take a place in the field of volunteer organizations to promote mutual aid before encouraging blacks to enter the business world.

From 1792, Prince Hall had emphasized the charitable obligations of Freemasons. This notion of obligation is not confined only to Freemasons, however; quite the contrary. In 1797 he stressed the duty of solidarity with the whole of humanity, without even giving the black community any special privileges, as his descendants would do.

> We see how necessary it is to have a fellow feeling for our distressed brethren of the human race, in their troubles, both spiritual and temporal. How refreshing it is to a sick man, to see his sympathizing friends around his bed, ready to administer all the relief in their power; although they can't relieve his bodily pain, yet they may ease his mind by good instructions and cheer his heart by their company.[1]

In 1793, when a yellow fever epidemic struck Philadelphia, Absalom Jones, worshipful master of the Prince Hall Lodge, mobilized his brothers as well as those from other lodges to give aid to the sick.[2]

It was, however, during the years of reconstruction following the Civil War that a large number of mutual-aid societies emerged, either directly connected with the Prince Hall Lodges or very close to them. The Odd Fellows, the Knights of Pythias, and the Knights of Tabor grew stronger during this time, as did two women's organizations: the Order of the Eastern Star and the Calanthe Sisters.[3]

In the eighteenth century the members of the first English lodges had the custom of attending the plays performed at the famous London theaters of Drury Lane in particular, giving them financial backing and writing prologues and epilogues in honor of Freemasonry that would be read on stage.

At the beginning of the twentieth century the Prince Hall Masons also had taken on the task of encouraging cultural activities, often for charitable ends. The brothers of the Carthaginian Lodge n° 47 organized variety shows for the purpose of collecting funds to support their needy members. In 1905 the lodge organized a ball in Brooklyn. In 1909, and again in 1910, the brothers, but also some profanes as well, most likely, were invited "to a ball and vaudeville show" by these "ladies," probably the wives of Masons, that took place in Brooklyn, then a noted black suburb of New York, all for the "profit of the lodge."[4]

Mutual-Aid Societies

The Odd Fellows appeared before the Civil War. It was originally a "friendly society" created in England during the eighteenth century. These numerous societies of mutual aid are intended to provide assistance to members and their families when they are struck by death or illness. The existence of these societies, in contrast to that of the first unions, was enthusiastically supported by the British authorities. They openly displayed their respect for the established order and religious morality. Contrary to all other associations in the United Kingdom, they were the only ones, other than the Masonic lodges, who were granted permission to hold meetings after 1795.*

The first American Odd Fellows lodge was established in Baltimore in 1819. The first black Odd Fellows lodge, the Philomathean Lodge n° 646, was created in New York in 1843 on the initiative of Peter Ogden, who obtained a charter from his own lodge in Liverpool. Ogden, a black steward aboard a British vessel, advised the New Yorkers to directly solicit his English lodge rather than the white American Odd Fellow lodges.

In 1847 there were twenty-two Odd Fellow lodges in the United States, only one of which was black. It so happens that the Odd Fellows enjoyed enormous success in the black community, for the number of black American lodges had climbed to around fifty by 1863.[5] By 1893 the black organization of Odd Fellows claimed some two hundred thousand members. These Odd Fellows were placed under the control of their high officers, who met in their Philadelphia headquarters in a fairly autonomous fashion, it seems, with respect to the white Odd Fellows lodges.

The Odd Fellows supplied aid primarily to their members and their families, but, as much as their means would permit them, they were open to take requests from outside the order into consideration. They defined themselves as a "vast mutual-aid society."[6] The members paid dues and, in exchange, received assurance for basic medical coverage. The family would receive a precise sum on a member's death. The members also received financial support while looking for employment. However, the society denied it was only useful on a material level and claimed it was working toward the perfection of its members.

> Those who speak of our Order as merely a sick society, betray an utter ignorance of the institution they undertake to criticize. . . . The object of this Order is to elevate the whole man, its provisions

---

*The Seditious Meeting Act of 1795 banned all public meetings. It was a conservative measure taken by the Pitt government in a desire to curb all the British reformers as a result of its fear of the French Revolution.

Fig. 7.1. District Grand Lodge nº 2, Grand United Order of Odd Fellows, Albany, August 2, 1921 (courtesy of the Chancellor Robert R. Livingston Masonic Library)

have reference to his intellectual, moral, and physical capabilities, it influences every circumstance of life, and it is calculated to modify the relations of society, both morally and politically. Its influence as a political safeguard cannot be overestimated.[7]

The black wing of the Odd Fellows association, which seeks to give social protection to its members, is also meant to protect their morality and thereby perform a favor for the political authorities, exactly like the friendly societies of eighteenth-century Great Britain. The black members of the Odd Fellows therefore undertake on their behalf the structure and goals of the white organization. The exact nature of the relations between the black and white lodges remains a mystery. It seems that the black American association of the Odd Fellows had an entirely autonomous means of functioning. There was also a women's branch of this order: the Grand Household of Ruth.[8]

No formal ties exist between the Prince Hall Masons and the Odd Fellows. However, both organizations had many members in common. For example, James Needham, who founded Unity Lodge n° 711 and the Grand United Order of Odd Fellows of Philadelphia, was also an influential member of the Prince Hall Grand Lodge of Pennsylvania. He was involved in the battle for civil rights as treasurer of the Penn-

Fig. 7.2. Grand Master John P. Scott, an educator whose name graces a Harrisburg elementary school, presided at a ceremony with several members of the Grand Chapter of Odd Fellows by the First Stone Church, Wesley Union AME Zion, situated at the corner of South and Tanner Streets, Harrisburg, Pennsylvania, Sunday, October 18, 1914. Tanner Street was populated by a large number of black Americans who participated in the Underground Railroad in the nineteenth century. (photo courtesy of John Slifko)

sylvania State Equal Rights League.[9] Similarly, according to the 1949 annals of the Prince Hall Grand Lodge of South Carolina, S. C. Moore was both a member of this grand lodge and grand master of this state's Odd Fellows.[10]

Odd Fellows meet in a lodge, following the Masonic model, and practice a ritual. They even claim to be more democratic than the Masons. This is how Charles Brooks, grand secretary of the order, put it in the preamble to his official history of the Odd Fellows.

> The Order of Odd Fellows is truly a Friendly Society, and always has been. Its fundamental principles and distinguishing characteristics are as different from those of Masonry as chalk is from cheese. The rich and poor, the high and low, the Prince and Peasant, men of every rank and station in life are and always have been admitted to odd Fellowship on equal footing. Not so with Freemasonry.[11]

This would make Odd Fellows somewhat the Freemasonry of the poor. This argument is quite significant. While Prince Hall Freemasonry was essentially perceived—and seemingly rightfully so—as a bourgeois institution, the Odd Fellows claimed a more popular recruitment. Nevertheless, the ties between the Prince Hall Grand Lodges and those of the Odd Fellows are quite real.

The Mechanics play a role providing mutual aid that is quite similar to that of the Odd Fellows. Numerous Prince Hall Freemasons are still members of this order today, in both the United States and the English-speaking regions of the Caribbean. In his history of Celestial Lodge n° 3 of New York, Harry A. Williamson notes that the worshipful master of this lodge in 1908 was able to hold in his own hands the original charter of the first Prince Hall Lodge during a gathering of Masons at Mechanics Hall in Worcester, Massachusetts. Williamson explicitly states that the local of the Mechanics was placed at the disposal of the Prince Hall Freemasons.[12] When one is aware of the symbolic importance of the charter granted to the African Lodge of Boston, we can measure the full importance of this event in the life of this New York lodge.

Charity or Mutual Aid?

Outside of the Odd Fellows and the Mechanics, many mutual-aid societies existed in a more or less temporary form in the black community. While naturally not all of them were connected to Freemasonry, the Prince Hall Masons did play a major role in a large number of them, either by founding autonomous societies modeled on the Masonic structure, with their own rituals, or by combining with already existing societies. The notion of mutual aid prevailed over that of charity, despite the opposition of some Masons who preferred the idea of spontaneous benevolence to that of mutual aid of an obligatory nature.[13]

Several Prince Hall lodges equipped themselves with bodies intended to provide direct assistance to their members or to those of the lodges in their region. For example, the Sumner Lodge of Springfield, Massachusetts, created the New England Masonic Mutual Relief Association, with an eye toward assisting the "indigent widows and orphans in our midst." The annals of the Massachusetts Grand Lodge make mention of this in the minutes for 1870.[14] During this same time the Celestial Lodge n° 3 created several mutual-aid societies: the Hiram Masonic Relief Association, the Masonic Mutual Relief Society (for a similar purpose), and the Masonic Memorial Burial Fund, to cover funeral expenses.*[15]

The Hiram Masonic Relief Association was active from 1888 until the mid-twentieth century.[16] Furthermore, the lodge stepped in to provide aid for the society at large, and not simply to give assistance to its own members. For example, in 1923 it donated ten dollars in assistance to Japanese earthquake victims and awarded an unspecified amount to the Citizens' Christmas Cheer Club for Widows and Orphans to give these individuals the means to celebrate Christmas.[17] Two years later this same lodge gave a ten-dollar grant to a day-care center maintained by a neighborhood Catholic church. In 1928 it offered financial support to a coed summer camp. In 1937 a donation was given to help the victims of flooding in the western United States.[18]

---

*On May 7, 1892, this last association came to the aid of a Celestial Lodge member, Rodriguez S. Dyer.

All these actions prompted commentary by Williamson: in his opinion the lodge had acted too generously on some occasions and sometimes lacked discernment. It had given assistance to various organizations that had no Masonic connections and even to a body that was under the jurisdiction of the Catholic Church! Williamson found accord here with the viewpoint of white American Masons who advocated the separation of church and state in the name of religious freedom inscribed in the American Constitution. Lodges should not pledge their faith to any particular church, although they preach religious values themselves. American Masons were particularly critical of the Catholic Church, which ran a large number of private schools. Williamson adopted a point of view that could almost be described as secular when he took offense at the assistance provided to a Catholic day-care center. In addition, he bemoaned the greed of several widows who attempted to shamelessly extort money from the lodge.

These observations offer a clear illustration of the mutual assistance that prevailed in the Prince Hall lodges. Although charity was advocated by almost all Masonic obediences, black Masons preferred to envision benevolence as a form of mutual aid. The brothers decided to lend assistance because they had decided to pay dues and equip their lodges with a specific entity with an eye toward having a minimal level of social protection that would mitigate the state's lack of support. It was mutual assistance far more than any kind of charity.

Other Masons feared that the Prince Hall lodges would not confine themselves to this role of assistance and would therefore be exposed to adulteration by losing their symbolic, if not to say philosophical, nature. Hence, the thousand precautions erected by George Crawford, author of a small practical manual for Prince Hall Masons, when speaking of mutual-aid societies. He takes pains to distinguish them from Masonic lodges and to show that in no case can they ever serve as a substitute for the lodge.

To a certain extent the difference between the provisions for relieving distress in Mutual Benefit Societies and lodges of Freemasonry is largely one of emphasis. In the one case the "care for the sick and burying the dead" provisions are the main object and fraternal and social features are incidental. On the other hand, in Masonic bodies the fraternal, moral, and social features are primary while for the needy, it is incidental. All of which is to say that help for the brother in need can and must be provided without compromising the great and paramount purposes of the Fraternity.[19]

The viewpoint expressed by Crawford is certainly quite representative of sentiments held by many of his fellow Masons. His alarm is revealing in any case of the strong tradition of mutual assistance among Prince Hall Masons. Some officials feared that the black obedience would be regarded only as the poor man's Freemasonry, or at least as a mutual-aid association that was more concerned with charity than symbolism and therefore probably less respectable. Perhaps this attitude can also be explained by a slight complex toward the white American Masonic obediences, which displayed unrelenting scorn for the black lodges.

The Other Forms of Mutual Assistance

Like their white "brothers," the Prince Hall Freemasons have always made the fields of education and health a priority. I have already mentioned in chapter 5 the scholarships they handed out to students of New York and Barbados. Similar examples are abundant throughout the United States. For the year 1982 alone, the southern jurisdiction of the Prince Hall Scottish Supreme Council gave grants totaling one hundred thousand dollars to black institutions of higher learning.[20]

The widow and the orphan attracted the attention of the Masons in particular; in the previous section I cited various actions taken by lodges and the associations they put in place to come to the aid of the families of deceased Masons. The same holds true for the elderly. The Prince Hall temple in the heart of Harlem is adjoined today by a retirement home supported by the grand lodge that is intended for Masons and their close relatives. The activities conducted by black grand lodges in the medical field are less spectacular than those of the white grand lodges, for want of financial means, but are significant nonetheless. Blood banks have been set up in several states by Prince Hall lodges; their use is primarily for Masons, but they are also open to the profane.

During the Second World War the Prince Hall Grand Lodge of New York formed a committee that would oversee the provision of material and moral support to Masonic soldiers and their sons, as well as a special fund, the Prince Hall Masonic War Fund. These funds continued to accept contributions after the war in order to provide assistance for the wounded.[21] Today, according to Joseph Walkes, the association of the Prince Hall Shrine, which is non-Masonic but operates closely with the Prince Hall Grand Lodges, regularly contributes "thousands of dollars" to the Prince Hall Shrine Health and Medical Research Foundation, formerly known as the Tuberculosis and Cancer Research Foundation. Additionally, annual scholarships of six thousand dollars are regularly awarded to hospitals and institutions of higher learning.[22]

According to Walkes, scholarships are also awarded to young women who are seventeen to twenty-four years of age to enable them to enroll in the universities of their choice. Can Prince Hall Masons still be accused of sexism?*

Finally, the Prince Hall Grand Lodges also seek to provide financial assistance to youth through a program that fights against drug use and delinquency.

The Mutual-Aid Banks

In the social sector the most specific and probably most spectacular action taken by the Masons of Prince Hall was certainly the creation of banks modeled on mutual-aid societies. Muraskin cites the particularly ambitious speech of the Alabama grand master who in 1909 bemoaned the fact that Prince Hall Masons confined their social activities to assistance to the ill and contributions to offset funeral expenses, in accordance with the tradition of friendly societies.

The eternal shame of Negro secret societies is that the most they are accomplishing is to take care of the sick and bury the dead. I

---

*This subject will be expanded upon in the next chapter, "Women and Black Freemasonry."

am of the opinion, that properly managed, through our Masonic lodges, reinforced by other societies, many of which most of us are members, farms could be owned, teachers trained to instruct us, soldiers trained to defend us.[23]

Obviously these goals were not attained. However, in 1911 the Grand Lodge of Texas founded its own bank, the Fraternal Bank and Trust Company. Individual members and the lodges themselves were encouraged to invest. Each lodge was expected to deposit at least 10 percent of its capital in the bank. The fraternal bank was administered by shareholders and not directly by the grand lodge. In the beginning the Texas Masons turned for assistance to the Odd Fellows and the Knights of Pythias, who bought 2,500 of the 5,000 shares. In 1930 the Grand Lodge of Texas was strong enough to take possession of the majority of shares and to set itself up as a lending body for black Masons. The bank was still in existence in 1953. The Grand Lodge of California was not able to follow the example of Texas but did create a loan organization through the Prince Hall Credit Union n° 1 in San Diego. It also financially supported an association to promote construction, the Liberty Building and Loan Association. Meanwhile, the Grand Lodge of Georgia encouraged all its members to invest in black banks as a priority.[24]

The goal of all these banking operations was to promote black companies and help the brothers make investments in the business world. Of course, the mortality rate for black businesses was particularly high, as noted by Muraskin, who does not conceal his admiration for the battle waged by the Prince Hall Lodges to assist them. Consulting the *Who's Who in Colored America* from the years 1933 to 1937, he drew up a list of the Prince Hall Masons who had found success in the business world. Among those he mentions are W. W. Allen, grand master of Maryland and sovereign grand commander of the Scottish Rite Masons, Southern chapter, who headed the Southern Life Insurance Company of Baltimore; and John Webb, grand master of Mississippi, director of the Universal Life Insurance Company of Memphis and the president and treasurer of another insurance company in Arkansas.

Other examples Muraskin gives include that of Grand Master

Theodore Moss of California, who owned the Independent Plumbing Works of California and organized a business club for blacks, the Modern Order of Bucks. According to Muraskin, 80 percent of the names listed in the black *Who's Who* of this time were members of Prince Hall.[25] This percentage testifies to the role played by Prince Hall Masonry in the advancement of the black middle class. The question can be raised, Did Masons attempt a formal translation of the tontine process, the traditional way capital was mobilized in African-style societies, which still survives in the Caribbean, as shown by the Haitian *sou-sou*?

The Difficult Relationships with White Organizations

The relationships between the mutual-aid or benevolent societies reflected the racism that, with few exceptions, raged in the various Masonic obediences. This will be the subject of part 4 of this book. I will only cite two examples here: that of the Odd Fellows, a mutual-aid society, and that of the Shriners, a charitable organization. These two organizations existed in white and black associations, but with no intermingling.

The history of the creation of the first black lodges of the Odd Fellows is significant. Boston women, most likely of the upper middle class, had stepped in unsuccessfully and encountered great difficulty in working with the city authorities. They had requested that blacks, in order to prepare the creation of an Odd Fellows lodge, be allowed to meet at Faneuil Hall, a shrine of the American Revolution and thus a symbol of freedom, but only freedom for whites. It so happens that it was the members of this mutual-aid society—until that time all white—who were trying to halt the movement of the association into the black community. When the black sailor Peter Ogden, who had long lived in Great Britain, tried to arrange a meeting with the New York Odd Fellow members, he ran into a wall. He recounts that incident.

On my arrival in New York, I wrote to them, informing them of my arrival and appointment, also my readiness to meet them for the purpose of effecting a union between them and our lodge.

I felt disposed to make every concession that could consistently be done; in about four days a man called on board my ship and enquired for Peter Ogden. I informed him it was my name; he said I was not the person he was looking for. I told him there was no other person of that name on any of the ships; however he left without saying anymore. In four or five days I received an answer to my letter, declining an interview on account of what do you think? On account of color.[26]

The second example of the strained relations between the two American communities is that of the benevolent society known as the Nobles of the Mystic Shrine, or simply the Shriners. Although this organization is not, strictly speaking, Masonic, the only individuals eligible to join it are Masons who have attained the 32nd degree of the high Scottish grades or the highest degree of the York Rite, that of Knights Templar. It is easy to see that this charitable organization is also, or especially, an honorific site where the highest grades of the Masonic Order can enjoy meeting each other, whether they come from the York Rite or the Scottish Rite.

While the plurality of rites is recognized, the same has not always been true for ethnic origins—quite the contrary. The first Shriners' association was created in New York in 1872 by white Masons. Blacks created a similar body for the first time in Chicago in 1893. Several Shriners' associations appeared in various states, separate, of course, founded by white and black Masons. In 1918 the white Shriners of Texas filed a suit on the pretext that the black Shriners were using the same name as theirs. The affair generated a nationwide controversy between white Shriners and their black counterparts. The Texas court found in favor of the white Shriners and forbade blacks from using the same name, which they were considered to have usurped.[27] There are no grounds to be surprised by this verdict, which is an illustration of the visceral racism of the Texans of that era. Unfortunately, the Texas Masons were not figures of exception on this occasion.

The history of the mutual-aid and benevolent associations is liberally sprinkled with racist incidents similar to the one described above.

EIGHT

Women and Black Freemasonry

American Freemasonry—white or black—is unanimous on at least one point. While Masons are happy to cite the example of the Queen of Sheba, not for a moment do they draw the conclusion that their female companions have the right to be initiated. Thus, King Solomon remains a safer value. Neither the white grand lodges nor the black grand lodges of the United States apply the principle of equality when it comes to women.

However, to humor them, and to get the best possible advantage from their assistance, they admit women into separate organizations and chapters, equipped with their own rituals, but which are not considered to be Masonic.

Masons give their female companions a completely subaltern role. Certainly, each chapter is presided over by a most worthy matron, who is seconded by a most worthy patron.[1] The presence of the latter proves to be still obligatory in those associations for women sponsored by the brothers. The prestigious names of these lodges for women are mind-boggling: when it is not the Order of the Eastern Star, it is the Order of the Amaranth or even the Heroines of Jericho. The same is true for the titles of the officers, each one more pompous than the one before it.

Here we have the international grand Adah, international grand Ruth, international grand Esther, international grand sentinel, and the international grand chaplain.[2] Adah represents quite simply the daughter; Ruth, the widow; Esther, the wife; Martha, the

Fig. 8.1. Hattie Pearl Prophet, grand worthy matron (Guiding Star, Historical Edition)

Fig. 8.2. Cassandra Wheeler, grand deputy, Chapter of the Amaranth, Ohio, 2012 (courtesy of the Chapter of the Amaranth)

sister . . .*[3] But in practice, with few exceptions, these women performed charitable works, in exemplary fashion, moreover, and worked this way for the brothers, as suggested by the few annals we have at our disposal.

History of Female Organizations

It was not women, but men, who took the initiative of creating these welcome centers. The Eastern Star is the oldest and most important of these organizations. The first chapters of the Eastern Star were founded in 1875 and 1876 by Thornton A. Jackson in Washington, D.C.[4] In fact, the Queen Esther Chapter n° 1 was opened on December 1, 1874, in Washington, D.C., in the home of Mrs. Georgiana Thomas under the dual leadership of Martha Welch, worthy matron, and this same Thornton A. Jackson, worthy patron.[5]

According to Harold Van Buren Voorhis, the first chapter in the state of South Carolina only became operational in 1880.[6] Jackson pursued his activity and in April 1890 founded the Queen of Sheba Chapter n° 3, and in October of that same year, the Gethsemane Chapter n° 4 in the District of Columbia. Under his impetus, chapters also appeared in Alexandria, Virginia; Maryland; and Pennsylvania.[7]

This means that the black organization appeared after the white organization bearing the same name and owes its existence to Freemason Rob Morris. The charter was then granted by C. R. Case, representative of Robert Macoy, famous publisher of Masonic books and, what's more, grand patron of the white organization of the Eastern Star.[8]

This was therefore done in complete legality, with the consent of the white Masons, who, oddly enough, did not protest against the creation of black chapters while at the same time the vast majority of them rejected the very idea of black Freemasonry. It is tempting to conclude that the question of women appeared to be completely harmless. This clearly shows that American Masons, whatever their skin color, never

---

*Andrée Buisine analyzed the white Eastern Star ritual. That of the black organization is identical.

granted much importance to these organizations reserved for their wives and close relations. Some Masons—black and white—encouraged these coed organizations. This was the case of Macoy as well as that of the publishing house bearing his name, which recently published the works of Joseph Walkes, the Prince Hall historian cited so often in this study.*

More chapters were created shortly after this time: the Eureka Grand Chapter in Louisiana on June 30, 1884, which was followed by the Eureka Grand Chapter of New York in 1895.[9] The membership conditions for the Eastern Star were set at an early date and were quite strict. The only women eligible for admission were those benefiting from a direct blood tie with a master Mason, as shown by the following details found in the Arkansas annals.

Can a Master Mason's half-sister become a member of the Order of the Eastern Star?

The fact she being only a half-sister does not entitle her to the degrees. None but whole sisters are entitled to the degrees.

Can a Master Mason's widow who has married a second time and her second husband not being a Mason, become a member of the O.E.S.?

The fact of her marrying again a man who is not a Mason would bar her from the rights of becoming a member. If she is married, she is not a widow.[10]

Some Masonic lodges created their own club in addition to the Eastern Star to exclusively recruit their members' relatives. For example, the Plumb and Level Club, which was attached to the Carthaginian Lodge n° 47 of Brooklyn, had recruitment criteria that were even more strict than that of the local chapter of the Eastern Star, the Queen Esther Chapter n° 9, which was open to all women who were kin to Masons, but not only lodge members.

---

*It should be noted that Macoy was particularly open to advances against discrimination, as shown by the fact that he published several black authors.

In 1922 the Carthaginian Lodge thus had two clubs, with one more restrictive than the other. The second club, Hiram's Circle, brought together the women of the Eastern Star from that chapter and those from neighboring chapters. This example allows us to assess the complexity of the relationships between the brothers and their female colleagues. By all evidence, the primary objective was to have total control over the recruitment of these various clubs. The Plumb and Level Club was directly connected to the activities of the lodge, and was in the service of this lodge, for the purpose of planning the entertainment and providing good stewardship.[11]

The Heroines of Jericho is an organization open to the wives and daughters of Masons of the Royal Arch, therefore of the high grades. They too exhibit their ties of kinship with the brothers. They are even proud of them, as shown by this song.

> *We are the Heroines of Jericho,*
> *The female relatives of Masons you know;*
> *We are the Heroines of Jericho,*
> *We shall not be moved.*

> **Chorus:**
> *We shall, we shall, we shall not be moved,*
> *We shall, we shall, we shall not be moved,*
> *Like the Rock of Gibraltar,*
> *We shall not be moved.*[*12]

The Order of the Amaranth was closely tied to that of the Eastern Star. It was also created by Morris and Macoy. The first supreme council was founded in New York in 1883. One had to be a member of the Eastern Star to become a member of the Amaranth. According to Harry A. Williamson, the Order of the Amaranth is only connected to the Eastern Star in the black obediences, and its rituals are very different.

---

*The text of the whole song can be found in appendix 2.

Is the Amaranth degree attached to the Order of the Eastern Star? If you will make a very careful comparison between the Eastern Star and the Amaranth rituals, you will observe the ceremonies of the former are based upon Biblical history while those of the latter are based upon modern political history, consequently there can be absolutely no relationship between the two sets of ceremonies.[13]

It was common to belong to the Eastern Star, the Heroines of Jericho, and the Amaranth at the same time. Instead of exerting any real power inside the Masonic institution, the members accumulated titles of distinction.

In 1857 the Eastern Star claimed "around 3500 chapters, with more than one hundred thousand members, and held in their combined treasury around half a million dollars," according to the grand matron of that year.[14] In 1925, according to Voorhis, the Eastern Star no longer held more than 3,434 chapters but had a total of some 121,101 members.*

According to Voorhis, the crash of 1929 had serious repercussions on recruitment. He gives the example of the Grand Chapter of New York, which numbered forty-one chapters of some 2,231 members in 1924, and had only thirty-nine chapters with some 940 members in 1936.[15] Since then the Grand Chapter of New York has grown again. In 1999, according to the sitting grand matron at that time, it included around three thousand members, whereas the Prince Hall Grand Lodge of this state numbered between five thousand and six thousand brothers. The exact figures are extremely hard to obtain, and it is necessary to be content with estimates.† It would seem that the members of the Eastern Star had diminished less proportionately than those of Prince Hall and the white equivalent female organization.

---

*In the 1925 edition of her book *The Story of the Illinois Federation of Colored Women's Clubs* (first published 1921), Elizabeth Lindsay Davis cites statistics provided by Eastern Star from probably around 1923 (the precise date is not given): 3,434 chapters and 120,101 members. The figures therefore agree with those provided by Voorhis.

†These estimates were given to me during my visit to the Harlem Temple in April 1999.

The Relations with the Prince Hall
Grand Lodges

The Prince Hall Masons asked themselves if they should consider the Eastern Star an adoptive Masonic order and therefore as a specific form of Freemasonry, or else as a completely separate association with no Masonic character. The same debate took place among white Masons. However, at its beginning, the Eastern Star was considered to be an adoptive organization. Albert Pike, a famous white American Mason who could never be accused of laxity, explained the validity of the female order in these words:

> Our mothers, sisters, wives, and daughters cannot, it is true, be admitted to share with us the grand mysteries of Freemasonry, but there is no reason why there should not be a Masonry for them, which may not merely enable them to make themselves known to Masons, and so to obtain assurance and protection; but by means of

Fig. 8.3. Albert Pike (1809–1891)

which, acting in concert through the tie of association and mutual obligation, they may cooperate in the great labors of Masonry by assisting in and, in some respects, directing their charities and toiling in the cause of human progress. The object of "la Maçonnerie des dames" is, therefore, very inadequately expressed when it is said to be the improvement and purification of the sentiments.[16]

Numerous Freemasons, both black and white, have since contested this rather modest notion about the role of women in Freemasonry. It seemed to grant far too many prerogatives to women. For a long time it was the most retrograde notion that appears to have prevailed: the Eastern Star lodges were not considered as associations practicing a Masonic ritual, not even the Rite of Adoption of eighteenth-century French lodges taken up by R. Morris. Williamson's position was perfectly clear-cut.

Is there any definite connection between Freemasonry and the Order of the Eastern Star?

Absolutely none . . .

Is the Eastern Star an auxiliary to Freemasonry?

Absolutely no . . .

Is there such an order in the United States known as the Rite of Adoption?

Absolutely no. The use of that phrase in relation to the Eastern Star has been a very grave error.[17]

However, the black grand chapters of the Eastern Star were clearly stated to be working at the "Rite of Adoption or Degree of the Eastern Star."[18] They aligned themselves with the rite of adoption that Jackson had granted them in the name of Macoy, "Supreme Patron of the Rite of Adoption in the World."[19] A white 32nd-degree Mason of the Scottish Rite even in 1997 observed that the black chapters of the Eastern Star had been more loyal to the original rite of adoption promoted by Morris than their white counterparts.[20]

Williamson felt, however, that the Prince Hall Masons had shown evidence of a shameful laxity with respect to the Eastern Star, contrary to the white American grand lodges, which always considered the Eastern Star chapters to be organizations entirely apart and non-Masonic. It is hard to believe that Williamson was unaware of the statements of Albert Pike and the Eastern Star founder, Rob Morris. It is amusing, moreover, that Williamson sought to refer to the practice of the Masons he was dealing with in a fairly scornful way as "Caucasians" (like several other authors, it is true), who he was not in the habit of admiring. Williamson also revealed himself to be particularly sectarian when it came to women and seems to have greatly feared their interference in the Prince Hall Lodges. He cites the example of Pennsylvania, where the Prince Hall grand master forbade the wives of master Masons to become members of the Eastern Star, because he found the bonds between the brothers and the sisters compromising.

> It seems the reason underlying the Edict was that the women of the Star were injecting themselves into the business of Lodges through their husbands if some one of them did not like the wife of some member, also, the same interference was reaching into election of officers in the Grand Lodge, etc.[21]

For this opinion as well, Williamson sought a model in white Masonry. He therefore cited the United Grand Lodge of England, which had also maintained its distance from the Eastern Star by rejecting any and all notions of a female Masonry.[22] After describing the danger represented by some sort of Masonic promiscuity with women he tends to consider as shrews, Williamson states that the Prince Hall Masons in turn should refrain from governing the Eastern Star. In consistency with his position, he thus condemns any attempt at interference in the internal crises of this organization. Williamson bemoans the fact that on several occasions members of the Eastern Star had attempted to call the brothers of Prince Hall as witnesses. He is probably alluding to an internal conflict that was disturbing the New York Eastern Star chapter, probably concerning a simple matter of succession in the leadership of the order.

It seems to have been motivated by certain women who had ambition to become the Grand Matron, but who could never procure the necessary majority of votes at any session of the Grand Chapter to be elected to this office.[23]

A rift then occurred inside the grand chapter: it would seem that these women were as incapable of resisting as their husbands those honors that are casually called "cordonite"* in the French Masonic milieus. Williamson bemoans the fact that the New York grand master of that time, George E. Marshall, became embroiled in this conflict by giving support to those who created the rift. Generally speaking, he found it regrettable that the Prince Hall Grand Lodges placed the members of the Eastern Star on equal footing with themselves![24] He was inclined to believe that the female organizations were essentially a source of irritation and that the Prince Hall Grand Lodges should not encourage their existence or at least should have the sense to keep a safe distance from them. However, his viewpoint does not seem to have been shared by the majority of Prince Hall Masons, who most often used the Eastern Star as a foil, the ladies having the courtesy to help them in material tasks to ensure the harmonious functioning of the lodge and its external standing.

Anxious to maintain good relations, the officers of the Prince Hall Grand Lodges paid numerous courtesy visits to the members of the Easter Star, Amaranth, and Heroines of Jericho.

For example, the Pennsylvania grand master, in his 1956 report, states he attended religious services organized jointly by the Heroines of Jericho and the Eastern Star with the First African Baptist Church.[25] The sisters, like the brothers, were heavily involved in local religious life and especially in the churches that specifically served the black community. They were enthusiastically encouraged by the Prince Hall Masons, even when they had not been founded by some of their fellow members.

---

*[From *cordon,* meaning "ribbon," as in the ribbons that customarily adorn medals, which means that members compete to become officers of the lodge because they consider offices as prestigious, and therefore earn the right of wearing the jewels attached to each office. In French we refer to "cordons," but in England and the States it is rather "jewels," or Masonic regalia. —Trans.]

The Women's Activities

Some women worked on behalf of a specific lodge. This was the case for the Plumb and Level Club, founded in 1922 by Mary Helps and Minerva Williams, wives or close relatives to members of the Carthaginian Club n° 47 in Brooklyn. The club organized a bridge and whist party at the home of Clarence G. Holmes, first supervisor of the lodge. The club met once a month at the private home of a brother and his wife, and the women did needlepoint under the guidance of Helps. Furthermore, the club was responsible for preparing the meal and various snacks for the brothers at the end of their sessions. In 1923 the club gave the lodge one hundred aprons that its members had made.[26]

It should be noted that Williamson, who wrote the history of the lodge and its club, did not utter the slightest criticism of the work performed by the women. It was likely that he found this kind of organization perfectly suitable, because the relatives of the brothers had a clearly defined role and did not meet in lodges that practiced a ritual, even an adoptive one. Williamson even expressed regret when the club disappeared several years later, as it had been a source of much dynamic energy for the lodge and especially supported the morale of the brothers, who then had to take personal responsibility for it.

> It was a rather unfortunate period when this Club began to become inactive because it had proved a great asset to the morale of the Lodge.[27]

Celestial Lodge n° 3 could also count on its wives' support. In 1892 mention is made in its annals of a benevolent women's society, the Ladies Helping Hand Society.[28]

The Supreme Grand Chapter of Boston was founded in 1907 for the purpose of "cooperating in the great labors of Masonry by assisting in and, in some respects, directing their charities and toiling in the cause of human progress," thus repeating almost word for word the statement by Pike cited earlier.[29]

It would seem that the lodges of the Eastern Star pursued activities quite similar to those of the Carthaginian Lodge club of Brooklyn. This is how it was possible to see the Eastern Star women at the Harlem Temple in April 1999 preparing lottery tickets for a benefit run by the Prince Hall brothers for the neighboring retirement home while the brothers were talking and drinking beer in the adjacent office of the grand master.* The old-fashioned nature of this women's association has not yet discouraged all those of goodwill, to the great relief of the brothers.

It would be unfair not to mention the role of Grand Matron Joe Brown in the early part of the twentieth century. In her 1924 speech to the order's grand officers she appealed to the women to use their right to vote and to work harder that way in their battle against racial discrimination, in particular by mobilizing to have a law enacted against lynching.

> And while I would not suggest the taking of our Order into politics, yet in this new day our women everywhere should be urged to make use of their right of suffrage, where they are permitted to do so and that when they vote not fail to place in office men and women who will safeguard the interest of our group as well as the public in general in both State and National Legislatures, and by so doing we may do away with the present status where our National Congress has failed for two sessions to pass the Dyer Anti-Lynching bill, because as the Senators declare there has been no demand for such legislation on the part of their constituents.[30]

The same Joe Brown rose up courageously against the position of several Prince Hall grand masters who seized the right to govern the chapters of the Eastern Star and even made their disagreements public by filing suit against the women's organizations. This was a wrong done to the entire black community, she stated, because it showed a total lack of confidence in women.

---

*Personally witnessed by this author.

In several Jurisdictions the grand master of Ancient Free and Accepted Masons seems to have conceived the idea that he is also grand master of the Order of the Eastern Star and has even gone so far as to carry his contention in this respect into the civil courts, thus proving to the members of the other race that our men have no confidence in their women or that we are not yet ready for our own leadership.[31]

This example is truly the exception that proves the rule. In fact, generally speaking, and in sharp contrast to the French female lodges, the Eastern Star chapters seem to have taken scant interest in the emancipation of women.

In 1923 the Eastern Star organization was officially invited by the NAACP to take part in the Third Pan-African Congress but was unable to accept this invitation as the inscription fees were too steep. This shows both that the Eastern Star was not a very wealthy organization and, on the other hand, that the NAACP probably got greater advantage from the presence of the Prince Hall brothers than that of their companions.

The Prince Hall wives were particularly sensitive to their image in American society. It is not impossible that they had informal ties with some of the white women members of the Eastern Star. These women frequently visited the black neighborhoods of New York. In Williamson's personal papers there is a story of the visit of Mrs. Estelle D. Caldwell, grand matron of the white Eastern Star of Mount Vernon, to the Bronx Masonic Temple on March 21, 1944, in the company of her officers.[32]

Many Eastern Star women would recognize themselves in the remarks of a member of the Indiana Grand Chapter who stated that on the day when "all the white Masons were as true to the principles of Masonry as the Christian women of the land we would soon extirpate from the face of the country all barriers of fraternal organization."[33]

Thus, to the extent possible, and even if it led them to collide with the resistance of the men of their community, not to mention those of the Prince Hall Grand Lodges, the female companions of Masons have sometimes performed a militant role in American society.

Recent Developments

The women of the Eastern Star and of the Amaranth sometimes are not satisfied to perform purely charitable activities and sometimes are heavily involved in the social sector. This is the account that Cassandra Wheeler, grand deputy of Ohio, gives of her own activities.

> Amaranth Grand Chapter is the state body for Prince Hall Eastern Stars. I am the Grand Deputy and have about 750 Eastern Stars under my jurisdiction. We are engaged monthly in several charity projects including Walks for all the different organizations such as American Cancer Society, Diabetes Association, Domestic Violence against Women. We serve meals at a local City Mission to the homeless and have food drives to re-stock neighborhood pantries that distribute food to low-income and homeless people. We have several scholarships to assist college-bound high school seniors and also ones for returning adults. I organize an annual Women's Seminar program, which features free mastectomies, speakers about financial planning, pre-need funeral services, issues concerning caregivers, blood pressure screenings, and preventive medicine—most of these are coordinated through social service agencies and local hospital community-outreach programs. Lately we have focused a lot on domestic violence against women and hazing in the gay community. I conduct quarterly Leadership Training for officers and assist them with personal development including resume writing, interview techniques for jobs, and team-building skills. It is honestly a full-time job—but very rewarding.[34]

It is easy to see that this woman is engaged in some very contemporary struggles, such as the fight against domestic violence and discrimination against homosexuals.

Furthermore, contrary to the sisters of the Eastern Star chapters attached to the white lodges, those of Prince Hall today consider their practice as that of the adoptive rite. This is an important subtlety, for the rite of adoption is a completely distinct Masonic rite and not an indulgence by the relatives of Masons doing charitable works in the name of the brothers. In addition, contrary to what is the case for the white Eastern Star, there is no autonomous Eastern Star chapter in Prince Hall Masonry. All chapters fall under the direct jurisdiction of the Prince Hall Grand Lodges. This clearly means that the chapters of the Eastern Star are related to Freemasonry and do not form some autonomous, distinct organization. Another significant difference concerns the ritual: the Order of the Amaranth today represents the 3rd degree awarded inside the Eastern Star and is not a separate degree, as it is for white women. In fact the Eastern Star awards three grades:

> The Eastern Star Degree
> The Queen of the South Degree
> The Amaranth Degree

This means that all these grades are awarded in the chapters that are themselves directly connected to the Prince Hall Grand Lodges. Because of this, the bond is much closer inside black Masonry between the male grand lodges and the chapters.

Furthermore, Paul Rich and Guillermo de los Reyes have clearly shown the importance of the Queen of the South ritual in the practices maintained by the black sisters of Eastern Star while it has been removed from those of their white counterparts. It so happens that this degree includes a dialogue between the Queen of Sheba and King Solomon on the specific place of women in Freemasonry.[35]

It would be a mistake to think that the Eastern Star chapters connected to the Prince Hall lodges have exactly the same mode of functioning as the grand chapter that is recognized as a simple charitable organization by the white American grand lodges.

Black women still have a long road ahead of them before they achieve equality, but it seems they have taken a few steps further in this direction than their white sisters. However, with only a few exceptions, the sisters, like the brothers, practice Masonry separately according to skin color in the American community tradition.

NINE

Jazzmen
and Black Artists

The visitors to the jazz museum* occupying a small hall on the top floor of a building on a small street in Harlem receive a warm welcome because they are rare. If, in addition, they are knowledgeable enough to ask a few questions about Freemasonry, they will stupefy their hosts, as it is still not common knowledge that Nat King Cole, Cab Calloway, Duke Ellington, and many others were lodge members. The jazz museum is currently undergoing renovation and will soon set up shop in premises much worthier of the cultural influence it seeks to have in the heart of Harlem.

The histories written about jazz do not mention the Masonic membership of many musicians, although there may be some exceptions. The same is true for the biographical sketches, although they are generally well informed, posted by American National Biography Online.[1] We are in Raphaël Imbert's debt for the first materials on jazz and Freemasonry.[2] Not only did he attempt to take a census of Freemason jazzmen, but he also deeply analyzed the spiritual dimension of jazz,† which has heavily influenced American society since its golden age in the 1920s and throughout the twentieth century.[3] This does not mean, he says, "that there is some kind of Masonic jazz. Or rather, there are no musical Masonic rituals that can be identified as jazz."[4]

---

*I visited it in July 2012.
†The word *jazz* appeared for the first time in written form in 1913.

Imbert breaks down the spiritual dimension of jazz into three tendencies: "religious, mystical, and metaphysical."[5] He rightly demonstrates that the religious dimension is an abiding presence for these musicians, much more than it is for most European musicians. The attitude of the American churches, which in most cases supported the fight against slavery and the civil rights movement, just like the lodges of Prince Hall, explains the attachment of many black Masons to the religious tradition, as I have tried to show in the preceding chapters.

I am not going to focus so much on the "spiritual" dimension of the bond between jazz and Freemasonry as on the social aspects. In fact the so-called royal art and the art of music have coupled harmoniously to accompany the social rise from poverty of a large number of artists who also had to confront a society that was still strongly gripped by racial discrimination.

The Racist Context and Social Ascent of Jazzmen

Several of these musicians were born in dire poverty. In his autobiography, *Satchmo,** Louis Armstrong describes the wretched conditions in which his family lived in New Orleans during the years 1910–1920, in a neighborhood where violence and prostitution got on well with each other. As a teenager he was sent to a juvenile home for firing a shot in the air to defend himself against a criminal threatening him, and he was also a small-time pimp for a while until he was able to make a living from his concerts.

Armstrong's father, a worker in a turpentine factory, abandoned him at an early age, and he rarely saw him. It so happened that his father was a member of the Odd Fellows, the mutual-aid society that often included the same members as the Prince Hall Lodges. Armstrong recounts with some pride how his father took part every year in

---

*It is not certain that Armstrong was a Mason, and some have claimed he was not the author of this autobiography, but this takes nothing away from the validity of the observations about society at that time.

Fig. 9.1. Louis Armstrong (1901–1971)

the great parade as a grand marshal.[6] He later explains that all the clubs paraded in New Orleans: "the Oddfellows, the Masons, the Knights of Pythias (my lodge)."[7] It is likely that, like his father, Armstrong joined fraternal societies and that "my lodge" refers to the Knights of Pythias and not the Freemasons. He says he was also a member of the Tammany Soul and Pleasure Club.[8]

It is certain that these societies or clubs played a very similar role to that of the Masonic lodges by affording their members social recognition that was all the more valuable as they were often of humble extraction and the victims of racial discrimination. At the end of the First World War, while playing concerts in New Orleans, Armstrong was still obliged to deliver carts of coal in order to make a living.

Membership in Freemasonry conferred a guarantee of respectability and good morality. This was of such import that Dizzy Gillespie wrote in his autobiography that he was not initiated because he was living with a woman out of wedlock and had neglected to mention it to the lodge members, who learned of it on their own.[9]

Chicago attracted many jazz musicians, and Nat King Cole took

*Fig. 9.2. Nat King Cole
(1919–1965)*

advantage of the fact that his family had decided to move there in 1923, when he was just four years old. The city, all the same, was not a haven from racist behavior, including that of "colored" people who wanted to assimilate completely into white society, as shown by the following incident that Cole experienced a short time later.

> Once in Chicago, I sat down on a bus next to this light-skinned black lady, and she turned to me and said: "You are black and you stink and you can never wash it off."[10]

These remarks, which were all the more hurtful coming from a black woman, left an indelible impression on Cole. Later, when the musician had successfully broken into an artistic milieu that was largely white, he had to confront many forms of discrimination, or at least some unpleasant incidents. When he tried to buy what was a veritable palace—a fourteen-room home—in one of the most bourgeois neighborhoods of Los Angeles, Hancock Park, a homeowners' association, tried to oppose it by suing the seller. A year later the B'nai Brith,* a Masonic-like Jewish organization, published a report denouncing the organizations guilty of discrimination against blacks. Among them they cited the homeowners' association that had harassed Cole and his wife: the Hancock Park Property Owners Association.[11]

When Cole neglected, it must be said, to pay his taxes, his Cadillac and house were confiscated, and the musician barely managed to hold on to his property by negotiating a repayment plan for his fiscal debts. Finally, during a concert tour in the South, he was physically attacked by four people in the middle of a concert in the city of Birmingham, Alabama. His assailants were arrested and convicted thanks to the support of the mayor of Birmingham and the determination of the judges, who were outraged by this openly racist assault.[12]

The Musicians in Society

To the extent that musicians released no public statements about their Masonic membership, and by reason that the Prince Hall Grand Lodges have never made their archives available to researchers in any systematic fashion, it is quite difficult to precisely evaluate the importance of Freemasonry in these men's lives. No jazz composition makes any allusion to Freemasonry with the exception of Albert Ayler's "Masonic Inborn," from 1964.[13] In *Great Black Men of Freemasonry,* Joseph Cox clearly tried to take an inventory of some of the big names, but without giving initiation dates or when these Masons were received into the higher grades, only the lodge names.

Several Internet sites offer lists of Freemason musicians, but without supplying any details and, more importantly, any evidence. I can only provide foundations for this argument based on several accounts, mainly those of Armstrong on those rare occasions he mentions Masons in his autobiography.

---

*The B'nai B'rith is an international organization founded in 1843 in the United States, which only accepts members of the Jewish faith and practices Masonic rites but has no official ties with any Masonic obediences. Its purpose is to fight anti-Semitism and discrimination. It is therefore no surprise that it stepped forth on Cole's behalf when he was the victim of a racist campaign.

As for the supposed fact that Duke Ellington relayed his impressions of initiation in the song "I'm Beginning to See the Light," all it takes is to read the words of this song to out a swift end to this fable, which has been peddled over the Internet as well as by a few American Masons with overactive imaginations.[14] On the other hand, *The Brotherhood*, the title of a concert he gave at Westminster Abbey on October 24, 1973, several months before his death certainly makes allusions to Freemasonry.

Imbert cites the testimony of bass player Milt Hinton, who, in his autobiography published in 2008, recalls the era when he played in Cab Calloway's band, which was composed of a large number of Masons, all of whom had been initiated at the Pioneer Lodge n° 1 of Prince Hall in Saint Paul, Minnesota.[15] The Pioneer Lodge still exists and has an Internet site on which it retraces its history. Created in Minnesota in 1866, the lodge successively obtained charters from the Prince Hall Grand Lodge of Missouri, then from the Prince Hall Grand Lodge of

Fig. 9.3. Pioneer Lodge n° 1 of Saint Paul, Minnesota

Iowa, before obtaining its current charter from the Grand Lodge of Minnesota* in 1894.[16]

Whether or not initiated (doubt persists in Armstrong's case), jazzmen often had an opportunity to rub elbows with Freemasons. It is common knowledge that Masons have always given great importance to funeral ceremonies. In his autobiography, Armstrong tells how his musician friends were hired for the funeral memorials of Masons killed during a hurricane that struck New Orleans shortly before the First World War.

> Joe Oliver, Bunk Johnson, Freddie Keppard, and Henry Allen, all of whom played trumpets in brass bands, made a lot of money playing at funerals for lodge members who had been killed in the storm.[17]

Armstrong tells a funny story about the performance of his group of musicians at the funeral for one of these Masons. He does not say whether the brothers of this lodge were white or black; most likely both would have displayed the same social derision, as the Prince Hall Masons were generally members of the black middle class. Whatever the case, these Masons, who had their own orchestra but needed backup, treated Armstrong and his friends haughtily until the moment when these latter threw the crowd into a frenzy with their fast-paced music and compelled their admiration. The lodge then called on them to play many times after that. He explains:

> The day of the funeral the musicians were congregating at the hall where the Lodge started their march, to go to the dead brother's house. Kid Ory and I noticed all those stuck-up guys giving us lots of ice. They didn't feel we were good enough to play their marches.
>
> I nudged Ory, as if to say, "You dig what I'm digging?" Ory gave me a nod, as if to say, he digged.
>
> We went up to the house playing a medium fast march. All the

---

*All of these changes correspond to the dates on which these Prince Hall Grand Lodges were created. The Minnesota lodge only came into being in 1894. This is why the lodge had to affiliate with lodges in other states before this time.

music they gave us we played and a lot easier than they did. They still didn't say anything to us one way or the other.

Then they brought the body out of the house and we went on to the cemetery. We were playing those real slow funeral marches. After we reached the cemetery, and lowered the body down six feet in the ground, and the drummer man rolled on the drums, they struck a ragtime march that required swinging from the band. And those old fossils just couldn't cut it. That's when we Ory boys took over and came in with flying colors. We were having that good old experience, swinging that whole band. It sounded so good! . . . and the crowd went wild.

After that incident those stuck-up guys wouldn't let us alone. They hired us several times afterward. After all, we'd proved to them that any learned musician can read music, but they can't all swing. It was a good lesson for them.[18]

Involvement in the Fight against Discrimination

Several jazz musicians who were Masons lent their support, more or less directly, to the NAACP, which in 1909 replaced the Niagara Movement, which was founded by the Prince Hall Mason W. E. B. Du Bois for the purpose of combatting racial discrimination.* Cole, in particular, dedicated several concerts to the group. However, as he long refused to become a member of the organization, some NAACP members accused him of being an Uncle Tom.† Criticisms were levied against Cole that he thought solely of his personal integration and his commercial interests in the white artistic world. However, when Cole did join the NAACP, he did it with no hesitation and became a lifetime member. It must be said that shortly before he took this step he had been the victim of the racial assault at the Birmingham concert (see pp. 108–9). In May 1956, he wrote a memorable letter to the editor regarding the NAACP.

---

*See chapter 6, "The Fight for Civil Rights."
†See page 33 for an explanation of the expression.

Detroit, Michigan

To the Editor:

I have been concerned over reports appearing in newspapers, which purport to represent my views on Jim Crow* and discrimination. These reports also attributed to me statements I was supposed to have made regarding the NAACP and its activities.

First of all, I would like to say that I am, have been, and will continue to be dedicated to the complete elimination of all forms of discrimination, segregation, and bigotry. There is only one position in this matter and that is the right one: full equality for all people, regardless of race, creed, or religion.

This has been my position all along, and contrary to any published reports, it remains my position. I have fought, in what I considered an effective manner, against the evil of race bigotry through the years. I had hoped that through the medium of my music I had made new friends and changed many opinions regarding racial equality. I have always been of the opinion that by living equality, living as a full American dedicated to the democratic principle that [I] was helping fight bigotry by example much as the NAACP and other organizations have fought through the courts.

I do not want to be defensive about my position. I stand on my record. I have always supported the NAACP and other organizations fighting segregation and discrimination. Only last November I played a benefit for the Las Vegas Branch NAACP. Roy Wilkins has in his files my written offer to help in the NAACP program in whatever manner I can. I have in my personal records cancelled checks of my contributions to several NAACP Chapters, as well as to the Montgomery bus boycott.†

Since it is obvious that those who are opposed to equality and dignity of all men have used the unfortunate Birmingham incident as a weapon against the NAACP, against me, and against the fight for first-class citizenship, I am today subscribing to the NAACP as a liege member.

---

*"Jim Crow" is an expression that designates racial segregation.

†Cole is referring to the famous bus boycott that followed the arrest of Rosa Parks. She had been arrested for refusing to give her seat to a white person on the bus. This was the beginning of the civil rights struggle. Martin Luther King Jr. was deeply involved in the support of this boycott.

I sincerely hope, that in a small manner, this will set the record straight and help bring closer the day when bigotry and discrimination are things of the past, wherever they exist.

Nat (King) Cole[19]

The use of the term *race* is naturally dated, but more so in France than in the United States, and there is nothing pejorative about its use by Cole here. It is worth noting that the musician emphasizes the fanatical form of discrimination by his use of the word *bigotry*. His references to equality regardless of religious belief or race are quite in accord with the Masonic concepts of his Prince Hall brothers. The white Masonic obediences could call themselves universal as much as they wished, but the fact remained that in 1956 none of them recognized their black brothers. In 1963, President John F. Kennedy (who was not a Mason) invited Cole to the White House. As a general rule, Cole did not like being questioned about civil rights, because he considered himself "a professional musician and not a professional Negro."[20]

Actor and singer Paul Robeson, on the other hand, was unambiguously committed to the fight against discrimination. Contrary to many artists of his time, he made a political choice. It was George Bernard Shaw, the famous English playwright, who initiated him into socialism. Robeson expressed enthusiasm, not absent of a certain naïveté, for the Soviet Union during a trip to Moscow in 1943. He lived there at several different times and even enrolled his son in a Soviet school. In 1938 he went to Spain to give support to the Republicans. During the Second World War he gave benefit concerts in London for the victims of fascism, in partnership with English militant organizations. Named best actor of the year for his performance in *Othello* in 1943, he was also rewarded by the NAACP, which gave him a prestigious award in 1945, the Spingarn Medal for his involvement in support of civil rights.

His socialist ideas earned him harsh punishment during the McCarthy era. He was labeled a communist by the House Un-American Activities Committee, kept under surveillance by the FBI, and stripped of his passport.[21] His artistic career was radically affected, and he had to sell

*Fig. 9.4. Paul Robeson
(1898–1976)*

his property in Connecticut. Although he had been awarded a medal by the NAACP, he criticized this organization's positions, which he deemed too moderate, and felt that blacks should lead the movement for civil rights, thereby foreshadowing the black power movement of the 1960s. In his autobiography, *Here I Stand,* he states:

> The artist must elect to fight for Freedom or for Slavery. I have made my choice. I had no alternative.[22]

It is quite noteworthy that the Prince Hall Freemasons, who ordinarily showed the wariness of a wild animal when confronted by political involvement, invited him to join their ranks. It is true that there was one precedent: Du Bois (see chapter 4).

Generally speaking, the members of Prince Hall Lodges were not open to separatism but favored integration into American society. Some exceptions prove the rule, such as the case of Martin Robison Delany, mentioned in chapter 3. I should also mention the coauthor of *The Auto-biography of Malcolm X,* Alex Haley, who attained the 32nd degree of the Ancient and Accepted Scottish Rite in the Prince Hall Chapter, Southern Jurisdiction.[23] Haley had published his book in 1965, several weeks before the assassination of the book's subject. This book, which advocates black nationalism and Islam (related to the Black Muslims movement), was based on a series of interviews with this famous black leader.

It is certain that jazz musicians' desire for recognition in American society generally encouraged them to moderation. In the main, however, they were incapable of bending their knees to racist behavior such as refusing to admit black spectators to some of their concerts and physical attacks like the one that befell Nat King Cole. It can be assumed that membership in a Masonic lodge offered support and reassurance.

Extensive research is still necessary to be able to precisely determine the affiliation of black musicians. The Masonic membership of a certain number has been established, although it is imprecise, so the dates of their reception and elevation into the higher grades are still mysteries. It is probable that several musicians belonged to Masonic lodges that were not recognized by the Prince Hall Grand Lodges. A great number of these lodges exist, but, in the absence of archives, whether this absence is dictated by a desire for discretion or the negligence of their secretaries, it is impossible to say anything more about them and to retrace the affiliation of their members.

Several Talented Mason Brothers

Louis Armstrong (1901–1971): A jazz trumpet player and singer, Armstrong, who was known universally as Satchmo, then Pops, was born in New Orleans, where he was raised by his grandmother. He began enjoying success as a musician in Chicago starting in 1922. In 1933 he began performing on the radio, the first black musician to host a broadcast on the airwaves.

Armstrong contributed to the advancement of black culture through the Harlem Renaissance. He stood up against racial discrimination, particularly when Alabama governor Orval Faubus tried to deny black children access to a public school in 1957 following Supreme Court desegregation. He was nicknamed the Goodwill Ambassador or Ambassador Satch during his tours through Europe and Africa in the 1950s, tours sponsored by the United States government. Armstrong is universally recognized as one of the great figures of jazz.[24]

His Masonic adherence has not been fully established. Some say that he was a member of Montgomery Lodge n° 18 in New York, affiliated with Prince Hall, but no Prince Hall Lodge goes by this name.[25] According to Joseph Walkes, Armstrong could very easily have been part of an association that Prince Hall did not recognize, so it would not appear on any of their lists.[26]

In his autobiography, Armstrong mentions his father, who was not a Freemason but an Odd Fellow, as well as the Masonic funerals for which he was hired to play as a musician. He states that he was a member of the Knights of Pythias, a fraternal organization founded in Washington, D.C., in 1864.[27]

Count Basie (1904–1984): This famous pianist and bandleader was born in New Jersey and there began his career in the 1920s before going to the Reno Club in Kansas City. He then moved to New York. He hesitated between the stage and a career in music and acted in vaudeville in New Orleans, then Kansas and Oklahoma. He was a member of the Blue Devils, a band that played boogie-woogie. He took on the name Count in imitation of the nicknames adopted by other Harlem

Fig. 9.5. Count Basie (1904–1984)

musicians and took on this title once and for all when he was a member of Benny Moten's band. He toured Europe on several occasions and recorded several records with Frank Sinatra.[28]

Basie was a member of the Medina Lodge n° 19, Grand Lodge of Prince Hall.[29]

James Herbert "Eubie" Blake (1883–1983): Blake was a pianist and a composer of ragtime music (most notably "Charleston Rag"). He was born in Maryland and the son of former slaves. He lived briefly in New York before moving into the Goldfield Hotel of Baltimore. In 1915 he met singer and bandleader Noble Sissle, with whom he collaborated for many years composing songs. Their vaudeville show, *Dixie Duo,* enjoyed great success. They both contributed to the creation of the Broadway musical comedy *Shuffle Along,* for which Blake was the bandleader. This musical launched the careers of several famous actors and actresses, among whom are Paul Robeson and Josephine Baker. At the age of sixty-three Blake enrolled in New York University, where he obtained a degree in music.[30] Blake was a member of the Medina Lodge n° 19, Grand Lodge of Prince Hall.[31]

Fig. 9.6. Eubie Blake (1887–1983)

McHenry Rutherford Boatwright (1928–1994): Boatwright was an opera singer who was mentioned in an article in the July 26, 1967, edition of the *New York Telegraph* for his role in *The Visitation,* an opera that brought the relations between New York blacks and whites to the stage.

Boatwright too was a member of the Medina Lodge n° 19, Grand Lodge of Prince Hall.[32]

Cab Calloway (1907–1994): This singer and bandleader was born in Rochester, New York. As a child he played as a soloist for the Bethlehem Methodist Episcopal Church; he then played for a number of jazz bands, including Armstrong's. He had countless love affairs, the first of which took place before he finished school and resulted in an illegitimate child. He was bandleader for the Missourians and played alternating dates with Duke Ellington at the Cotton Club of New York, as well as in Minnesota. He was the inspiration for the character of Sportin' Life in George Gershwin's 1935 opera *Porgy and Bess*. He was extremely popular and made many tours across the United States and Canada.[33]

Calloway was a member of the Pioneer Lodge n° 1, Minnesota Grand Lodge of Prince Hall.

He is depicted in a photograph published in Milt Hinton's autobiography, in the company of that author, trumpet player Keg Johnson, and another unidentified Mason, all wearing their gloves and aprons.[34]

Fig. 9.7. Cab Calloway
(1907–1994)

Nat King Cole (1919–1965): A pianist, bandleader, and actor (he appeared in several films, including *Cat Ballou,* starring Lee Marvin and Jane Fonda, and on television), Cole was born in Montgomery,

Alabama. He studied piano, first with his mother, then with a music teacher. He became friends with Armstrong in 1935 and in 1937 formed the King Cole Trio, which performed and recorded in Los Angeles, New York, Chicago, and London. He also worked with several bands, including that of Count Basie.

Cole died of lung cancer at the age of forty-five on February 15, 1965. Just before his death he was planning to bring James Baldwin's play *The Amen Corner* to the stage. His widow, Maria, took over for him. Both his daughters followed in his footsteps, Carol as an actress and Natalie as a singer. His son, Kelly, works in film production. Maria Cole, in collaboration with Louie Robinson, wrote her father's biography: *Nat King Cole: An Intimate Biography*.[35] He was a member of the Thomas Waller Lodge n° 49 of Los Angeles, California, Grand Lodge of Prince Hall.[36]

Edward Kennedy "Duke" Ellington (1899–1974): Ellington was born to a middle-class family in Washington, D.C. He did not get a high school diploma, and he tried his chances in the music world at an early age. He debuted at a Harlem cabaret. His breakthrough came when he opened a new club on Broadway, the Kentucky Club. From 1927 to 1931 he led the house band at the Cotton Club. In 1933, Ellington left

Fig. 9.8. Duke Ellington (1899–1974)

for his first tour of England and Europe. According to his biography at American National Biography Online, his work enjoys greater success after his death than when he was alive. He wrote an autobiography, titled *Music Is My Mistress,* in 1973.

Ellington does not discuss his Masonic membership in this autobiography but includes a photo of himself wearing a Shriner's fez. Membership in this organization is restricted to high-degree Masons, but, paradoxically enough, it is not considered Masonic. Contrary to what has often been claimed, "I'm Beginning to See the Light" is a love song and has nothing to do with his impressions of initiation.[37]

Ellington was a member of Social Lodge n° 1 in Washington, D.C., and also a 32nd-degree Scottish Mason, Supreme Council of Prince Hall, Southern Jurisdiction. He was also active in the Acacia Grand Lodge in Washington, D.C.[38]

Lionel Hampton (1908–2002): Hampton was a pianist, drummer, and singer and also played the vibes. He was born in Louisville, Kentucky, although efforts were made to convince him that he was an Alabama native, born five years earlier than his actual birth date.[39] He played in several bands, including the band Louis Armstrong headed at Frank Sebastian's Cotton Club in Culver City, California. He also played in small groups with Benny Goodman, then in 1940 founded the Lionel Hampton Orchestra, in which he trained young talent such as Charles Mingus. Hampton also headed a record company and was involved in philanthropic work that included the construction of low-income housing in Harlem. In 1985 he began providing consistent financial backing for the Lionel Hampton Jazz Festival, and in 1987 he sponsored a music school at the University of Idaho: the Lionel Hampton School of Music. He was given what is presumably an honorary degree from Pepperdine University in California.[40] The composer of many well-known pieces of music, his "Stardust" achieved legendary status. A sometime-Republican, sometime-Democrat, he performed at the inaugurations of Presidents Truman, Eisenhower, Nixon, G. H. W. Bush, and Clinton (he was eighty-eight years old when he played for the last).

Hampton was a member of the high grades of the Scottish Rite:

Fig. 9.9. Lionel Hampton (1908–2002) (photo by William P. Gottlieb)

King David Consistory n° 3, Valley of New York (one of the many supreme councils of the Scottish Rite for the Prince Hall lodges).[41] He was also a member of the Prince Hall Research Lodge of New York.[42] It is not known when he was initiated, or where.

William C. "W. C." Handy (1873–1958): This composer, who wrote "Memphis Blues," "St. Louis Blues," and "The Beale Street Blues," among others, and a collection of Negro spirituals, was born in Alabama.

Fig. 9.10. W. C. Handy (1873–1958)

Handy was a lifetime member of the Hiram Lodge n° 4, Prince Hall Grand Lodge of New York, and a 33rd-degree Mason of the Supreme Council of the Scottish Rite, Northern Jurisdiction, of Prince Hall.[43]

J. Rosamond Johnson (1873–1954): Johnson was a ragtime composer. A student of the Boston Conservatory in Massachusetts, he went on to become the musical director of the oldest music school in New York, the Music School Settlement. He directed a musical comedy in 1913 at London's Lyric Hammersmith Opera House, which enjoyed great success.

Johnson was also a member of the Hiram Lodge n° 4, Prince Hall Grand Lodge of New York, and a 33rd-degree Mason of the Supreme Council of the Ancient and Accepted Scottish Rite, Northern Jurisdiction, of Prince Hall.[44]

Fig. 9.11. J. Rosamond Johnson
(1873–1954)

"Mississippi" Fred McDowell (1904–1972): McDowell was a native of the Mississippi Delta. He played slide guitar* in Tennessee, specializing in the blues.[45] We do not know what lodge he belonged to, but he was photographed in his coffin wearing his Mason's apron. Furthermore, a square and compass are carved on his tombstone in the Hammond Hill Methodist Baptist Church Cemetery, in Como, Panola County,

---

*Slide guitar means that the musician plays it while wearing a glass bottleneck on a finger, which he slides on the strings to get a gliding sound from note to note.

*Fig. 9.12. "Mississippi"
Fred McDowell (1904–1972)*

Mississippi. He is buried there with his wife, Ester Mae McDowell (1906–1980). It is likely that he belonged to Prince Hall.*

Paul Robeson (1898–1976): Robeson was a singer, actor, and lawyer. He studied law at Columbia University in New York, where he financed his education by playing professional football. He was considered brilliant as both a student and athlete. When he finished his studies he worked for a New York law firm but after being the victim of discrimination opted to pursue an artistic career. He performed in Eugene O'Neil plays at a Massachusetts theater. He was introduced to socialism by the famous playwright George Bernard Shaw in 1928 and visited the Soviet Union in 1934. He also lived in London for several years, probably to escape the racism of American society of that time. In any case, he first achieved recognition in the United Kingdom before finding success in his native United States. He was the first black actor to play the role of Othello, on the London stages in 1930 and on Broadway in 1943. He was also an actor in Hollywood (*King Solomon's Mines,* 1937) and the author of a book titled *Here I Stand* (1958), his autobiography.

---

*This is the opinion of Martin Cherry, librarian of the Library and Museum of Freemasonry in London, although he was not able to get any answers from the Prince Hall Grand Lodges. This does not exclude the fact that McDowell may have belonged to a black obedience that Prince Hall did not recognize. He is not among the Masons listed by Joseph Cox.

He was a Mason on sight,*[46] an honor granted by a Prince Hall Grand Lodge, but Cox does not identify which one.[47]

Noble Sissle (1889–1975): A violinist, bandleader, and composer, Sissle was also a lieutenant in the U.S. Army. He was born in Indianapolis, Indiana, where his father was a Methodist minister and his mother a teacher. He pursued his university studies in his home state. He was the first bandleader to perform at the deluxe Ritz-Carlton Hotel in New York. He worked in partnership with Eubie Blake, with whom he wrote the music for vaudeville shows performed in New York. He helped found an association for black actors, the Negro Actors' Guild, of which he was the first president. He also received the honorary title "Mayor of Harlem" in 1950.[48]

Like Eubie Blake, Count Basie, and McHenry Rutherford Boatwright, Sissle was a member of the Medina Lodge n° 19, Grand Lodge of Prince Hall.[49]

*Fig. 9.13. Noble Sissle
(1889–1975)
(Photo taken in 1951
by Carl van Vechten)*

---

*"Mason on sight" means a Mason who was invited to join by the lodge, as was the case for Booker T. Washington and W. E. B. Du Bois. Raphaël Imbert thinks Robeson was initiated into the Beta Kappa Lodge, but when seeking verification from the Livingston Masonic Library of New York, I was told there is no lodge of this name. There is though a student fraternity, Phi Beta Kappa, and Cox mentions that Robeson was a member.

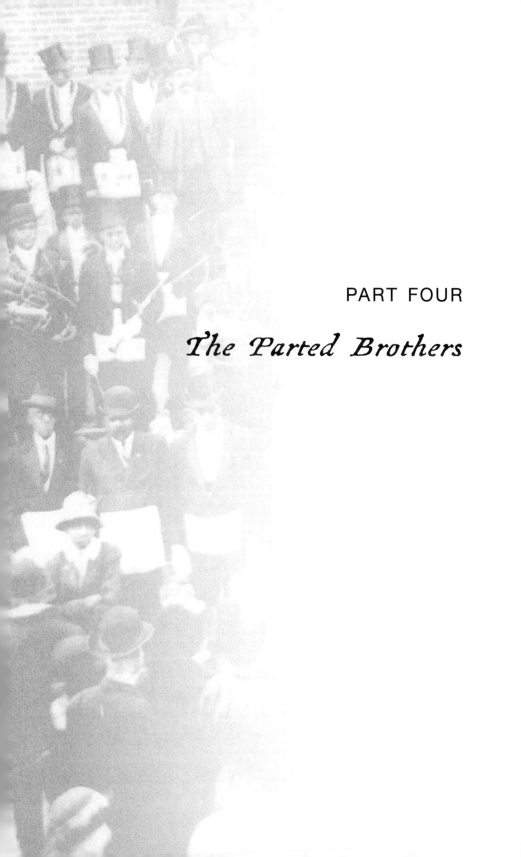

PART FOUR

The Parted Brothers

TEN

The Brothers Who Were Excluded in the Name of the Great Principles

Article III of Anderson's *Constitutions*

Freemasonry can proclaim both its fraternal and universal natures all it likes, but the fact remains that it had no fear about excluding blacks in the name of some very odd principles. American Masonic obediences have long evoked the famous article 3 of Anderson's *Constitutions,* which casts the same discredit on women and slaves.

> The Persons admitted Members of a Lodge must be good and true Men, free-born, and of mature and discreet Age, no Bondmen, no Women, no immoral or scandalous Men, but of good Report.[1]

It is how the text is read that has turned out to be the most crucial thing. It so happens that the white American grand lodges chose the most restrictive reading, while the Grand Lodge of England opted for a more flexible interpretation. This is a good illustration of the fact that the text does not always have the force of law and often inspires subjective interpretations that can conceal inadmissible motivations, which, in this case, would be racist.

In fact, when the freedman Prince Hall, an emancipated slave, requested that he and his friends be accorded the right to found a lodge in Boston, he obtained the charter from the English without Anderson's famous article ever being invoked in opposition. Neither John Rowe, grand master of the Saint John Grand Lodge of Boston, a lodge affiliated with the English Modern Grand Lodge, nor Joseph Warren, worshipful master of the Saint Andrew's Lodge and grand master of the Massachusetts Grand Lodge, felt any need to invoke Anderson's *Constitutions* to definitively shut the door to the former slaves, even though neither granted the famous charter.

Prince Hall maintained excellent relations with the Grand Lodge of England in the years following the African Lodge's obtaining of the charter, so excellent, in fact, that Grand Secretary William White asked him to lead an investigation on the whole of Freemasonry in Massachusetts, both the black and white lodges that were affiliated then with the Grand Lodge of England. White therefore granted no importance whatsoever to his correspondent's skin color, as shown by the letters they exchanged in 1792. Prince Hall completed his task and brought White abreast of the situation of lodges n° 12, n° 88, n° 91, n° 93, and n° 142, white American lodges that appeared on the register of the Grand Lodge of England at the side of African Lodge n° 459. Prince Hall verified that all were meeting regularly with the exception of lodge n° 91.[2]

White could have turned to the worshipful master of any one of these lodges to perform this task. However, it was Prince Hall specifically he chose to do this work, probably because he knew him personally, contrary to the others. Perhaps White also desired to show the confidence he had in Prince Hall by this gesture and show the white lodges the legitimacy of the African Lodge.

The English decision to grant a charter to a black lodge created a precedent, even before the 1847* change that replaced the expression "free-born" with "free." Starting at this date it would no longer be necessary to be "free-born," it would be sufficient to be free at the time one requested admission. As it happens, American Masons did not think it good to make the same alteration. To the contrary, Albert Mackey

---

*This is the date when that change took place in the text of the *Constitutions*.

gave new strength and vigor to the exclusion of slaves, and therefore all American blacks, in Landmark n° 18.*

> Certain qualifications of candidates for initiation are derived from a Landmark of the Order. These qualifications are that he shall be a man—unmutilated, free-born, and of mature age. That is to say, a woman, a cripple, or a slave, or one born in slavery, is disqualified for initiation into the Rites of Freemasonry.[3]

There was never any question of following the English brothers onto this slippery and dangerously tolerant terrain. Throughout the nineteenth and twentieth centuries the Americans took shelter behind Anderson's text, then Mackey's Landmarks, to exclude blacks.

The Validity of the Charter

There is no doubt that the charter of the first Prince Hall Lodge held symbolic value for both black and white Masons. Martin Robison Delany gives it such importance that he stated in his 1853 speech, without the slightest evidence, that Joseph Warren, the Massachusetts grand master, had granted them one but that it had been lost when he was killed on the battlefield of Bunker Hill in 1775. Delany claimed that the black Masons kept their charter in a secret place due to their great reverence for it and that, in despair at losing it on Warren's death, they had the grand master's body exhumed, thinking he might have carried it with him to his grave. Here legend ends, to be replaced by history.

> It is said, that at an early period of its existence in this country, entertaining a kind of superstitious idea of its sacredness, the

---

*The notion of a "landmark" is subjective because it was subject to a certain number of variations. Anderson was the first to use the term *ancient landmark* in 1723, meaning by that a fairly vague set of principles in force among operative Masons and considered inviolable, but which he took no pain to identify by name. Subsequently, Mackey listed twenty-five, followed in 1893 by the grand secretary of the Grand Lodge of Kentucky, who drew up a list of fifty-four Landmarks.

Masonic warrant was kept closely in some secret place, prohibited from the view of all but Masons. Consequently when General Warren—who was the grand master of Massachusetts—fell in the revolutionary struggle, the warrant was lost, and with it Masonry in Massachusetts. All Masons are familiar with the fact that Grand Master Warren was raised from his grave and a search made, doubtless, supposing that the warrant might have been found concealed about his person.[4]

It is naturally impossible to state that any such document ever existed, but it is likely that Warren had made promises. It would seem likely that at the very beginning of black Freemasonry, Grand Master Rowe of the Saint John Grand Lodge of Boston granted the black brothers a permission in the place of a charter. No one contests today that the African Lodge n° 459 obtained a proper charter from the Grand Lodge of England dated September 29, 1784. However, because Prince Hall and his friends did not receive this charter until 1787 (see chapter 2, "The Birth of Black Freemasonry"), because of travel mishaps, Prince Hall took the trouble to dissipate any misunderstanding on the matter by sending the following communiqué to the local press.

The Columbian Sentinel—May 2, 1787; "African Lodge," Boston, May 2, 1787.

By Captain Scott, from London, came the charter, etc., which his Royal Highness, the Duke of Cumberland, and the Grand Lodge have been graciously pleased to grant the African lodge in Boston. As the brethren have a desire to acknowledge all favors shown them, they, in public manner, return particular thanks to a certain number of the fraternity, who offered the generous reward in this paper some time since, for the charter supposed to be lost; and to assure him, though they doubt of his friendship, that he has made them many good friends.

Prince Hall[5]

In this way Prince Hall brought to a definitive close the debate on the charter's existence. It can be guessed that tongues were wagging and that the Prince Hall Lodge was the butt of some Bostonians' jokes, because the announced charter never arrived. It is likely that the brother mentioned in this communiqué had derisively offered a reward for the lost charter. This unrefined gesture on the part of a Mason would have given some publicity to the Prince Hall Lodge and earned it some sympathizers, as Prince Hall seems to be saying with tongue in cheek.

Whatever the case may be, no one could deny the existence of the charter dated 1784. Unfortunately for the Prince Hall Masons, and probably because of the same financial negligence that caused the first delay, the lodge vanished for good from the rolls of the United Grand Lodge of England in 1813.* In 1784 some brothers with few scruples had neglected to deliver the money intended for the charter to the grand secretary of London. It would also seem that subsequently the Prince Hall Lodge was not consistent in paying its dues to the English lodge. According to author John M. Sherman, the lodge number was changed in 1792, and African Lodge n° 459 was given the number 370. This seems quite likely given the fact that a large number of English lodges vanished from the rolls of the Modern Grand Lodge for nonpayment of dues.[t6]

So there is no need to see any ill intent directed at the African Lodge in particular: the English simply did not wish to keep any undesirable members, that is to say, those who were bad payers. The peremptory tone adopted by John M. Sherman in *Ars Quatour Coronatorum* in 1980 is therefore cause for some surprise.

---

*Like many other lodges, that of Prince Hall vanished from the rolls of the United Grand Lodge of England; the new grand lodge was created from the Modern and Ancient Grand Lodges in 1813.

†Following the construction of the prestigious Freemasons' Hall in London in 1776, the grand lodge had demanded quite substantial financial contributions from its lodges. Because a large number refused to pay the sums that were asked, they were removed from its rolls.

In 1813 . . . the African Lodge was erased from the rolls of the
Grand Lodge of England for failure, since 1797, to submit returns
to the Grand Lodge and to make any payments to the charity fund.
This "striking from the rolls" automatically made the Charter void
since its Grand Lodge sponsorship had been withdrawn; the fact
that the lodge had retained the certificate made no difference to
its status. Therefore the certificate was nothing more than a historic document, having no force and the lodge, meeting without
authority, had become clandestine.[7]

Sherman should have acknowledged that the Prince Hall Lodge
was not the only one to be erased from the rolls at that time, thereby
minimizing the significance of the British Masons' decision. With this
snap judgment he instead did a favor for the American grand lodges
that had excluded blacks and continued to follow a racist policy toward
them. Sherman adds that in 1824* the African Lodge had formulated
a new request for the renewal of its charter but that the United Grand
Lodge of England denied it on the grounds that the lodge was asking
for the authority to confer the 4th degree, that is to say, that of the
Royal Arch, and that the English obedience did not practice this degree
in its lodges.[8]

The white American grand lodges based their argument that the
Prince Hall Lodge was irregular on the fact that it had been stricken
off the rolls in 1813. They employed this argument for two centuries, probably because it seemed impossible to wear down. Examples
abound. I will simply cite that of the New York Grand Lodge in 1898.
William A. Sutherland, grand master of that lodge, was outraged at
the intention of the Washington Grand Lodge to recognize black
Freemasonry and ended his letter to his colleague, Washington grand
master William H. Upton, with these words:

---

*Only the white American grand lodges mention the 1824 episode; the Prince Hall
Grand Lodges do not.

My dear brother,

There are some essentials in the making of a Mason. One of these is that he must be made in a duly constituted Lodge. Another of these is that Lodge must be furnished with the Great Light of Masonry, and still another is that it must be furnished with a proper charter.[9]

These remarks reveal that the New York grand master was deliberately ignoring the existence of the charter awarded to Prince Hall and his friends. Close to a century later a group of white Masons, the Masonic Research Associates, published a collection of violently racist statements that had been made against black Freemasonry and ended their pamphlet with an official condemnation of all Prince Hall members. The presentation brings to mind those well-known wanted posters that Western sheriffs posted against outlaws. This text does not open with the word *WANTED* in capital letters, but it does start with this warning written in bold letters.

IMPORTANT FOR REGULAR MASONS (READ CAREFULLY).[10]

The authors believe that the charter held by the African Lodge is nothing more than "a worthless scrap of paper devoid of any Masonic authority, validity, force, or effect."[11]

The bad faith of white Masons was shattered even further, for, as observed by the committee of the Massachusetts Grand Lodge, the charter sent to Prince Hall is undoubtedly the sole charter granted by the Grand Lodge of England to Masons meeting on American soil that has been preserved to this day.

That charter is in existence today in a safe deposit box in the City of Boston, Massachusetts, and has been inspected by members of your Committee. There is no question of its authenticity. Moreover, it is believed to be the only original charter issued from the Grand Lodge of England which is now in possession of any Lodge in the United States.[12]

This statement cannot be described as chauvinism as it was issued by a committee named by the white Massachusetts Grand Lodge.*[13] Loretta Williams confirmed this information in 1980 in her book *Black Freemasonry and Middle-Class Realities.*[14] She specifies that the charter survived several mishaps—including a serious conflagration—thanks to the dedication of the African Lodge brothers. Here too history is erased for the benefit of several fine legends. Some claim that a brother heroically entered the building where the lodge customarily met to rescue the charter (kept in a metal tube) from the flames. Others maintain that it was hidden for four years in the trunk of a tree, an oak tree to be precise, to protect it from the evil designs of white brothers who wanted to steal it! Whatever the true circumstances may be, the fact remains that the charter was physically preserved, and no one can challenge its existence today.

The Principle of Territorial Exclusivity

With the independence of the country, commenced the independence of Masonic jurisdiction in the US.

MARTIN ROBISON DELANY,
THE ORIGINS AND OBJECTS OF ANCIENT FREEMASONRY
AND ITS INTRODUCTION INTO THE UNITED STATES
AND ITS LEGITIMACY AMONG COLORED MEN

Delany made the above declaration somewhat casually in 1853, as if the principle of exclusive territorial jurisdiction was self-evident. He did not take into account all its consequences for the black Masonic obediences. Yet he was right in presenting it as a typically American principle. This doctrine does not appear in such stark terms in the British texts, no doubt because the geopolitical context is different. Each American state was concerned with preserving its full Masonic autonomy.

---

*The Massachusetts Grand Lodge did not recognize as such the black Prince Hall Grand Lodges until 1995, but the naming of this committee represented a first step in this direction. The committee's report is signed by Grand Secretary H. Hilton.

Consequently, only one grand lodge was proclaimed legal, which, in actual circumstances made the coexistence of a white grand lodge and a black grand lodge totally impossible. In the United Kingdom, on the other hand, the grand lodges seem to have adopted a more flexible policy. This is what prompted Harry Davis, a black Mason and lawyer, to say in 1946 that the British advocated the doctrine of "rivalry" and not territorial exclusivity, a statement that is probably more demagogic than scientific.[15]

History shows once again that texts are interpreted in accordance with immediate needs. Some American grand lodges flout these geographical restrictions today. Mackey, who could never be accused of Jesuitical tendencies, only mentions the quarrels with the Grand Orient of France under the heading of "exclusive territorial jurisdiction."[16] Mentioning the exclusion of the black Masons in the name of this principle would have only allowed the specter of the white grand lodges' racism to rear its ugly head again.

The grand master of the white obedience in New York, William H. Upton, rightfully noted that the doctrine of territorial exclusivity did not exist in Prince Hall's time, so it is dishonest to criticize the African Lodge, in the name of a principle that was still up in the air, for granting a warrant to the Pennsylvania Masons.

> Inasmuch as it has been assumed and asserted that granting this "license" was an "invasion" of "the exclusive territorial jurisdiction of the Grand Lodge of Pennsylvania," it may be well to note that— assuming that such a thing as exclusive territorial jurisdiction existed at that day, which I do not think any Masonic scholar will admit to have been the case—there were no Lodges or Grand Lodges in Pennsylvania at that time which the Grand Lodge of England—of which Prince Hall was for twenty years a member—admitted to be "regular" bodies.[17]

Let's salute the perseverance of this white grand master who spent his life trying to rehabilitate black Freemasonry in the eyes of his compatriots. Upton clearly shows how specious the argument of territorial exclusivity is. Applying it a posteriori to the first black lodges amounts to writing a biased history, which has often been the case.

The viewpoint of a German Mason, Gottfried Joseph G. Findel, is not lacking in interest, be it only for the fact that he obtained the recognition of black Masons. In 1860, on the eve of the Civil War, the Prince Hall Grand Lodge of Massachusetts named him past grand master of honor and delegate of all the Prince Hall Grand Lodges in Germany as thanks for working to achieve the recognition of the black American obediences. This is a unique example in Masonic history.[18]

Findel, to counter the negative report on the Prince Hall Grand Lodges written by the representative of the white New York Grand Lodge in Germany, Brother von Mensch, compared the theory of territorial exclusivity to the Monroe Doctrine. Just as this famous 1823 doctrine stated any European interference on American territory between the Arctic and Tierra del Fuego would be deemed inacceptable, the white grand lodges sought this pretext to preserve their monopoly over any competition from the black lodges. There is nothing Masonic about this attitude, says Findel.[19]

The Prince Hall Masons condemned the harmful effects of this doctrine on several occasions. In 1877 the Grand Lodge of Arkansas performed an extensive study of this matter. It listed in great detail all the Masonic incidents attributed to the said doctrine, not only among blacks but whites as well. For example, a white lodge of Nebraska was reprimanded by a white Indiana lodge for organizing the Masonic funeral of a member of the Indiana lodge who lived in Nebraska. The black Ohio Grand Lodge obtained the recognition of foreign obediences in France, Italy, Hungary, Germany, Peru, and the Dominican Republic but not that of the white Grand Lodge of Ohio.*[20] Not without humor, the author of the report wrote:

---

*I have not been able to verify these statements, so I am leaving all responsibility for them to their author. Even if they are not all precise, they do clearly show the scope of the problem posed by the principle of territorial exclusivity and the many controversies it triggered.

We have thus far given a brief sketch of the controversies relative to Jurisdiction, which agitated our Grand Bodies during the past year, and as the first result, are driven to wonder how Brothers Solomon, Hiram of Tyre, and Hiram Abiff managed to "rock along" so easily when they exercised concurrent jurisdiction over the temple. . . . It is an American doctrine, or rather a United States, white man's doctrine, for the forty colored Grand Lodges of the United States repudiate it, and the Grand Bodies of other portions of North America know it not, excepting the Canadian Grand Lodge to a partial extent. . . . A nation may acquire jurisdiction by force; a Masonic organization only by concession.[21]

It was precisely during this era that the problem of the existence of a black federal grand lodge, the Compact Grand Lodge, or National Grand Lodge, arose.[22] I have already mentioned the reservations about the lodge of many Masonic historians, such as Joseph Walkes. Even the Alaska Grand Lodge, which denied that there were any good grounds for the principle of territorial exclusivity, seemed in agreement with the convention of the Prince Hall Grand Lodges that met in Chicago on September 4, 1877, and voiced their desire that this national organization would put a halt to its activities.[23] Despite their repeated condemnations of the doctrine of territorial exclusivity, paradoxically, black Masons did not want to be caught red-handed. In other words, they sought an utterly convincing historical justification for the expansion of the first Prince Hall Lodges on American soil, but in 1877 they were sticklers on maintaining exemplary behavior. To show that they were attached to Masonic principles, even henceforth that of territorial exclusivity, they demanded the Compact Grand Lodge to cease its activities.

Subsequently, Prince Hall Masons repudiated "irregular" black Masons in the name of this same principle. With only a few lines between his statements, Williamson pulled off the trick of condemning the white doctrine of territorial exclusivity, then referred back to it to exclude the black Masons who were not members of the Prince Hall Grand Lodge. It seems that whatever weapon comes to hand is good: even the dullest blade.

What effect does the "Doctrine" have upon Prince Hall Masonry?

Absolutely none. The American Grand Lodges refuse to initiate men of color into their Lodges, consequently they have absolutely no control over men in our racial group as Masonic Material. . . .

Why does the Prince Hall Order adhere to that same "Doctrine" of exclusive territorial jurisdiction?

Because the records prove that the Prince Hall Fraternity is a direct descendant of a Grand Lodge of legitimate origin, while there are no records extant which prove any of the "unrecognized" bodies are such descendants.[24]

Williamson then provides a list of "irregular" black Masons who have organized lodges outside the Prince Hall obedience.[25]

This clearly reflects the consistent and highly ambiguous attitude of black Freemasons. They condemned the white grand lodges who opposed them with a certain number of principles in order to exclude them. They were fully aware that these principles were only pretexts. But in their turn they used the same procedure against the black Masons they considered undesirable in order to prove their own concern for legitimacy, at the risk of being extremely legalistic and intolerant themselves. One always needs to find someone weaker than oneself.

The principle of territorial exclusivity still fueled many polemics during the twentieth century, always in a fairly delusional way. While the British appear to be less imprisoned by this doctrine than their American brothers, they invoked it in fairly crude fashion in 1941 to turn down a gift of fifty dollars from the New York Prince Hall Grand Lodge for the London Hospital on the grounds that the United Grand Lodge of England had formal ties with the white grand lodge of this state only.[26]

It was still in the name of this doctrine that the Rhode Island grand master refused to recognize the Prince Hall Grand Lodge of his state in 1992.[27] This grand lodge reconsidered this decision in 1998. During the 1990s the Congress of North American Grand Masters, which represented the white obediences, established the Commission on Information for Recognition. Although aware of the hindrance to the recognition of the black obediences formed by the doctrine of territorial exclusivity, this commission released the following statement.

> There can be no question about Exclusive Jurisdiction. It is a basic principle that a Grand Lodge must be autonomous and have sole and undisputed authority over its constituent Lodges. This cannot be shared with any other Masonic council or power. But the question of exclusive territorial jurisdiction is not so clear-cut. In some European and Latin American countries, a geographical or politically self-contained unit may be served by two or more Grand Lodges. If these Grand Lodges and hence their constituent Lodges are working in amity, and both are worthy of recognition in all other respects, this joint occupation of a country, state, or political subdivision should not bar them from recognition.[28]

The commission's statement clearly shows that the doctrine of territorial exclusivity made it possible to exclude the black obediences, which, paradoxically, they themselves used in turn to expel "irregular" Masons. Masonic principles have given rise to the widest variety of interpretations. Some brothers have invoked an article from Anderson's *Constitutions,* others the validity of a charter through the ages or the doctrine that Mackey made popular. All have sought bad pretexts to drive away black Freemasons without displaying their racist motives.

ELEVEN

The Racism of White Freemasons

In his 1792 speech, Prince Hall asked, in the guise of a joke, if the Knights of Malta rejected their travel companions because of their skin color.

> Query. Whether at that day, when there was an African Church, and perhaps the largest Christian Church on earth, whether there was no African of that Order; or whether, if they were all whites, they would refuse to accept them as fellow Christians and brother Masons; or whether there were any so weak, or rather so foolish as to say, because they were blacks, they would make their lodge or army too common or too cheap.[1]

Prince Hall explains that black Masons fought in the American army.[2] Those who attack Masons on the basis of their skin color alone are therefore insulting the Creator, he concludes. Vain speech, if we take history at its word. John Walkes makes the following cruel but undoubtedly well-founded observation about American Freemasonry:

> Some years ago, a Civil Rights leader notes that "the Church was the most segregated institution in America," but he was mistaken. Freemasonry is the most segregated institution in America, and this to its shame.[3]

This is how Freemasonry, which was one of the first institutions to emancipate itself at the time of the American Revolution,* would also be the most racist institution. It would be helpful, of course, to qualify Walkes's remarks by taking into consideration the attempts of some white Freemasons to combat this state of affairs (see chapter 12). However, we really need to begin by studying what jumps right off the page at you: the racism of the vast majority of white grand lodges until the end of the twentieth century.

The Living Legends of White Freemasonry

The extreme case is obviously that of Nathan Bedford Forrest, one of the first members of the Ku Klux Klan, who was received into Freemasonry seven years later (see chapter 6 on the battle for civil rights). Unfortunately, Forrest does not stand out as an exception. Equally grotesque, at least from the context of the concept of Masonic fraternity, certainly a remote ideal, is the case of Albert Pike, figurehead for the Scottish Rite. His example is all the more shocking, for, contrary to Forrest, who did not pursue a career in the Masonic institution, Pike is considered a monumental figure of American Freemasonry, a living legend.

A poet, teacher, and adventurer who took part in the winning of the West in the 1830s, then an Arkansas lawman, Pike also fought on the Confederate side in the Civil War—all of which are respectable activities, if we so choose. According to Walkes, Pike also pulled off the tour de force of combining the duties of the sovereign grand commander of the Scottish Rite and chief justice of the Ku Klux Klan. As the author of the renowned *Morals and Dogmas,* a veritable Scottish Rites' bible, Pike would have been wrong to have the slightest doubt, as no white Mason would criticize this dual membership. Denslow does not mention it, though, in his biography of Pike.[4] Mackey makes no allusion whatsoever to it in his *Revised Encyclopedia of Freemasonry.* There is nothing that has emerged to stain Pike's reputation in the eyes of white

---

*The Grand Lodge of Massachusetts declared its independence from the Grand Lodge of Scotland one year after the Declaration of Independence, thus in 1777.

American Masons. We should note, however, that Mackey mentions the Ku Klux Klan,* but only to asset that there was never any connection between this organization and the American grand lodges.[5] It is permissible to wonder if Mackey was lying outright or by omission. It is hard to accept that he could not have known of Forrest's Masonic membership and Pike's double game. Furthermore, he describes the Ku Klux Klan with discreet sympathy.

> The Ku Klux Klan began at the end of the Civil War as the general name for a constellation of secret societies and associations during the anarchy of the Reconstruction Period. The Ku Klux Klan proper was constituted in 1867 AD, with General Nathan Bedford Forrest as its first Grand Wizard—and the power it began immediately to wield was remarkable, seeing that most of the societies, clubs, etc., which formed it had begun as amusement societies—a fact which explains the Halloween Character of its nomenclature. The general movement was on the whole a success, in the sense that it carried out its purpose.[6]

Mackey trivializes this organization by explaining its purpose was to protect the property of Southern whites and ensure their safety during a period of "anarchy," which means after the abolition of slavery. In the beginning it was a simple "amusement," but finally the whites had been well protected and the Ku Klux Klan was therefore a success! The whites were simply pretending to be wizards; it was Halloween every day! Big children playing innocent games—just like Harry Potter. Not a word about Forrest's Masonic membership, not a word about the odious acts perpetrated against the black people by the Ku Klux Klan. The author of this glowing portrait of the Ku Klux Klan, the worthy Albert Mackey, who accumulated the highest Masonic distinctions, stands as the authority as a historian of the order.

Walkes's assertion about Pike's dual membership remains to be

---

*Mackey wrote, "Neither the old Klan nor the new ever received any support from the Masonic Fraternity, nor ever had any connection with it." With "old" and "new" Klan, Mackey is referring to the banning of the movement and its resurgence.

verified, but nothing allows us to dismiss it as erroneous.* We should note that Walkes only offers that information in the form of a footnote[7] and thereby abstains from making any commentary about it, as if seeking to spare the tender sensitivities of white Masons. This can probably be explained by the aura of Albert Pike and also by the fact that the Prince Hall Masons practiced the Scottish Rite, thereby referring to Pike, without any regard for history.

Knowing Pike's personality, there is no cause for surprise in this peremptory statement: "I took my obligation to white men, not Negroes. When I have to accept Negroes as brethren or leave Masonry, I shall leave it."[8]

Thus spoke the sovereign grand commander. All the same, for political purposes, Pike displayed the acumen to not reject the Prince Hall Masons but, to the contrary, to encourage them, albeit to exist in a separate fashion. This is why in 1877 he offered a copy of the ritual of the Supreme Council of the Scottish Rite to a black friend, Grand Commander Thornton A. Jackson,† to assist him in founding the Supreme Council of Prince Hall in Washington D.C.[9] Pike was already a complete convert to the American communitarian tradition: each community is respected provided that it remains separate.

These two examples are hardly better than caricatures and materializations of the prevailing racism of the South. The silence of Masons on Forrest and Pike, as well as the many statements of the grand lodges of the Southern states, provides sufficient evidence, as seen later in this chapter.

Oddly enough, in 1853, Martin Robison Delany complained about the Masons of the Northern states, finding them much more racist than those of the South. He said that members of the Southern lodges gladly fraternized with black Masons and gave a specific example, that of a Kentucky city where a municipal councilor and a judge, both white Masons, enjoyed good rapport with the author, a free-

---

*I regret that I did not have access to the Ku Klux Klan archives in this regard.

†It was this same Thornton A. Jackson who received from C. R. Case the adoptive rituals of the Eastern Star so that he could create an equivalent black grand chapter.

born black man.[10] Nevertheless, this took place before the Civil War. Also, nothing implies that Delany's observation could be extended to other Southern states. Free blacks like Delany were so sufficiently few in number that white Masons could feel no threat by showing proof of civility toward them. On the other hand, during the years following the emancipation of the slaves, resentment toward blacks was amplified. In 1899 the grand master of the Prince Hall Grand Lodge of New York went on at length about the racial prejudices of which blacks—whether or not they were Masons—were victims in the Southern states.

> I cannot conclude without making some reference to the present state of the South, where the life of an Afro-American is not secure. These acts of violence have become so common and colored men killed by the half dozen, and for no crime sometimes but sheer pretext. I hope this Grand Lodge will put in its protest before we adjourn.[11]

While the more racist statements seem to have come from the Southern grand lodges, several grand lodges of the North adopted the same attitude. I will make a distinction between two kinds of remarks: those that we will label, certainly somewhat derisively, as civil, and those that are overt expressions of racism.

Civil Remarks

In 1898 the white Masons of Washington, under the leadership of Grand Master William H. Upton, recognized the legitimacy of several black lodges in their state, without going so far as to establish any formal ties with the Prince Hall Grand Lodge. This prudence spared them in no way from the criticisms of the other white grand lodges. A correspondence, which remained polite, was established between Upton and William A. Sutherland, grand master of the New York Grand Lodge. Sutherland scolded Upton for having acted thoughtlessly, but from the first defended himself against any charge of racism.

The race question has no place in this discussion. To introduce it as an argument for or against the steps taken by the Grand Lodge of Washington is only to confuse the real question.[12]

Sutherland brings up the traditional argument of white Masons for calling the Prince Hall Grand Lodges irregular: the black lodges do not hold bona fide warrants. This is naturally a vicious circle, as the black lodges that bestowed the charters were not recognized by the white organizations. He also mentions the principle of territorial exclusivity and states that the New York Grand Lodge refused to recognize the existence of the Boyer Grand Lodge. To prove that the motives of the New York Grand Lodge were not the least bit racist, its grand master recalled that the Pythagoras Lodge was declared irregular because it was affiliated with the Grand Lodge of Hamburg. Then he reminded his correspondent that, according to the principle of territorial exclusivity, only one grand lodge had the right to officiate in each state. Sutherland took this opportunity to make a joke: by recognizing the lodges affiliated with the Prince Hall Grand Lodge, the Grand Lodge of Washington brought to mind the example of Utah.* Sutherland was implying by this that the New York Masons were behaving like polygamous husbands, as they had contracted several unions![13] Apart from these legalistic remarks, Sutherland gave free rein in his January 19, 1899, letter to frivolous chitchat that is extremely revealing of his own feelings about the black community.

I have seen upon the streets of my own city colored men wearing regalia in processions and calling themselves Free Masons. Not long ago, I was informed that the barber who was then shaving me was the grand master of the so-called Colored Masons in the State of New York. These circumstances sufficiently put me upon warning as to the existence of clandestine bodies in the State of New

*Sutherland gives the example of Utah as it was the state where polygamy was accepted (at least during that time) because of the predominance of the Mormon religion among its people.

Fig. 11.1. Procession of Freemasons of Prince Hall of New York, Enoch Grand Lodge, Brooklyn, June 21, 1953, from the Edward R. Cusick Collection, Artifact Storage, AIS815f (courtesy of the Chancellor Robert R. Livingston Masonic Library)

York. I use the designation "clandestine bodies" because this is the way I was taught to regard them.[14]

When one grand master cuts the hair of another grand master . . . the Masons cannot make head nor tail of it. Whoever said a barber could rise to the rank of grand master? Considerations of social status become grafted to the problem of race and give it particular acuity. We can sense that Sutherland was annoyed that a simple barber could perform the high functions of Freemasonry.

Fifty years later Thomas Harkins, former grand master of South Carolina, followed his colleague Sutherland's example and condemned the decision of the Massachusetts Grand Lodge to extend recognition to the Prince Hall Grand Lodge of their state in 1947. He wrote a treatise, a pamphlet rather, titled *Symbolic Freemasonry among the Negroes of America. An Answer to Their Claims of Legitimacy and Regularity.*[15] Harkins attacked Prince Hall the individual in a way that was especially malicious. He claimed that the man was initiated irregularly in an itinerant Irish lodge. These itinerant lodges, attached to an army, did not have the right, according to him, to initiate the profane. Harkins reminded his readers that the lodge created by Prince Hall no longer appeared on the rolls of the United Grand Lodge of England in 1813. To discredit the black lodges, Harkins stated that it took them several years to realize Prince Hall had died. Finally, he implied that Prince Hall was tempted to follow the British Army in the Revolutionary War. Harkins's tone was particularly aggressive.

> By relating this circumstance in this discussion, I do not mean to charge Prince Hall and his associates with any intention of disloyalty, but it is not unreasonable to believe that the soldiers of the Irish regiment may have thought that they could use these Negroes in the British cause in the conflict that was rapidly approaching.[16]

Harkins imputes very specific intentions to the Irish lodge this way. Of course this scenario is not completely unlikely. However, the conclusion he draws concerning Prince Hall appears entirely exaggerated, as it seems, to the contrary, that he enlisted in the Continental Army. On the other hand, Harkins forgets that the British Army was extremely appealing to slaves as it promised to emancipate any who joined its ranks. As free black men, Prince Hall and his friends did not have any particular reason to find this tempting. Somewhat short of arguments, Harkins guesses that if the Modern Grand Lodge truly granted Prince

Hall a charter it was because it would do whatever it took to expand its influence and sought to rival the competing English obedience, the Ancient Grand Lodge.

This is probably partially true. However, we should not underestimate the English desire to annoy American Masons, who had claimed autonomy from the British Grand Lodges, sometime directly after the Declaration of Independence. Harkins takes great joy in mentioning an article from the Boston press that derisively referred to the African Lodge as "St. Black's Lodge," alluding in this way to the two regular and very respectable lodges of that city, Saint Andrew's Lodge and Saint John's Lodge.[17]

From all these considerations of a more or less historical nature, Harkins draws conclusions for the modern era. He feels that the position of the Grand Lodge of Massachusetts is ambiguous to the extent that it recognizes the regularity of the Prince Hall Grand Lodge in that state but not the right of mutual visits, for reasons of "social status." It must be acknowledged that there was a serious flaw in the behavior of the Massachusetts Masons. They seemed anxious to repair an injustice by recognizing the regular status of the black Masons, but by the same token they were not prepared to fraternize with blacks, arguing on the basis that these latter were of inferior status and that would cause discomfort in the life of the lodges. Harkins dives right in to this flaw and uses it as a pretext for ridiculing the idea of mutual recognition of the white and black grand lodges.

> The Stupidity of the Grand Lodge of Massachusetts can be fully appreciated, I think, when we consider what will happen when this Negro Freemasonry, which has been recognized as being regular by Massachusetts, begins to initiate white members, which they have a perfect right to do if they are regular. Will the Grand Lodge of Massachusetts then say to these white Masons who have been initiated in the Negro Lodges which they acknowledge as regular: "Yes, you belong to a regular Lodge of Freemasonry, but we cannot admit you into any of our Lodges because of your association with the Negroes in the Lodge which initiated you, and because we have

refused the right of visitation to the members of the Lodge on the grounds of social distinction." Such position is un-Masonic, wholly unjustified, and can result only in bringing confusion, disorder, dissention and disruption into regular Freemasonry in America.[18]

Finally, the problem that disturbs Harkins most is that white Masons will go astray in the black lodges. Now, oddly enough, the Grand Lodge of Massachusetts had the same apprehensions as they openly wished to extend formal recognition to black Freemasonry but, in practice, wished to avoid any mixing of the races in the lodges. Harkins states that he has black friends and is not a racist but that he will always oppose recognition of the Prince Hall Grand Lodges.

I have no controlling bias or prejudice against Negroes. The leading Negroes of my community, as well as the rank and file, recognize me as their friend, but this relationship could never under any circumstances induce me against my conviction to recognize as regular and legitimate any Masonic organization which has no better claim than that of the Prince Hall Affiliation.[19]

As a postscript, the author of this pamphlet states that since he distributed this text to all the lodges of his state, several grand lodges had condemned the position taken by the Grand Lodge of Massachusetts. Some of these lodges, those of Texas, Alabama, and Florida, even officially severed relations with the Grand Lodge of Massachusetts. Others threatened to follow suit if the lodge did not go back on its decision. Finally, the Grand Lodge of Massachusetts, after a change of grand master, revoked its decision to recognize the black Freemasons of its state, to the great satisfaction of the white Masons of America.[20] Harkins's pamphlet, which was quite clever on a tactical level, had therefore borne its fruits. It was republished in 1963 with the support of the sovereign grand commander of the Southern Jurisdiction of the 33rd Degree of the Scottish Rite.[21] The Prince Hall Masons would be kept at a distance for many more years.

Not all white grand lodges went to the trouble to hone their weapons with such finesse. Some were satisfied to make the crudest kinds of attacks without trying in any way to conceal their racism, contrary to Harkins's approach.

Openly Racist Remarks

The attack waged during 1898 and 1899 by the Grand Lodge of New York against that of Washington was moderate when compared with the one that came out of the Grand Lodge of Kentucky. This lodge also employed legalistic arguments but much more aggressively. It mentions the creation of the African Lodge, then the charters that it granted to other lodges in these terms:

> From this bastard progeny of an illegitimate and spurious body sprung [*sic*] the Prince Hall Grand Lodge. . . . In 1827 they declared themselves independent of the Grand Lodge of England, and free from all Masonic authority, and from that day to this they have enjoyed the freedom of the wild ass and rejoiced in the liberty of an unbridled and unrecognized existence—a freedom, which the committee of Washington Lodge seems anxious to emulate, when in order to convince the outside world of the catholicity of their Masonry they take unto their embrace the unctuous and unwilling African, ignore the facts of history and insult the intelligence and challenge the honesty of the Grand Lodge of Massachusetts, in fact the whole body of American Masonry, by denouncing the candid judgment of impartial men, acting under the sanction of Masonic obligation, as the unworthy result of race prejudice and cowardly prudence.[22]

The reader will appreciate the choice of adjectives used by this respectable committee to describe black Freemasonry, as well as the openly racist description of Africans.

If we were to have the bad taste of offering a prize for racism, we would have to hesitate between several laureates: The Grand Lodge of Alabama? The Grand Lodge of Mississippi? Unfortunately, a plethora of other candidates has also emerged. In 1866, just after the abolition of slavery in the United States, the Alabama Grand Lodge proclaimed the absolute impossibility of initiating blacks and did not hide its aversion to a race it deemed inferior. This white Mason is particularly odious when expressing the veritable physical aversion he feels toward blacks:

a) We know that Masonry is not only close in fellowship, but is perfect in morals and intricate in science. And we know that the Negroes of the south are wholly incompetent to embrace it. They are ignorant, uneducated, immoral, untruthful, and, intellectually, they are more impotent than minority in age or dotage—both of which we exclude. It would be rare if any locality could furnish the requisite number of sufficient capacity to open a lodge. Therefore, to have lodges exclusively composed of Negroes, would be dangerous to the high character of our Order. And, to associate with them in lodges with white brethren, would be impossible.

b) But the violation of the right of jurisdiction is not all; it is to make Masons of Negroes, an inferior species of man, with whom brethren generally, neither North nor South, will ever associate on terms of equality; a class of men whose very smell is alike the stink of a menagerie of wild animals, to say nothing of their moral, mental, and other qualifications.[23]

In 1908, irritated at the existence of Alpha Lodge, a black lodge in the white Grand Lodge of New Jersey (a veritable exception, it is true), Edwin J. Martin, grand master of Mississippi, broke off all relations with the New Jersey Grand Lodge. It was no longer a matter of invoking the irregularity of the Prince Hall Grand Lodges, as this was a lodge that had been constituted in regular form by a white American obedience. He therefore wrote an openly racist letter that stated blacks were incapable of being initiated as Masons solely on the basis of their skin color. Martin did not take any oratorical precautions to conceal the discriminatory nature of his opinion.

Yours of August 25th, advising me that Negroes are initiated and affiliated in your Grand Jurisdiction is received.

Our Grand Lodge holds differently. Masonry never contemplated that her privileges should be extended to a race, totally and intellectually incapacitated to discharge the obligations which they assume or have conferred upon them in a Masonic Lodge. It is no answer that there are exceptions to this general character of the race. We legislate for the race and not for the exception.[24]

This poor excuse for a gentleman carried the weight of the Southern states' racism on his shoulders. No gleam of light could dispel this darkness. To the contrary, he took Masonic principles as his pretext for closing the door to the temple forever to a part of the American populace he had no hesitation about labeling inferior. The quarrel between the North and the South was still not over forty years after the war ended. Affiliation with Freemasonry changed nothing of the visceral nature of the South's racism.

We should not be mistaken in viewing this sinister Martin as an exception. A year later the grand secretary of this same grand lodge, Frederic Speed, drew an even more exaggerated caricature.

But Scipio Africanus* is simply a brute, with no revenge or resentments, and no regard for truth and purity of his women. Whiskey and cocaine and miscegenation are his bane and until some remedy is found to these great evils, the poor fellow will continue to go down lower and lower in the social scale until finally the time will come when he and the white man must part company.[25]

The word *miscegenation* is emphasized. As a general rule, contrary to French colonial tradition, the British have always made sure to avoid miscegenation, based on an argument of respect for the communities and lifestyles of every people. The term *race* is used frequently among the English and Americans, who have no hesitation about taking a census based on the different ethnicities. Speed says aloud, and in fairly

---

*[The choice of this prestigious name is, of course, intended ironically. This is how the author describes the degenerate black type. —*Trans.*]

crude terms, what many Southern Americans were then thinking—that it was necessary to preserve the purity of the white race.

Along these same lines, when in a 1913 letter addressed to the Grand Lodge of Virginia, the Grand Lodge of West Australia dared speak of the equality of all men in Freemasonry, whatever their color, their Virginia correspondent responded in these words:

> Now, to a brother in Western Australia, and equally to one in Maine, no doubt it is natural that a Negro seems to be simply a black white man, with like impulses and instincts, who, under like auspices, would have like moral sense and similar, if not identical, reasoning powers. No arguments we (who have known them well for a lifetime, as free and slave) could advance, would change their fixed views, but how utterly wrong they are in their disregard of scientific ethnology. No Negro ever born is the social or moral peer of a white man. . . . To return to the question above, we will say "the colored folk" are the creatures of the same Creator as ourselves, but so are Kentucky mules. The Negroes have many good traits, but they cannot make good Masons any more than they would make good husbands for our daughters.[26]

Some Southern grand lodges were particularly explicit: there was no question of accepting the whitest mulatto or receiving Masons with any black blood, no matter how little was in their veins.

> That this Grand Lodge is unqualifiedly opposed to the admission of Negroes or mulattoes into Lodges under this Jurisdiction (Grand Lodge of Illinois, 1851).
> A man possessing one-eighth to one-sixteenth degree of Negro blood cannot be made a Mason (Grand Lodge of Kentucky, 1914).[27]

No half or fourth breed would be authorized to receive the light. This exclusion from Freemasonry struck blacks in particular; Indians, for example, were only victims of it temporarily.[28] Walkes reports that an Illinois lodge was harshly reprimanded for this in

1846.* It must be pointed out, however, that the lodge had the poor taste to initiate the son of an Indian woman and a mulatto.[29] However, in 1847 the Grand Lodge of Arkansas, known as the Grand Lodge of Indian Territory, was born. The current Grand Lodge of Arkansas dates from 1909, following the merger of the first grand lodge with a rival grand lodge. When formed in 1909, essentially consisting of Indians, it was immediately recognized as the sole Grand Lodge of the state of Arkansas by the other American grand lodges.[30]

These examples of white Masons' racist attitudes toward their black brethren (and those of other minorities) can be multiplied. It will be sufficient to cite one last example that dates only from 1952. The body of a black soldier killed during the Korean War was stored for five weeks at a Phoenix morgue because that city's cemetery belonged to the white Lodge n° 2 of Arizona, which refused to let him be buried there for all that time. It took the intervention of several veterans' groups for the lodge to finally allow the burial to proceed, albeit in a well-marked-off section of the cemetery reserved for blacks, Chinese, and Japanese.[31]

Whether the speech was muted or overtly racist, white grand lodges excluded blacks throughout the nineteenth century and almost all of the twentieth. In the 1960s an association of Masonic researchers went to the pains of drawing up an inventory of the official statements forbidding the acceptance of black Masons in white lodges. This collection of forty-nine quotes, corresponding to the number of all the states at that time, ends with the following recommendation to all "regular Masons."

None of the 49 Grand Lodges of the United States has ever recognized one single black or colored lodge in the United States.

Consequently, all black or colored Grand Lodges of the United States, as well as their lodges and members, are illegitimate and irregular.[32]

---

*Walkes also cites the following statement released by the Grand Lodge of New York in 1851: "A resolution was adopted declaring that men of the Indian race were unfit material for Masonry."

On the other hand, there is no consensus on this from a historical perspective. Harry A. Williamson drew up a list of the books hostile to Prince Hall Grand Lodges. Among them, those by Albert Mackey figure in good place. The list is most likely not exhaustive.[33]

Several authors have tried to restore black Freemasonry's legitimacy. Williamson pays homage to William H. Upton, John D. Caldwell, and several other historians for their impartial judgment. These few individuals strove in vain to combat against the ambient racism; it was a superhuman task, and "the ashlar was far from perfect." It would not be until 1989 that a significant evolution in this regard would occur.

TWELVE

Some Attempts to Come Together

The attempts made by two grand lodges, that of Washington, followed by that of Massachusetts, to officially recognize the lodges of Prince Hall in their states were quite exceptional and all the more meritorious as the pressure from the other grand lodges of their time caused them to lose the first match. The fact remains that they mark a point in the battle against segregation. On the other hand, individual initiatives were more numerous.

As the history of Freemasonry reveals, simple Masons have often shown more good sense than their leaders. When, in the eighteenth century, the Modern and Ancient Grand Lodges forbade their members from visiting each other, these latter braved the interdiction on several occasions, which, over the long term, encouraged the joining of the two rival lodges. The same was true in the United States. Despite the official declarations, despite the opprobrium cast on black Freemasonry, some white Masons trusted in their own judgment and displayed a desire to fight against the most flagrant injustices.

Individual Initiatives

Harold Van Buren Voorhis cites several examples of blacks who were received in regular white lodges. According to him, formal proofs are lacking before 1844, but individual cases, isolated ones, of course, had existed since 1821.[1] However, the Civil War encouraged the Confederates to redouble the strictness of the racial discrimination practiced in white lodges. Naturally, the acceptance of black Masons remained very much an exception.

It will be recalled that Joseph Warren, an influential member of Boston's Saint Andrew's Lodge, is said to have promised Prince Hall and his friends a charter, but his premature death in the Battle of Bunker Hill put an end to this hope. Tradition has it that members of Saint Andrew's Lodge attended the inauguration of the first Prince Hall Grand Lodge in Boston in 1791.* Furthermore, Saint Andrew's Lodge, to its credit, initiated black Masons over the next century. According to Joseph Walkes, eight blacks who had become Masons under their aegis requested the authority to create their own lodge, Thistle Lodge, in 1871.[2] This fact is corroborated by the Saint Andrew's Lodge annals.

The Grand Lodge of Massachusetts did not accede to their request, no doubt for two reasons: The first being, of course, that they were not white, and the idea of a specifically black lodge seemed incongruous to the grand lodge. The second was the fact that Saint Andrew's Lodge, which had initiated them, had chosen to follow its own path. In fact, since it had come into existence it had refused to affiliate with the Grand Lodge of Massachusetts, preferring to maintain its ties with the Grand Lodge of Scotland.

That the lodge, which was once the most patriotic one in the city, should single itself out this way, first by refusing to break its ties with Scotland and then by initiating blacks, could not help but irk the Grand Lodge of Massachusetts, which eventually got its way. In fact, on the one hand, Saint Andrew's Lodge reluctantly rejoined its ranks in 1809, and on the other, it never managed to create Thistle Lodge. Despite this defeat, Saint Andrew's Lodge remained proud of its past, as shown by the story in the lodge publication *An Ancient Tale Told New*, published at its bicentennial in 1956.[3] Not only did this lodge accept blacks, it also encouraged them to seek the highest Masonic offices. This was the case of Joshua Bowen Smith, who was initiated in 1867, right after the

---

*This fact has not been established with full certainty, but the members of the St. Andrews Lodge alluded to it in 1956 in *An Ancient Tale Told New*.

Civil War. Smith was a member of the Royal Art of Saint Matthew's in Boston in 1869 and also attained the 32nd degree of the Scottish Rite. The Boston press wrote two articles about him in 1867 and 1870.[4]

Thistle Lodge would never come into existence, thereby leaving to another lodge the task of initiating blacks into a white Grand Lodge. This would be Alpha Lodge, the sole black lodge considered to be regular within a white American obedience at the end of a long, hard struggle. It was a particularly enlightened grand master, William Silas Whitehead, who headed the New Jersey Grand Lodge at the end of the Civil War and who created an atmosphere conducive for this tolerant action. A dyed-in-the-wool abolitionist, he was one of those who deemed that the Masons should not be the last to fight against racial discrimination.

When he stepped down from his charge in 1867, Whitehead gave a very notable speech on "universal fraternity."[5] Judging the time was ripe, twelve blacks requested to be initiated into a New Jersey Lodge, Alpha Lodge n° 116 of Newark, which was created on January 27, 1871.[6] A white schoolteacher had joined with them on this step. A petition was immediately sent out against these requests for initiation: in this letter, dated February 24, 1871, and addressed to the grand master, two hundred New Jersey Masons demanded that this lodge be closed. John Moon, the white schoolteacher, was initiated while the dozen black men were turned away. The lodge was temporarily closed.

A year later its charter was restored, despite the protests of Trenton Lodge n° 5, which was radically opposed to the initiation of blacks. In 1873 the Jurisprudence Committee proclaimed the regular status of Alpha Lodge against the recommendation of Trenton Lodge. The first blacks to be initiated were teachers, clerks, and two ministers of a church—all members of the middle class. The argument of inferior social status could therefore not be used in the specific case of this lodge. This permitted Donn A. Cass, who told the story of Alpha Lodge's creation, to emphasize the major role Masons could play in improving relations between ethnic communities.

Freemasonry can play a very important part in shaping the future development of the Negro race. The grand masters of Negro Grand

Lodges, as well as Negro Freemasons, generally represent their highest type of men, and by friendly cooperation and assistance can, with the help of white Masonic leaders, make this transitional period considerably less difficult for both Negroes and Whites.[7]

Certainly the Grand Lodge of New Jersey ran into some very hostile reactions, like those of the Grand Lodge of Delaware, which, in 1872, forbade its lodges from having any relations with Alpha Lodge. I have already cited, in chapter 11, the statement of the grand master of Mississippi in 1908. It appears that the Delaware grand lodge initially maintained relations with its New Jersey counterpart, contrary to the opinion voiced by its committee on external affairs. Following the grand master's intervention in 1908, the Grand Lodge of Mississippi officially broke off relations with the Grand Lodge of New Jersey and did not restore them until 1928. The Grand Lodge of New Jersey did finally manage to impose the existence of a black lodge, but this example is the only one of its kind on American territory.

Voorhis has listed the names of several black Masons received into white lodges.[8] He cites the example of John William, initiated by Lodge n° 55 of Newark, and that of William Hancock, initiated by Saint John Lodge n° 3 of North Carolina in 1846. He also mentions the lodge in Greensburg, Indiana, the one of Mount Hope, Massachusetts, Simonds Lodge n° 59 in Shoreham, Vermont, and Union Lodge n° 2, also in Vermont. These few lodges all initiated one black man, rarely more than that, between 1870 and 1942.[9]

The reverse was also true, still on a small scale. Black lodges accepted white Masons. Cass mentions the case of Marshall Field, a white merchant and philanthropist of Chicago, and L. Fish, another white businessman, who were both members of the North Star Lodge n° 1 of Chicago.[10]

Williamson cites several other examples from the twentieth century. William J. Anderson, the second black man* to serve in the Vermont

---

*[The first was Alexander Twilight, who was also the first black man to be elected to public office in the United States. —*Trans.*]

legislature, was a leading member of a white lodge. Williamson states that his own lodge was disposed to initiate white men.[11] He gives a list—a very brief one—of the Prince Hall lodges that accepted white Masons in New York: Downshire Lodge n° 12, founded in 1870, was composed almost entirely of Jews, with the exception of the secretary. The Carthaginian Lodge n° 47 in Brooklyn conferred the grade of master to a white man of German origin in 1905. In 1910 the El Sol de Cuba Lodge n° 38, also affiliated with Prince Hall, included among its members several white Hispanics, while Saint John's Lodge n° 29 had several Italians.[12]

All of these confirm the hypothesis maintaining that on an individual basis both white and black lodges tried to fight against segregation. Of course these were extremely isolated cases, but they all probably contributed to help change people's thinking on this matter.

For example, in 1946, Grand Master of Vermont Conant Voter wrote a letter to Voorhis, then New York grand master, to congratulate him on his book *Negro Masonry in the United States* as well as to impart some information concerning "Brother Curtis McDowell." Voter emphasizes the intellectual refinement of this brother as well as his light skin. He deplores the fact that his departure for the Southern states put an end to his Masonic activities.

> I received your letter of March 2nd asking for information regarding Brother Curtis Mc Dowell. Brother Mc Dowell was born on January 20, 1919, at Talladega, Alabama. His father was a very successful missionary and a very cultured gentleman. I believe the Negro blood came into the Mc Dowell family through a marriage of Curtis' grandfather to an African Negress. Curtis was not very dark and does not show very many of the Negro features. He was a very good friend of mine and was very well liked in college. Because he was so completely accepted by the student body, we seldom were conscious of his origin. He was elected into Union Lodge n° 2 on April 2, 1940, received the first degree on April 9, the second degree on May 7, and the third degree on June 14. He demitted on May 5, 1942. At the time he requested a demit, he was working in the South where

obviously he could not visit the white lodge. I hope that someday he will reaffiliate with us and pick up his Masonic work again.[13]

A militant separatist would certainly be horrified by these remarks, which attempted to erase this brother's negritude and show how he was perfectly integrated into white society. However, if we recall the virulence of the remarks tendered by almost all the white grand lodges, we cannot help but salute this grand master's open-mindedness.

The Attempts by Two Grand Lodges to Recognize Prince Hall Freemasonry

These attempts were mentioned in the previous chapter, which examined the racism that once prevailed in the United States. The statement issued by the Grand Lodge of Washington prompted an outcry from all the other white grand lodges. But just what was this grand lodge advocating in 1898? William H. Upton explained his grand lodge's declaration in a letter to New York Grand Master William Sutherland, dated December 8, 1898. To summarize, here is what Upton said: First of all, the Grand Lodge of Washington had formulated a declaration of principle against racial prejudice, which could not help but shock the more racist Southern states. Second, it recognized that the first black grand lodge was the lodge of Prince Hall. Upton hoped that each of the white grand lodges could form its own opinion on this subject without having to obtain authorization beforehand from the Grand Lodge of Kentucky and its friends. Third, the Grand Lodge of Washington voiced its wish that both black and white grand lodges in the state of Washington could enjoy good relations. However, the Grand Lodge of Washington would have preferred that only one sole grand lodge existed and declared itself ready, so that this might happen, to recognize as regular and take under its wing a certain number of black lodges, following a serious investigation.

Naturally Sutherland did not find these explanations at all satisfying. He persisted in seeing in the steps taken by Washington's grand lodge the desire to immediately extend recognition to all the Prince Hall Grand Lodges and thus cause harm to the autonomy of other white grand lodges. The reality was different, however. While the steps taken by Grand Master Upton were of symbolic importance, they were not followed by immediate effects.

Not without some rancor, in his will Upton stipulated that no stone should be erected over his grave as long as black and white Masons did not extend full recognition to each other.

> In passing I will say that Brother Upton specified in his will that no monument should be erected over his grave until at such a time the white and colored Masons in America should be able to stand beside as "brothers" in the fullest sense of the word.[14]

When we know the importance granted by Masons to funeral rites we can grasp the full extent of this gesture. By rejecting posthumous honors, Upton expressed all the ill will he felt for the racism of his Masonic brothers and tried, this way, one last time, to arouse their guilty consciences.[15]

Thomas Harkins's condemnation pamphlet appeared shortly after the 1947 declaration of the Grand Lodge of Massachusetts in favor of black Masonry. This position was adopted on the recommendation of the Committee of Past Grand Masters of Massachusetts,* so no suspicions can be entertained that it was a passing whim. It relied on the history of the African Lodge and the Prince Hall Grand Lodge of Massachusetts to demonstrate the legitimacy of black American Freemasonry.

The committee showed it was acting with extreme prudence.

> The Very Respectable Melvin M. Johnson [one of the past grand masters] would like to draw attention to the fact that Committee is not recommending what is technically called "recognition" in Freemasonry. It is not recommending mutual visits. The simple notion of legitimacy does not incur any of these measures.[16]

---

*Official title given to former grand masters.

This ambiguity was mercilessly pointed out by Harkins and other detractors of the Grand Lodge of Massachusetts. Harkins saw it as an expression of social scorn for blacks. What it was, however, was tactical prudence. Frank Hilton, the grand master, explained his and the committee's viewpoint: "The real opposition to Negro Freemasonry is rather social than legal."[17]

Once this observation had been aired, the committee drew from it the conclusion that it was appropriate to recognize the legitimacy of the black lodges but to limit, initially, the contacts between white and black brothers, no doubt to avoid incidents and also to more easily overcome the reservations of the white Masons. Even if this attitude may appear pusillanimous today, it should be analyzed in the context of its time. Given the racism that then prevailed throughout white Masonry, the efforts of the Grand Lodge of Massachusetts were remarkable, and the steps it took seem realistic. The grand lodge adopted the committee's report unanimously. It was not capable, though, of resisting the immense pressure exerted by the other grand lodges following the publication of Harkins's pamphlet, and it backed down from its position.

Only two grand lodges tried to counter the racism of white American Freemasonry. Their efforts were in vain as both ended up renouncing their positions.

According to Joseph Cox, during the time of Franklin D. Roosevelt, the Grand Lodges of New York made an attempt to come together, but these plans were abandoned with the death of the Mason president.[18] The real advances are extremely recent. They have been made with great caution and in accordance with different modalities.

Several Foreign Masons to the Rescue

Direct intervention on the part of several foreign grand lodges certainly accelerated the process of recognition among white American Freemasons. I have already mentioned, in chapter 10, the laudatory reports by the German Gottfried Joseph G. Findel to his original grand lodge on the Prince Hall Grand Lodge.[19]

In 1912, J. Junck, a Luxembourg Mason of the 33rd degree of the

Scottish Rite of the Supreme Council of the United States and holder of the title of international grand master,* wrote a short treatise on universal fraternity, condemning the separation of white and black brothers in the United States. He referred to several European Masonic Congresses, particularly the one held in London in 1912, and openly criticized the attitude of white American Freemasons while offering an example of French democratic principles.[20] He repeated the words of a senator from Guadeloupe, Monsieur Béranger, in *Le Matin* newspaper in November 1912:

> When France declared all French citizens equal before the law, she gave the Black people to understand that they had become "French citizens. . . ." I do not think that is only through a simple incident that our adventurous France has become the decisive rendezvous between the Black and the White races and in civilization; but I think that in all countries and to all nations in the fair Archipelago of the Antilles, as well as in the wide African Kingdoms, also to the Black race and in the year 1912 as well as it was in 1793, the Tricolor Flag must proclaim the universal rights of man and citizen as these: Freedom, Equality, Brotherhood.[21]

It is no sure thing that all Guadeloupians would express themselves in such Jacobin terms today. The French democratic model could, though, exercise a certain fascination for the United States. Whatever the case may be, Junck quoted the words of this Guadeloupian to compare the French egalitarian vision to the American vision, which he labeled as segregationist. Junck also gave the example of the Belgian Congo, which he claims practiced no racial discrimination. It is hard to measure the influence of these Masonic congresses on white American Freemasonry. It was most likely quite weak, but considerable from a symbolic perspective, particularly for the high grades of the Scottish

---

*We do not know whether Junck was black or white. This European Masonic Congress took place under his aegis in 1912. Black Masons who had risen to the high degrees of the Scottish Rite took part in it.

Rite. Junck reflected back at Americans and Freemasons in particular a hardly flattering vision of their society, yet theirs was a land that was traditionally considered as a welcoming one.[22]

The Ambiguities of the United Grand Lodge of England

Relations between the Prince Hall Grand Lodges and the United Grand Lodge of England were not lacking in ambiguities. We know that the Modern Grand Lodge had granted the African Lodge its charter, after some twists and turns. However, the adversaries of black Freemasonry made much of the fact that the United Grand Lodge of England, created in 1813, did not include the lodge of Prince Hall on its rolls. In the context of the Revolutionary War, England had granted legitimacy to a black lodge. It subsequently did not seek to maintain these ties on the basis, which is quite likely, that the black brethren were not in good standing with its treasury. The United Grand Lodge of England certainly was not lacking an administrative reason for striking the lodge from its rolls. It is, however, possible that they could have demanded of their black brethren that they regularize their situation if they truly wished to maintain a connection with Prince Hall's successors.

English Freemasonry, however, retained a highly symbolic value in the eyes of black Americans, to such an extent that a Mason as nationalistic as Martin Robison Delany suggested in 1853 to appeal to English arbiters to settle, once and for all, the differences between the black and white brethren.

> That all of the Prince Hall lodges of the United States and the National Grand Lodge meet in a National Grand Lodge Convention, for the single purpose of petitioning the Grand Lodge of England for a settlement of the question of the legality of colored Masons in the United States, claiming to have originated from the warrant granted to Prince Hall, of Boston. This should at once be done, to settle the controversy as it would to us be a great point

gained, because it would be the acknowledgment and establishment of a right among us as a people, which is now disputed, but which legitimately belongs to us. . . . We are either Masons or not Masons, legitimate or illegitimate; in the affirmative, then we must be so acknowledged and accepted—in the negative we should be rejected . . . whatever undue and unwarrantable obstructions may be thrown in our way by American Masons; and they are many—though there are some honorable exceptions—it is within the power of the Grand Lodge of England to decide in the matter, and at once establish our validity.[23]

This exhibited a complete misunderstanding of the United Grand Lodge of England. As good Britons, the Masons of His Majesty were first and foremost excellent diplomats. Granting a charter to some blacks was inconsequential in the context of the War of Independence and had, to the contrary, given the English a certain sense of satisfaction, as it pleased them to appear more generous than the American patriots this way. On the other hand, after the cessation of hostilities, the maintaining of official relations with this lodge had become more uncomfortable.

This was not necessarily the sign of an entente cordiale between the English and the Americans but was without a doubt evidence of greater prudence on the part of the English. Furthermore, as the crisis of increasing membership had been resolved by the unification of the two English grand lodges in 1813, the loss of a remote lodge in America occasioned little regret. As good humanists, the English Masons took the trouble to accept blacks and brothers of all ethnicities, provided they believed in the Great Architect of the Universe.*

For this reason the United Grand Lodge of England was never accused of racism, in contrast to its American counterparts. On the other hand, it was not in any way set on seeing the proliferation of

---

*It will be recalled that the United Grand Lodge of England had substituted the expression of "free man" for that of "free-born man" in its *Constitutions* in order to open its doors to emancipated slaves.

autonomous black lodges. As the Premier Grand Lodge, it gave its support to one grand lodge of each country and one alone. For a very long time it refused to grant recognition to the Grand Lodges of Prince Hall.

This explains why the United Grand Lodge of England had no reservations about refusing a gift from the Prince Hall Grand Lodge of New York in 1941, during the Second World War (see chapter 10). That same year, the Londoners refused to let a Prince Hall Mason enter the Temple of Great Queen Street.[24] There was no question of British Masons ruffling the feathers of the white Grand Lodge of New York, the only lodge with which they maintained relations. The British showed evidence of their humanism whenever possible, but never when it would be to the detriment of their interests. Like Edmund Burke, they always sought to save institutions without giving the slightest credit to the Jacobinic notion of the rights of man. The United Grand Lodge of England accepted blacks, but on an individual basis, without compromising its relations with the white American grand lodges.

Joseph Walkes noted that on many occasions the United Grand Lodge of England did not respect the principle of territorial exclusivity, so it had no reason to use this rule as a pretext to refuse recognition to the Prince Hall Grand Lodges. He shared Harry A. Williamson's opinion about English Freemasonry: it was an "aristocratic institution," and not "democratic," that had put in place a "caste system" and entrusted its governance to the nobility.[25] A judgment it is hard to contest . . .

Recent Developments

It was necessary to wait until 1989 for an American grand lodge, the Grand Lodge of Connecticut, to officially recognize the Prince Hall Grand Lodge of its state. Contrary to what was the case when Massachusetts had tried to advance this in 1946, this decision does not seem to have inspired any outcry from white Freemasons. If there was any gnashing of teeth, it could not be heard outside the temple.

Furthermore, the Grand Lodge of Connecticut set an example, as a year later the Grand Lodges of Nebraska, Washington, and Wisconsin made the same decision. Following that time, every year has marked new progress in the recognition of the black grand lodges.

It is to Paul Bessel, longtime curator of the George Washington Masonic National Museum in Alexandria, Virginia, to whom we owe regular updates on a website, with a chart of official relations between the white and black grand lodges, followed by a sales pitch in favor of mutual recognition: Masonic universalism, to make it short. The importance of this site is major and not only from a technical point of view. All American Masons have been able to have access to complete information on the state of relations. It is likely that the recalcitrant grand lodges were gradually influenced by the successive stances and that the diffusion of this information has played a decisive role. In other words, by developing communication, Bessel's initiative encouraged ideas to evolve.

The very term *recognition* is far from being unanimously accepted; black Freemasons tend to think that it implies a somewhat condescending approach on the part of white Masons. It is, however, the term generally used by the white grand lodges. The stances taken recently, very recently it must be said, by white Masons represent such an advance in ways of thinking that it appears somewhat pointless to attach excessive importance to the word itself. While it is understandable if black Masons show signs of being overly sensitive, it would be simplistic to deny the recent efforts made by white American Freemasons.

Furthermore, the term *Masonic recognition* forms part of the official vocabulary of the United Grand Lodge of England. If it poses any problem, it is therefore to all the obediences and not simply toward the black grand lodges. We can certainly question the privilege the United Grand Lodge of England assumes in this way with respect to the rest of the world in discerning labels of Masonic regularity as it pleases. The white grand lodges are only copying the British approach.

Bessel distinguishes different types of recognition by the white grand lodges of the United States as follows:

First there is full recognition, of the same nature as that of all American and foreign Grand Lodges that have established official relations. The brothers have the right of mutual visitation as well as that of belonging to the two Grand Lodges of their state, the white lodge and the black lodge.

This type of recognition has been adopted by thirty or thirty-two grand lodges. The others have not specified anything (things are a little hazy here).

Four grand lodges, those of Wisconsin, Colorado, Ohio, and Pennsylvania, have adopted a recognition that authorizes mutual visits but not dual membership. However, Bessel believes this category no longer exists but does not have solid evidence to back this assertion.

Bessel thinks that three lodges still fall into the category of mutual recognition, but without visitation rights or dual membership.

Furthermore, eleven grand lodges have adopted the principle of "blanket recognition," automatic recognition, one might say, of all the Prince Hall Grand Lodges from the time they are recognized by the white grand lodge of their state. This means that the Prince Hall Grand Lodges do not have to take any specific steps to be recognized. These eleven states that are in the forefront, relatively speaking, are Illinois, Connecticut, Nebraska, Colorado, Washington, Idaho, Hawaii, New Hampshire, Montana, Nevada, and the District of Columbia.

All in all, forty-two of the fifty-one white grand lodges have, therefore, recognized black Freemasonry. The majority of them have given absolute recognition without any restrictions. The three grand lodges that have most recently joined the "abolitionist" camp are those of Texas (2007), North Carolina (2008), and Kentucky (2011).[26]

The nine states that persist to this day to maintain a segregationist position are located in the South: Alabama, Arkansas, South Carolina, Florida, Georgia, Louisiana, Mississippi, Tennessee, and West Virginia.* Bessel very wisely places two maps on his site, one that shows which

*The last update posted by Bessel on his website was in 2012.

states have recognized black Freemasonry and one that shows the former slave states. For a long time the map of the states that allowed slavery in 1861 was almost exactly the same as that of the states that refused to grant recognition to Prince Hall Masonry.[27] But now the gap between these maps is filling in, slowly but surely.

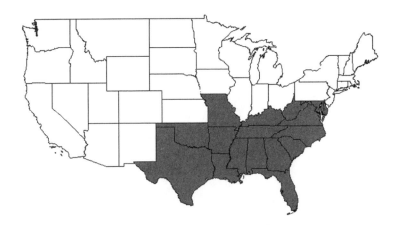

Fig. 12.1. The states (shaded) where slavery was legal in 1861 (map courtesy of Paul Bessel)

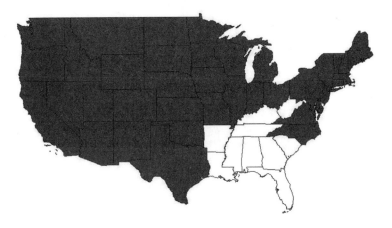

Fig. 12.2. The states (shaded) where Prince Hall Freemasonry is "recognized" (map courtesy of Paul Bessel)

Even if it has always forbidden itself from "playing politics," Freemasonry has never swum against the current of history. Superimposing these two maps, the profane and the Masonic, gives us additional proof of this. It has always faithfully reflected the great social divisions. It has allowed some ideas to hatch. It has often served as a school of democracy for its members. It has inspired them to assume their full place in society, but it has never gathered together anything more than men, with all their flaws and prejudices.

THIRTEEN

Prince Hall and the French Masonic Obediences

Paradoxically, wars have sometimes brought people together. For example, wars inspired American and French Freemasons to form ties that they had never seriously thought of forming before. This was the case during the First World War, and even more significantly so during and after the Second World War.

Just like the white American grand lodges, the Grand Lodges of Prince Hall had more comfortable relations with the Grand Lodge of France than with the Grand Orient of France, essentially for ideological reasons. It seems that the Great Architect, far from playing a unifying role, was the source of discord—and continues to be one today. Nevertheless, a dialogue was begun between the Prince Hall Masons and those of the Grand Orient of France during the Second World War, even though not much has come of it. Reason seems to prevail during times of crisis, and differences of a ritual nature take a backseat. Men are thrown together, and Masonic organizations are obliged to take this new state of affairs into account.

Several Attempts during the First World War

In 1917 the Prince Hall Masons of Massachusetts deplored the chilly relations between French and American Masons.

At the present time, while France and the United States are so closely allied in defense of human interests, it seems unfortunate that the Masonic relations of the brethren of the two countries should not be of the most intimate character.[1]

This same journal cites another article, which focuses on the position adopted by the Grand Lodge of New York, on the controversy surrounding the Grand Orient of France. The black Grand Lodge of New York recalls that it was white American Masons who deemed it wise to break off relations with the Grand Orient of France.

The Grand Lodge of Louisiana did so in 1868. It was, in fact, scolding the Grand Orient of France for having created a Supreme Council of Higher Degrees* on the soil of its state, thus violating the principle of exclusive territorial jurisdiction advocated by American Masons. Furthermore, this new French-like high-grade organization had the bad taste to accept black Masons.

All the white American grand lodges followed in the footsteps of the United Grand Lodge of England after 1877 and condemned the Grand Orient of France when its members were no longer obliged to believe in "the immortality of the soul." Several Prince Hall Grand Lodges had taken a very clear position against the Grand Orient of France. Let's cite, for example, the Prince Hall Grand Lodge of Arkansas, which felt the "French brethren were completely mishandling the inviolable landmarks established by Mackey" by removing from their constitution the obligation to believe in God and the immortality of the soul, but also by eliminating the office of the grand master in no longer recognizing the principle of territorial exclusivity.[2]

Indeed, the Grand Orient had voted to remove the function of grand master in 1870.[3] As temporary as this measure proved to be, it profoundly shocked both white and black American Masons, who felt a strong attachment to the hierarchical principles. On the other hand, it

---

*The lodges practiced the first three degrees (apprentice, companion, master). There are more organizations of higher degrees for the seasoned Masons wishing to study the symbolism more extensively (from the 4th to 33rd degrees in the Scottish Rite).

was fairly daring for a black grand lodge to criticize the Grand Orient on the basis that it was treating Mackey's Landmarks too lightly, particularly the principle of territorial exclusivity, when this very Landmark had been used as a pretext by white Masons for years to exclude black Masons. It is an excellent example of mimicry defying all logic.

It was only in 1917, during the First World War, that the black Grand Lodge of New York expressed any doubts. It wondered for what mysterious reason Prince Hall Grand Lodges should align themselves with the position of the white American grand lodges who had never shown signs of any sympathy toward them and adopted all their grievances against the Masons of the Grand Orient of France while refusing to hear the French organization's side of the story. It even went so far as to quote the remarks of Frédéric Desmons.

> Let us leave to churches and theologians the discussion of dogmas. Let us leave to accredited church authorities the formation of systems. Let Masonry continue to be what she ought to be, an institution open to progress of every sort, welcoming all moral ideas, all elevated ideas, all large and liberal aspirations. Let us never descend into the arena of theological discussions, which discussions have never, believe me, resulted in anything but troubles and persecutions.[4]

Frédéric Desmons, a pastor in his home region, had actually preached for the elimination of the mention of "the existence of God and the immortality of the soul" in article 1 of the Constitutions of the Grand Orient of France. Now, the Grand Lodge of New York came to the conclusion that the opinion of Desmons, a man who had been the target of Catholic persecution in his land, like all French Protestants, had at least as much authority as that of any white English or American Mason. It lent the following remarks to a "famous American Mason" who preferred to keep his identity secret as if he never existed. Perhaps this was simply an oratorical precaution that would allow him to take a greater liberty of tone.

Who do you think was the best judge of what French Masonry ought to do in 1877? Frédéric Desmons, scholar, public man, devoted patriot, disinterested and self-sacrificing Mason, Protestant minister in a Roman Catholic community, or you, who know no more about France than about the back side of the moon, who can't know what it is to sacrifice anything for Masonry, who justify yourself to your own conscience for being a Mason by figuring up the material advantages you can get out of it?[5]

It is no coincidence that the Grand Lodge of New York made reference to Desmons's remarks in 1917, during the First World War, looking in this way to justify the position adopted by the Grand Orient of France that earned it the scorn of white English and American Freemasonry. American Masons, undoubtedly some New Yorkers of both skin colors, found themselves in battles that brought aid to France in 1916. The Grand Lodge of New York urged its members to overlook the rifts and fraternize with French Masons. Not only did it encourage the creation of military lodges to uplift the morale of its members, but it also authorized New York Masons to visit French lodges.

Full liberty was given to all New York Masons in France to hold Masonic intercourse with French Masons and visit their lodges, the question of formal correspondence, to report next May.[6]

This statement specifically mentions the Grand Lodge of France but not the Grand Orient. It is likely that, in practice, black American Masons visited Grand Orient lodges without incurring any penalty. However, it was with the Grand Lodge of France that the New York Grand Lodge of Prince Hall envisioned establishing formal relations. In fact, it was the Grand Lodge of France that took the initiative to send an appeal to the Grand Lodge of New York on July 20, 1917.

The landing in our country of the vanguard of your army, which is crossing the ocean to unite with us in the great struggle for the freedom of the world, is an event of momentous import. It has aroused within us the thought that it is highly desirable that our ancient institution, which has always stood for liberty, should celebrate this manifestation of brotherhood by a drawing together of the bonds of fraternal esteems and affection, which unite Freemasons, all over the world.[7]

In this same statement the Grand Lodge of France expressed the wish that other grand lodges would establish ties with French Masons. It recalled that the Supreme Council of Louisiana, created by the Grand Orient of France, no longer existed, so American Masons no longer had any cause to nourish any grievance against France. The Grand Lodge of New York did not seem to advocate adopting a different position toward the two French obediences, the Grand Lodge of France and the Grand Orient. The main concern clearly seemed to be a chance to allow American and French Masons to bond and soften in this way the hardships of war.

A Favorable Context for the Coming Together of Prince Hall and the Grand Orient
World War II

It would seem that the Prince Hall Grand Lodges and the French obediences barely corresponded between the two wars. In contrast, the exchanges of letters with the Grand Orient of France resumed shortly after the Second World War.

Harry A. Williamson described the situation of the occupying troops in Germany. He strongly recommended to black Masons that they frequent the German lodges, which, according to him, had no racial prejudice, rather than join the only black lodge in the American occupied zone, which was recognized by a grand lodge of which he did not think highly.

Williamson probably had a white grand lodge in mind but did not want to say so explicitly![8] He encouraged the black Masons to form bonds with the local population, with German Freemasonry, which was painfully being reborn from its ashes, and also with the Masons of the Grand Orient of France in Germany. He was outraged that French Masons were not recognized by the Americans when they had paid such a heavy price during the war.

> Incidentally, these French Masons who are not recognized by us, paid the greatest price ever demanded of members of our Order for remaining steadfast in their allegiance to their Hiramic* obligation, since during the Petain-Germanic regime, thousands of them perished before firing squads, in liquidation camps at Dachau and Buchenwald, or were murdered in their homes (such as the three highest-ranking G.O. officers of Belgium) thus paying with their life the crime of being a Mason—yet we refuse them that title.[9]

For Williamson the concentration camps were not just a "detail," as a far-right French leader said a few years ago. Precisely at the time he wrote these lines, the grand master of the Prince Hall Grand Lodge of Michigan, William O. Greene, was invited to visit Volney Lodge of Laval, associated with the Grand Orient de France (GODF). Greene gives a long account of this visit in a series of letters addressed to Harry A. Williamson and to Marius Lepage, 33rd degree of the REAA (*Rite ecossais ancient et accepte* = Ancient and Accepted Scottish Rite) officer of the Grand Orient of France, who was trying to broker a rapprochement between the two obediences.

Greene was all the more appreciative of the warm welcome he was given at the French lodge in the summer of 1951 as in June of that same year he had been greatly humiliated when he went to the headquarters of the United Grand Lodge of England on Great Queen Street. Despite the support of Frederick Adams, worshipful master of Glittering Star Lodge n° 322 of the Grand Lodge of Ireland, the same lodge that was said to have initiated Prince Hall in his day, Greene had been given the

---

*The reference to Hiram is symbolic. In the ritual of the third degree, Hiram, the master Mason murdered by three evil companions, sacrificed himself to save the secrets of Freemasonry.

boot by an employee of the grand secretary, who could not be bothered to do so himself. "Mr. Greene does not belong to a Lodge whose constitution we recognize" were the words used as he was politely shown the door. When he was received a month later by a French lodge with all the regard due his position as grand master, he could not help but be struck by the contrast, which entirely favored the French.

> The reception into the meeting of this Lodge was a magnificent experience. All honors were bestowed according to our rank. An apron was presented and we were able to view an Entered Apprentice Degree, after which a lavish banquet was spread at the local hotel. These Masons noted their knowledge of the non-reception pattern prevailing in our Masonic relationship with American Masons (white). They were very emphatic in their attempts to make comparisons between the Frenchman's lack of prejudice and the American attitude. Following the experience, a new idea built on comparative practices between English, American, and French Masons developed. Naturally, having been subjected to the distasteful experience of the two former groups, and having the desire as a Man, and incidentally a Mason, to be recognized first as a Man without any distinction of being anything other than a first-class citizen of the United States; and in the latter instance, being received and respected because of my legality and regularity as a Mason, I was and still am very grateful to the Frenchmen of Volney Lodge. The matter of status of this Lodge and its non-recognition by the American and British Lodges was of little moment for certainly with the information at my disposal, with implicit faith in the Masonic wisdom and integrity of the person responsible for this visit, Brother Harry A. Williamson, I had little cause to suspect that this chance visit would have an impact of any sort on Masonry or potential repercussions that may affect the cause of Prince Hall Masons.[10]

This visit, far from going unperceived, would give rise to a huge controversy among Prince Hall Masons. It nonetheless testifies to the favor that a certain number of black Masons were predisposed to feel for the French lodges in the postwar period. Greene took shelter behind the authority of Williamson,* who had retired from active duties but had been most importantly the adjunct grand master of the Prince Hall Grand Lodge of New York.[11]

A year later, on January 26, 1952, this same Harry A. Williamson received a visit at his home from a member of the Grand Orient of France, in the presence of several Prince Hall brothers.[†12] On January 12, 1953, Williamson, in the company of four other Prince Hall Masons, visited the New York lodge of the Grand Orient of France, L'Atlantide.[‡] Williamson gives a detailed account of this evening reception, during which he and his friends were treated with all the honor they were due. The Masons of L'Atlantide formed the "vault of steel" when they entered the temple. On this same day they also received a visit from a member of the representatives at the United Nations. Williamson gave a speech that lasted more than an hour to the most attentive audience, according to his description.[13] The lodge worshipful master, after noting that for the first time in fifty years the labors of the lodge took place in English, asked Williamson if the Prince Hall Lodges would accept initiating white Masons. Williamson happily answered in the affirmative.

> The most important question put to me following the conclusion of my remarks was, would our Lodge initiate a white man; my answer was the one word "yes." I stated that at no time had my jurisdiction ever drawn the color line, also, that we would not be practicing

---

*Williamson was adjunct grand master from 1918 to 1921. According to William R. Denslow in *10,000 Famous Freemasons*, Williamson would have been grand master, not adjunct grand master. According to Joseph Cox in *Great Black Men of Freemasonry*, he was only adjunct grand master. I am prone to believe Cox, who was perfectly familiar with the New York Grand Lodge as one of its members. Williamson was also grand secretary and grand historian. Most importantly, he put together a huge archive of papers that are now collected together at the Schomburg Center in New York.

†Williamson notes that he received this member of the Grand Orient of France in the presence of Daniel O. Braithwaite, Samson Lodge n° 65; Hussein A. Adeeb, Jethra Lodge n° 89; and Buxter F. Jackson, Prince Hall Lodge n° 38, all in New York.

‡This lodge still exists; I had the pleasure of visiting it in 1999.

Masonry nor be consistent when we charge the white grand bodies with discrimination.[14]

This visit was both historic and unique. Williamson did not lose interest in this matter. He attempted to convince his Prince Hall brethren of the legitimacy of the Grand Orient of France and mainly to deal with the most delicate question, that of freedom of conscience.

The Obstacles

The Michigan grand master was received by the French Masons of Laval, but it was impossible for him to return the favor. Greene bemoaned this fact several times in his 1952 correspondence. Only Williamson, he stated, had foreseen some difficulties. Williamson was certainly the one who knew his brothers' minds best. On March 29, 1952, Greene received a telephone call from the Convention of Grand Masters, informing him of fears prompted by the visit of Marius Lepage. The grand masters as a group felt that an official meeting between the Grand Lodge of Michigan and Lepage, worshipful master of Volney Lodge and officer of the Grand Orient of France, would compromise the attempts at reconciliation with the white American grand lodges. In fact, the latter had not recognized the Grand Orient since 1877, and the Prince Hall leaders did not want themselves to be accused of laxity, so they acted extremely cautiously. After consulting George Crawford, author of a book proving the legitimacy of black Freemasonry, which had led to negotiations with the white grand lodges, the Convention of Grand Masters begged Greene to cancel Lepage's visit. Williamson analyzed this incident in 1952 in the didactic style he loved so dearly, which took the form of questions and answers.

Did the grand master of Michigan invite officials of sister jurisdictions to meet the prospective visitor?

He did and several of these not only approved the idea but indicated they would attend the session to meet the visitor.

What then happened?

Rumors to the effect the grand master of Michigan was about to commit a serious Masonic crime began to circulate among Prince Hall Masons.

What happened next?

Several of those who had accepted the invitation apparently "got cold feet" and found excellent excuses for not being present.

Did the French Mason come to Michigan?

He did, but because of the fuss, which had arisen, the visitor did not meet the Grand Lodge officially.

What was the cause of the fuss?

Word was passed around that because the white Grand Lodges refused to recognize the Grand Orient, the Prince Hall group should imitate them.

What is the reason for the non-recognition?

All of the English-speaking Grand Lodges throughout the world claim the teachings of the Grand Orient are atheistic due to the fact the latter does not require the presence of the Holy Bible upon the Altars of its Lodges.

Is such a requirement an ancient and fundamental regulation in Freemasonry?

No. The introduction of the Holy Bible as a part of the necessary furniture of a Lodge, is a comparatively modern requirement among the English-speaking bodies.[15]

The position of the Prince Hall Grand Lodges toward the French obediences has always been ambiguous because it was modeled on that of the white American grand Lodges, even when these latter unanimously scorned black Freemasons, whereas the French never exhibited any racist attitudes toward them. After the Second World War, black Masons appeared ready to make any compromise to obtain recognition from the white American grand lodges. Furthermore, these latter enjoyed an aura of superiority as they set themselves up as guardians of the temple in 1877 by excluding an entire section of Freemasonry— the French lodges. There are, therefore, no grounds for surprise at the rigidity displayed by the Convention of Grand Masters in 1952. Better to be impolite to Marius Lepage than incur the disapproval of white American Freemasons.

Some Prince Hall Masons acted more royalist than the king. For example, Henry E. Davis, 33rd-degree Mason and author of a history of black Freemasonry, rose up against the very designation of Great Architect of the Universe. He felt it was a continental invention and there were good grounds for distrusting all European Freemasons. He drew up the history of the higher degrees of the Scottish Rite among white American Masons. To do this he discussed the Scottish Rite Convention that met in Lausanne, Switzerland, on September 22, 1875, which brought together the North and South Supreme Councils of the United States, as well as most of the Supreme Councils of Europe. The Americans seem to have been opposed to the establishment of an International Conference of Supreme Councils on the basis that European Masons could give such an assembly an overly secular orientation.

> This hostility was induced by a fear that the European councils might involve them in religious and political controversies characteristic of continental Masons. Also, the Lausanne declaration of principles asserting a belief in a creative principle—the Great Architect of the Universe—did not satisfy their requirement of a belief in God asserted by English and American Masonry.[16]

In this way even the principle of the Great Architect was deemed too fuzzy and fanciful! This higher-degree Mason demanded a return to dogma and thus rejected all symbolism. God must be invoked, and Masons should abstain from using any other name. Such rigidity automatically excluded the two great French obediences, the Grand Orient and the Grand Lodge of France.

Not all Prince Hall Masons, however, displayed such dogmatism, as shown by the attitude of some grand officers like Williamson and the members of several grand lodges.

Attempts at Rapprochement

Williamson recalled by example that the Grand Orient of France had broken relations with the Grand Orient of Brazil in 1869, because "the latter not only recognized human slavery but would not confer degrees upon a Negro."[17] Williamson sought in this way to show the Prince Hall Masons that this French obedience was waging a battle against racism.

Several Masons of the Grand Orient of France, Marius Lepage in particular, and of the Grand Lodge of France, like Oswald Wirth, were part of an American research society, the Philalethes Society, which was initially presided over by Allen E. Roberts. All were working toward coming together with black Freemasonry.[18]

However the American grand lodges, both black and white, kept their distances from the Grand Orient of France. Several exceptions confirm this rule. For example, in 1877, a date that marks a turning point in the relations between French Freemasonry and English-speaking Freemasonry, the Grand Lodge of Mississippi opposed the fraternal attitude exhibited by the Grand Orient of France with the sectarianism of the white American grand lodges. In 1869 the Grand Lodge of Missouri, which most certainly suffered from the ostracism of which it was a victim, sought to establish official relations with foreign grand lodges and asked for official recognition from the Grand Orient of France. A letter from the council president of the order, "Brother Caubet," confirmed the desire of the Grand Orient to accede to the Missouri Masons' request. "Pledges of friendship" were named by the Grand Orient and the Grand Lodge of Missouri through "Brother Caubet" and "Brother Moses Dickson."[19] Caubet was a friend of Massol, the pioneer for secularism in the Grand Orient of France. We should note that fifty years later relations between the Prince Hall Grand Lodges and the French obediences were still at this same point.

Williamson is certainly the author of the greatest number of attempts to find common ground with the Grand Orient of France. He wished to acquaint black Masons with this obedience and explained the French developments, even when he did not approve of them personally. While he claimed to remain attached to the invocation of the Great Architect of the Universe, he did his utmost to explain the various points of view.

Williamson was first surprised to learn that the Grand Lodge of England had recognized the Grand Orient of France from its inception in the eighteenth century, whereas this latter only imposed the belief in the Supreme Being in 1849.[20] It was only on this date that the explicit mention "of the existence of God and the immortality of the soul" was introduced in article 1 of the Constitutions of the Grand Orient of France. Later, during the 1864 convention, Massol tried to remove this reference, but his theories would not prevail until 1877, thereby marking the secularization of the Grand Orient Constitutions.

Williamson rightfully noted that the extremely Christian period of the Grand Orient was quite brief, and if the English were logical they should only have granted their recognition of the French obedience between 1849 and 1877. It seems, though, that the English were completely indifferent to the French reality until 1877. It would be wrong to draw the conclusion from this that they had shown greater religious tolerance until this point.

Williamson enlightened the Masons of his obedience about the specific nature of the French context. He explained that Freemasons were the constant targets of the Catholic Church's hostility and that the charitable attitude of American Protestant Churches could not be compared with the sectarianism of French papists. Williamson even claimed that Pope Pius IX would have been a Freemason but that he wanted to get his revenge on the Italian general and politician Giuseppe Garibaldi, "a 33rd degree Mason," as well as the emperor Napoleon III, "who, too, was a Mason." Pius IX was treated as a "renegade" who chose to cast opprobrium on his former brethren by cowardly excommunicating them.[21]

Williamson seems to have initiated popes and emperors with a certain casualness. His intention was laudable, although it was a matter of proving the sectarianism of the Catholic Church and justifying the Grand Orient's decision to free itself of all dogma and proclaim freedom of conscience. Furthermore, by removing the Bible from their ritual the French Masons, according to him, were demonstrating they were not its rivals. Williamson was most likely generalizing a little on this final point. Furthermore, he explained that if the French Masons were so discreet and cautious, forbearing to even decorate the outsides of their temples, it was to protect themselves from potential reprisals on the part of the papists. American Masons had to realize that France was not as free a country as the United States, by virtue of the omnipresence of the Catholic Church.[22]

Following the visit of Michigan Grand Master Greene to the Laval lodge and the refusal of the Prince Hall grand masters to officially receive Lepage, a member of this lodge, and to thus return the favor to the French, Williamson, Greene, and the grand secretary of the Grand Orient of France, Paul Chevalier, began an extremely interesting correspondence, as it dealt with ideological problems, not merely administrative ones. In the letter he wrote Greene, Chevalier clearly raised the question of official relations between his obedience and the Prince Hall Grand Lodges. Such relations were not conceivable unless the latter accepted the principle of absolute freedom of conscience and refused all dogmatic assertions.[23]

On the other hand, Chevalier wrote an extremely courteous letter to Williamson in which he maintained that the sole "obligatory book" was Anderson's *Constitutions* but that each lodge could additionally choose to place on its altar an "optional book," which could be the Bible, the Qur'an, or any other "sacred" book.[24]

Williamson responded at length to Chevalier. He believed that a sacred book was obligatory on the altars of the lodges but that this "Volume of the Sacred Law" did not necessarily have to be the Bible and could be the holy book of another religion. Williamson did not wish to restrict access to the lodges to Christians alone, but he did exclude atheists.[25] He would not budge an inch on this point. This did not prevent him from defending the Grand Orient of France to the Prince Hall grand master of Louisiana, and he deplored both the rigidity of American Masons and the toadying displayed by some of his black brethren toward them.

> The white grand bodies refuse to declare that we are a regularly constituted Masonic Fraternity merely upon the fact of the color of our skin and irrespective of the fact that we, like themselves, make use of the Volume of the Sacred Law. I ask is there any vestige of consistency in this attitude when they refuse to admit men of color into their organization thereby declaring to the world that American Freemasonry is a white man's institution in direct conflict with the teachings of the ritual as observed in all English-speaking grand jurisdictions? In the face of this, there are some among us who wish to kiss the boots of the white Fraternity for a crumb thrown from their table. The above is, in my opinion, the grossest kind of hypocrisy.[26]

Relations with the Grand Orient of France barely evolved over the course of the twentieth century. We can see the same goodwill exhibited by both sides as well as the impossibility of taking the step toward official recognition by reason of holding notions that remained divergent. When the Masons of the Grand Orient proclaimed absolute freedom of conscience, those of Prince Hall tirelessly aligned with the Great Architect.

During the 1950s the magazine *Symbolisme* (the predecessor of *Renaissance traditionnelle*) opened its columns to Williamson in order to familiarize its readers with black American Freemasonry, which was still then little known in France. Williamson notably discussed the military lodges* established by the Prince Hall Grand Lodges in Germany, which were, like that of Oklahoma, "attached to the 75th Medical Battalion stationed in Bamberg."[27] In the 1970s, *Renaissance traditionnelle* gave the floor to Harvey Newton Brown, a grand officer of the white Grand Lodge of Texas, who was favorable to recognizing black Freemasonry. He was the author of a response to Thomas Harkins's 1963 pamphlet[28] in which the North Carolina grand master attacked Prince Hall Freemasonry.[29] Brown, to the contrary, proved the regularity of black Freemasonry. He dedicated his response to his great uncle John Churchman Brown, a soldier who died during the Civil War after being captured by Southerners, so that "his sacrifice and those of others like him, who died for the Rights of Man, may be eternally remembered."[30]

Brown was also a member of Berlin Lodge n° 46, attached to the Grand Lodge of Rhode Island. It is likely that this retired lieutenant colonel had been in the company of black American Masons during and after the Second World War.[31] Brown criticized the attitude of the United Grand Lodge of England, which only maintained good relations with white American Masons. He added that if the whites recognized the Prince Hall Lodges it would help limit the power of black extremists like the Black Panthers by legitimizing the "honest and loyal Blacks."[32] Furthermore, Brown was an extremely lucid writer. Far from idealizing Freemasonry, he made the following observation.

> You state that I consider both the GODF and the black Masonry of Prince Hall as "regular." Let's say "yes" and "no." I think that both should be recognized, but the Masonry of Prince Hall is only

---

*Williamson describes the "Periodic Bulletin" of this military lodge and says, "Courses on the Masonic ritual took place at the Nuremburg Study Club. During the month of December 1954, this club made a donation of 200 marks to the German orphanage in Augsburg; the armed forces newspaper *Stars and Stripes* mentioned it while recalling that the 'Lodge of Overseas Residents' had also created a 150 Marks fund to send ten poor German children to Kitzingern Summer Camp in Rotherburg. The Prince Hall Grand Lodge awarded its military lodge with an honorable mention in December 1954, for having given salary raises to 19 of its members."

a simple copy of the American Masonry of the Whites and has not produced a single Masonic scholar—for a variety of reasons. All they do takes the form of grievances against the non-Masonic attitude of the Grand Lodges.*[33]

Although little known today, this white American Mason had the merit of working to reconcile the white American grand lodges with the Prince Hall Masons and, more modestly, with those of the Grand Orient of France. His efforts proved to be more fruitful for the former than for the latter.

The Current Situation

The relations between the Prince Hall Grand Lodges and the Grand Orient of France have barely evolved since the time of Harry A. Williamson and Paul Chevalier, which is to say the period after the Second World War. The annals of the conferences of the Grand Orient contain very few references to the Prince Hall Grand Lodges. The collection of memorandums is hardly any more informative. However, a September 5, 1963, memo mentions the designation of four "pledges of friendship of the Grand Orient of France to Prince Hall: Brothers Jacques Mitterand, Ravel, Dumont, and Corneloup."

There has never been any official agreement between the two obediences. It seems that the situation has not changed a bit since the 1950s. Prince Hall Masons remain attached to the obligation of believing in God, both out of conviction and more importantly out of a concern not to attract criticisms from the white grand lodges, whereas the Grand Orient of France still remains loyal to its secular principle.

As the Grand Lodge of France has maintained the obligation to believe in the Great Architect of the Universe, relations with the Prince Hall Masons have been facilitated, although it has not led to a stable, official relationship. The fact that the United Grand Lodge of England,

---

*The situation has changed since then. It is no longer true to say that there are no black scholars related to Prince Hall.

and thus also the white American grand lodges, only recognizes one grand lodge per country as regular, does not seem to have presented a major obstacle. In fact, the Prince Hall Masons seem to regard official recognitions as unpredictable at all times, often linked to the problem of territorial exclusivity from which they suffered for so long. On the other hand, they remain quite touchy on the obligation to believe in God, most likely because of the Christian convictions of the black community as a whole; convictions that seem to have left a deep mark on their culture. One need only think of *soul music* and, more specifically, *gospel.*

It would seem that the United Grand Lodge of England and those American grand lodges that have recognized the Prince Hall Grand Lodges have closed their eyes to the fact that for a time the latter had established official relations with the Grand Lodge of France. The French grand lodge had adopted the principle of systematic recognition of all the Prince Hall Grand Lodges in the 1950s. It would seem that Prince Hall has ended these official relations.

The fact that the Grand Orient of France now maintains good, if not official, relations with the Supreme Council of the Scottish Rite in the United States (which is white) should facilitate relations with black Freemasonry, which itself has only recently enjoyed total recognition by American Freemasons from the Northern United States. This, however, confirms my hypothesis: whatever their past grievances toward the white grand lodges, the Masons of Prince Hall will never take any initiative that risks compromising their improved relationship with white American Masons. This was the case when Lepage visited. For obvious reasons, the Prince Hall Grand Lodges have always valued good relations with American Masonry over good relations with foreign obediences, with the exception, naturally, of the United Grand Lodge of England.

FOURTEEN

The Perspective of Prince Hall Freemasons

The Separatist Temptation

Only a few Southern states still refuse to consider the Prince Hall Grand Lodges as entirely autonomous Masonic obediences. A long road has been traveled since the battle waged by Prince Hall and his friends to wrest their charter from the Grand Lodge of England.

The Prince Hall Grand Lodges today are recognized institutions, both by the black community and by American society as a whole, even if things have not developed as far as they might have wished. In 1973 black Freemasonry even endowed itself with its own research body, the Phylaxis Society.* The Prince Hall Grand Lodges are certainly satisfied to be considered legitimate by a large number of white Masons. Nonetheless, their main concern clearly appears to be recognized first and foremost by the black community, then by the whole of American society.

---

*The society's primary activity appears to be the publication of a magazine with the same name. Joseph Walkes retraces the history of the creation of this society and mentions several polemics from the Prince Hall Grand Lodges about it. It would seem that several lodges, jealous of their prerogatives, feared their power would be halved by a body that was not directly dependent on the Masonic jurisdictions. Whatever the reason, this society has helped give a certain prestige to black Freemasonry.

The Status of the Prince Hall Grand Lodges
in American Society

Prince Hall Masons are constantly striving to show proof of their patriotism. They constantly refer to Anderson's *Constitutions* and to article 2, concerning "civil power." One will recall Prince Hall's desire to rejoin the Continental Army, his repeated requests to "brother" Washington for the latter to accept blacks fighting by his side in the War for Independence. In both Boston and Philadelphia, Prince Hall Masons gave assistance to their ill fellow citizens.

In 1786, Prince Hall, using Anderson's *Constitutions* for his model, reminded his brothers that Masons were loyal and in all circumstances respectful of governmental authority. To illustrate his contentions, he actively supported the Massachusetts authorities in their battle against Daniel Shay's supporters.[1] That same year this individual had organized a riot in protest of the situation of small farmers drowning in debt and targeted by rich merchants threatening to seize their lands. Anxious to demonstrate his attachment to the authorities and to distinguish himself from what today would be labeled "white trash," Prince Hall flew to the assistance of the authorities and wrote this letter, which one may find a touch servile.

Boston, November 26, 1786
To His Excellency James Bowdoin,

We, by the providence of God, are members of a fraternity that not only enjoins upon us to be peaceable subjects to the civil powers where we reside, but it also forbids our having concern in any plots or conspiracies against the state where we dwell; and it is the unhappy lot of this state at the present day, and as the meanest of its members must feel the want of a lawful and good government, and as we have been protected for many years under this once happy Constitution, so we hope, by the blessing of God, we may long enjoy that blessing; therefore we, though unworthy members of this Commonwealth, are willing to help and support, as far as our weak and feeble abilities may become necessary in this time of trouble and confusion, as you in your wisdom shall direct us. That we may, under just and lawful authority, live peaceable lives in all godliness and honesty, is the hearty wish of your humble servants the members of the African Lodge; and in their name I subscribe myself your most humble servant.

Prince Hall[2]

Being looked on favorably by the authorities was most likely a necessity for Massachusetts's blacks. Prince Hall did his best.

The "Troops"

Ordinarily numbers speak when one is assessing the weight of an institution in American society. For black Masonry it happens to be relatively difficult to obtain precise data, especially for the beginning period. Estimations are often vague. In 1866, John Jones reckoned the number of black Masons in the United States to be seven thousand.[3] Thirty-two years later Grand Master William A. Sutherland of New York, famous for his hostility toward recognition of black Freemasonry by the white grand lodges, estimated that the Prince Hall Lodges, which he did not believe had regular charters, had about thirty thousand Masons.[4] The years following the abolition of slavery were quite favorable for the expansion of black Freemasonry.

We do not have figures between those given by Sutherland and those given by Harry Davis in 1946. According to Davis the Prince Hall Grand Lodges had 500,000 members at this time, divvied up among 5,500 lodges, "one eighth of American Freemasonry."[5] The figures became more precise in the 1950s. In 1955, Harry A. Williamson found 311,048 members in 4,729 lodges.[6] The reduction in numbers could be partially explained by the losses suffered in World War II. In 1965, George W. Crawford announced 4,301 lodges with 229,481 Masons,[7] which would confirm a drop over the long term, unrelated to the consequences of the war. The NAACP, who can be assumed to be well informed about the black community, provided precise statistics for 1983: 4,675 lodges with 288,303 members.[8]

The white Grand Lodge of Maine mentioned 300,000 members on May 8, 1996.[9] This figure matches the one provided by the Phylaxis Society.[10] In 2001, 300,000 Masons were spread through 4,500 lodges and 44 grand lodges.* This includes the grand lodges outside the United States, such as those of the Caribbean. If we compare these figures to the ones issued by the Maine Grand Lodge in 1996, which applied only to the United States, we will see a slight drop.

Black Freemasons are most numerous in Alabama, with 30,822 members in 593 lodges; this represents 15 percent of the global membership of the Prince Hall Grand Lodges in 1997. Three grand lodges contain between 15,000 and 20,000 members: North Carolina, South Carolina, and Mississippi. Three others have around 10,000: Virginia, Texas, and Georgia. The weakest lodges are those of, in descending order, Minnesota, Arizona, Nebraska, Rhode Island, Alaska, Nevada, and Oregon, with fewer than 500 members. Paul Bessel counts 203,307 Prince Hall Masons in thirty-eight states.[†11] It is significant that Alabama represents the bastion of black Freemasonry. This state with a deeply troubled racial history is also where the civil rights movement was born.

The drop of the number of members is not confined to the black grand lodges. It reflects the malaise that affects the whole of American Freemasonry. It would even seem that black Masons have been less affected by this recruiting crisis than their white counterparts. In fact, white Freemasonry would have lost, since 1964, more than half of its membership, from 4 million to 1.5 million today.[‡12]

---

*This figure was sent by a grand officer of the Grand Lodge of the Caribbean (Prince Hall), April 30, 2001.

†This figure was obtained by adding up all the members of the Prince Hall Grand Lodges in the United States and using data from the U.S. Census Bureau. Bessel listed thirty-eight grand lodges. He does not make the figures available for the Prince Hall Grand Lodges of Illinois, Iowa, and New Mexico.

‡This evaluation dates from 2007, according to Gilbert Savitsky, grand secretary of the Grand Lodge of New York. The numbers are from the lodge's proceedings of May 2007. The exact numbers are 1,511,333 members in 11,594 lodges. In 1964 there were four million Masons, in 1986, three million.

American Freemasons as a whole are suffering from the aging of their institution. The dated nature of their notion of the relations between men and women has probably affected the Freemasons. Their wives are probably no longer content to stay in the kitchen cooking their meals, and this is but one reason . . .

Black Masons in Their Community

Prince Hall Masons pay close attention to how the white community sees their brand image. They do this by imitating white Freemasonry, which is not the least of the paradoxes. They have an obvious desire to give the impression of being an elitist society. This means they do their utmost to display the importance of their social role in the black community, but they also proudly sport the external signs of their symbolic distinctions. For example, a 33rd-degree Mason of the Scottish Rite has no qualms about wearing a fluorescent purple jacket in public, one that has been embroidered with golden numbers and letters that clearly indicate to all who see him what grade he has attained.*

The notion of secrecy is fundamentally different in the United States from how it is conceived in France. This has a bearing on the rituals but not on individuals. The Masonic rank is so closely associated with the notion of social success that Masons gladly display it. The harder it is to rise through the ranks of a society, the more pride is involved in showing one's ascent in another context. It is therefore perfectly normal that black Freemasons would sport their Masonic insignia more than whites. Proud of their success as Masons, they enjoy showing it off to their community. The feelings of envy this can inspire do not displease them.

Paradoxically, they do not seem to have learned their lesson regarding the sectarianism that white Masons displayed toward them. In turn they have not failed to cast anathemas on the black Masons they consider as irregulars or clandestine because they did not seek a place

---

*I was given a very friendly welcome by the worshipful master of a New York Prince Hall lodge, who was dressed this way in public.

beneath the banner of the Prince Hall Grand Lodges. They imitate white Masons and reject from the onset all those not holding a charter delivered by a Prince Hall Grand Lodge, as if savoring an almost too easy revenge. They rely on a failed argument, that of territorial exclusivity, in which each state should only have one single black grand lodge. Crawford wrote a small book in 1965 carrying the very significant title: *The Prince Hall Counselor, A Manual of Guidance Designed to Aid Those Combatting Clandestine Freemasonry.* In it he declares that all the black lodges in the United States that are not under the authority of the Prince Hall Grand Lodges, with the exception of the Alpha Lodge, which is under the authority of the white grand lodge of that state, are "spurious, irregular, and illegitimate."*[13]

The Prince Hall Lodges felt a constant need to assert their legitimacy, both in the overall Masonic community and in civil society. The Masons had a heartfelt need to show their respectability and good morality. They wished to behave in an exemplary manner in their communities, as shown by the speech of the Missouri grand master in 1877. Like Prince Hall in his first speeches to the African Lodge Masons, he opened by recommending sobriety to his brothers, without going so far as advocating the transformation of Freemasonry into a "temperance society of complete abstinence."[14] His motivation was likely to avoid being associated with the first movements in favor of prohibition. He next prescribed a code of good morality for his listeners.

> I desire once more, before the expiration of my official relation, to call your attention to the fact that the true Mason is required to be a gentleman at all times and at all places. Therefore the common use of coarse, profane, and vulgar language is utterly inconsistent and unmasonic. . . . Remembering that of all things human we hold sacred is character and reputation. . . . We as a masonic body ought to represent the intelligence, the influence, the manhood, and the gentility of the community in which we live.[15]

---

*Apparently not all black Masons share this point of view about the New Jersey lodge.

The grand master draws one practical conclusion from his remarks: as every Mason is a respectable individual, he must be able to pay his lodge dues. He cannot be indigent.

There is no need to show additional proof of the overwhelming importance attached by black Masons to education. In addition to Booker T. Washington and W. E. B. Du Bois, many lesser-known educators contributed to helping the youth of their communities.[16] I cited in chapters 5 and 7 the freely given effort by numerous lodges to award scholarships to the most deserving students. Furthermore, organizations under the direct control of the Prince Hall Grand Lodges and endowed with their own ritual were created for the purpose of training future Masons, to provide an education conforming to the order's principles for the children of Masons, or just simply to better supervise black youth. It was in this spirit that the Order of Saint Joseph was created on December 11, 1923. The preamble to the ritual, which opens with a prayer, defines the goals of this organization.

> To the Glory of God, Amen.
>
> After a thorough consultation with our most worshipful Grand Master, C. C. Kittrell, and believing the brethren would consent this plan was laid before our Grand Lodge as above noted. The purpose being to form, expand, and perpetuate an auxiliary of male juveniles ages fifteen (15) to twenty-one (21) in order to inculcate within the hearts and minds a reverence toward God. A purpose and proper regard for development; intellectually, morally, and industrially. A duty to self and humanity. The time now being ripe to gather in the youths, throw around them a shield of care, that by having them feel and know that the future holds bright prospects for them, the willing and earnest.[17]

An article in the *Pittsburgh Courier* in 1945 mentions the establishment of "two summer camps for black children."[18] The Masons wanted to render service to the whole black populace and not only their children. They also maintained close relations with the famous U.S. organization for youth, the Young Man's Christian Association

(YMCA).*[19] Organizations close to Prince Hall, such as the Eastern Star and the Heroines of Jericho, met on the premises of the Chicago YMCA, as shown in the bulletin of the Former Elders of Illinois in 1945.[20] The Christian aspect of the YMCA, as well as the role of social integration played by this association, met with the approval of black Freemasons, who were equally anxious to impart moral values to the young.

The Prince Hall Grand Lodges made considerable efforts to encourage the social success of their members, including the facilitation of their professional advancement or helping them build companies, thanks to the creation of savings and loan institutions (see chapter 7). Even though the development of the Prince Hall Lodges was not as striking as in years past, they still represented a magnet for the black middle class. Rightly or wrongly, they were perceived as the symbol of a rise in social status. On the other hand, some members of the black community regarded them as too close to white authority, too prone to making compromises, even collaborating with the oppressors. This would certainly explain the reservations felt by the Prince Hall Grand Lodges about becoming too close-knit with the white grand lodges, although they still set great store on how these white lodges viewed them.

Relations with the Other American Grand Lodges Today

The relations between the white and black grand lodges remain ruled by ambiguity. Prince Hall Masons are unable to abandon the mimetic attitude they have adopted toward the white grand lodges, and they persist in viewing the white lodges as models when it comes to jurisprudence and symbolism. At the same time, they have asserted their own unique qualities and their desire to do without white recogni-

---

*The YMCA was an organization imported from England in 1851. It enjoyed enormous popularity in the United States, with two hundred chapters in 1861, and two thousand in 1900.

tion if the only way they can get it is through begging. They even seem to have hardened their position. This has given rise to a relatively recent separatist reaction: the Prince Hall Grand Lodges have determined to retain their full autonomy and have squarely refused to merge with the other American grand lodges. They are now striving to distinguish themselves from white Freemasonry, probably to allay the suspicions of those who persist in considering them to be Uncle Toms. They have become sufficiently self-assured to do without the "recognition" of the whites. Some of the white grand lodges have gotten the message and given blanket recognition to all Prince Hall Grand Lodges, without waiting for the black Freemasons to ask (see chapter 12).

We should certainly not pass over in silence the signs of openings that have been seen here and there over the course of the centuries. In 1905 a white visitor was received by the Celestial Lodge, an event that was sufficiently exceptional to warrant explicit mention in the annals.[21] During his visit to the New York L'Atlantide Lodge of the Grand Orient of France, Williamson stated he was ready to initiate whites in his own lodge. To be sure, but Williamson was not just any worshipful master. In addition to his responsibilities in the Prince Hall Grand Lodge of New York, he was the primary architect of the reconciliation with the French obedience (see chapter 12). More recently, in 1999, Joseph Cox offered the example of the Prince Hall Grand Lodge of Texas, which now initiates white Masons—but only those who have married black women![22]

These few exceptions only prove the rule. Overall, Prince Hall Masons prefer to remain among their own company. Not only have they shown evidence at times of the same intolerance that white Masons have shown them by refusing to initiate whites, but they have even rejected Masons who became too close to the white obediences. The most flagrant case of this sectarianism would be that of the black Mason expelled from his original lodge, a Prince Hall Lodge, for joining the Alpha Lodge. The Alpha Lodge, a dependency of the New Jersey Grand Lodge, was at that time the only white lodge that was open to blacks. However, its membership was almost entirely black.[23]

This position of withdrawal has two likely explanations. First and foremost, the Prince Hall Masons are weary of going cap in hand to beg recognition from their white brothers. Next, they are sick of being constantly accused by some members of the black community of trying to assimilate and mold themselves after whites.

In the 1920s they sought to parry this attack by turning toward the Republic of Liberia, founded in 1821 by freed black slaves. In 1919, Nathaniel H. B. Cassell, grand secretary of the Grand Lodge of Liberia, wrote of courtesy visits made to several American Prince Hall Grand Lodges, those of New York, Washington, D.C., and Maryland. On September 22, 1919, the minister and future president of Liberia, C. D. B. King, was officially received by the Prince Hall Grand Lodge of New York. Arthur Schomburg, who gave his name to the famous Schomburg Center for Research in Black Culture in New York City,* presided as grand secretary over the banquet that the New York Masons organized in King's honor.

The event was reported in detail in an article in the *Masonic Quarterly Review*. The report's author was unstinting in his praise for the Liberian president. He reviewed his speech and appreciated the hand he held out to black Americans, who King said would always be welcome in Liberia, which hoped to play a pioneering role in spreading the benefits of civilization across the African continent.

> The Africans are the founders of the present Occidental civilization, and, perhaps, were the originators of the civilization idea. . . . President King made it clear that Liberia held out a welcome hand to Americans of African descent. . . . In Liberia lies the hope and future of Africans; it is the key to the domination of African affairs by Africans for Africans.[24]

This openly expressed desire for African supremacy and the implicit feeling of superiority over other ethnic groups is likely not foreign to

---

*It is this research center, located in the heart of Harlem, that is home to the Williamson Fund (among other collections) dedicated to black Freemasonry.

the serious crisis that has been roiling the Liberian republic for the past several years. In the 1920s there appears to have been a perfect complicity between black American Freemasonry and the Republic of Liberia, probably because they both viewed themselves as the elites of their respective communities.

Nonetheless, black Masons were living on American soil and could not ignore their white counterparts. Their relations had long been stagnant, essentially because of the racism displayed by the white grand lodges toward the Prince Hall Lodges. However, the Prince Hall Lodges never regarded recognition as some kind of ideal. In 1914 Crawford put his brothers on guard against an attitude he deemed paternalistic and said he wished to write "a book, which, while stating strongly the case for Prince Hall Masonry, shall be free from any assumption, conscious or unconscious, of the inevitableness of white patronage."[25] Requesting "recognition" presumed, in his opinion, acceptance of the superiority of white Freemasonry in hopes it would condescend to bestowing its label on a black organization. Crawford used a grandiloquent yet familiar style to express the depths of his thought.

> The only recognition that Negro Masons could ever accept without self-stultification would be recognition coupled with union with them under the white baldachin of universal Masonry, from which the white brethren have drawn themselves apart. As to recognition on any other basis—a fig![26]

In 1946, Harry Davis, a 33rd-degree Mason of the Scottish Rite, expressed his fear of seeing Prince Hall Masonry absorbed by the white American grand lodges and said that so long as relations between blacks and whites remained so tense in the United States, it would be better to remain separate and autonomous, while preserving their distinct identities and histories. He advocated for an entente cordiale between white and black Masons, a kind of establishing of diplomatic relations between equals.

Amalgamation or absorption is inexpedient at this time; such an event will have to wait the slow attrition of time for the solution of the entire question of race relations in America. Moreover, the Prince Hall Mason is not especially eager for a solution that would destroy his historic institution.[27]

Loretta Williams states that black institutions operate according to the "pillarization" principle and applies this theory to Prince Hall Freemasonry. According to her, to be effective, black institutions must exist next to white ones but without ever merging, thus forming the pillars of society next to the white pillars.[28] It seems that Prince Hall Masons have increasingly adopted this operational model.

Institutional autonomy and greater maneuvering room is the official reason Prince Hall Masons put forth against a merger of black and white obediences. A New York Mason said, in very colorful terms, "There is a risk of the big fish swallowing the little one."* However, the basic reason, which does not contradict the preceding one, is perhaps of a social nature. The remarks made by Williamson in the 1950s remain quite meaningful in my opinion.

The Prince Hall Mason has never sought, nor does he seek "social intimacy" with any individual or group who may not desire such contact.[29]

Long before the civil rights movement, Williamson feared that *equality* would be a vain term inside and outside the lodge. He therefore preferred that blacks gain self-confidence inside their own organization among themselves, at least initially. In 1999, Cox expressed very similar feelings, although in a less stark fashion: "The successful would say yes, those who are struggling would say no."[30]

Only the blacks who have succeeded in American society would

---

*This is what I was told by a worshipful master during my visit to the Harlem Prince Hall Lodge in March 1999.

draw any real benefit from integration, according to Cox. As a general rule, black Freemasons have enjoyed more success than the majority of the other members of their community. All the same, they still have reservations and prefer to keep their distance from men whom they see as socially distant, even if they are Masons like themselves.

FIFTEEN

The Caribbean Masonic Space

Between Prince Hall and Europe

The Planters' Lodges on the Sugar Islands

Freemasonry closely followed in the footsteps of growing empires. We shall only examine the French and British sugarcane islands here, without claiming any exhaustive study but merely to outline several broad tendencies.

The first observation is that the lodges were made up almost exclusively of colonists until the time of emancipation. For the most part these colonists were planters, cultivating sugarcane thanks essentially to very inexpensive manual laborers consisting almost exclusively of slaves from Africa.

The first lodges of these islands were established by the British or French, depending on the context and sometimes in rotation, according to colonial conquests. The first Caribbean lodge came into being on Antigua in 1738. In 1739 there are supposed to have been three lodges on this small island, all placed directly under the aegis of the Grand Lodge of England, while a fourth was a dependent of the provincial Grand Lodge of New England, which was also under the authority of the Grand Lodge of England.[1]

Jamaica was the second island of the archipelago to witness the

204

appearance of Freemasonry, followed closely by Barbados. Unfortunately, the archives of the Kingston lodge have vanished. We do know, though, that a large number of Jews from Europe and South America made up the bulk of its membership. An Englishman, Alexander Irving, who had recently settled there, founded the lodge Saint Michael's n° 94 on Barbados, on March 12, 1740. Contrary to other islands, Barbados, nicknamed Little England, remained British from the colonial period until its independence was declared. A great consistency is therefore found among the members of the first lodges, who were generally planters, sailors, and slave traders. The Albion Lodge, with its well-chosen and distinctive name, became a veritable institution starting in 1790 and still exists today, proof of its ability to adapt to local political developments.[2]

The first steps taken by Freemasons were quite different in Jamaica, Barbados, and Trinidad for reasons that owe more to differences of contexts than to idiosyncrasies connected to their rituals. Planters wielded much greater power in the chartered colonies, like Barbados and Jamaica, than in the more recent colonies that were directly under the authority of the British crown (crown colonies), like Trinidad or Guyana. The lodges reflected these differences and were dependent on the high mobility at this time of their members, who hopped from one island to another, based on economic and political circumstances.

La Sagesse Saint Andrew Lodge n° 243 was the first to be formed in Granada in 1764 by the English, but it was removed from the rolls of the United Grand Lodge of England in 1813.* Its distinctive French name can be explained by the fact that Grenada was alternately under French or English domination. It was still inhabited by a large number of French people and only became English once and for all a short time later. In fact, in 1795, Julien Fédon, a mulatto and the owner of a farm,

---

*Like a good many lodges at this time, such removal was often for nonpayment of dues. When the United Grand Lodge of England was created in 1813, resulting from the union of the Modern and Ancient Grand Lodges, it took advantage of the merger to clean up its financial situation and remove from its rolls all lodges that were not in good standing with its treasury. We saw earlier that the African Lodge created by Prince Hall was a victim of this purging of the rolls.

attempted one last time to place the island under French control by freeing his own slaves with an eye toward following the example of the Jacobins and the first emancipation in 1794. With the slaves he freed he managed to besiege the island and terrorize the English for a full year from atop a hill and even managed to kill the British governor.[3]

We know little about the beginning of Freemasonry in Granada, but Robert Freke Gould mentions the existence of two French lodges in the 1780s as well as the creation of a third in 1828, the Loge La Bienfaisance (Charity Lodge), under the banner of the Grand Orient of France.[4] The fact that a lodge could be attached to France when the island was then British is worth pointing out, but it is not surprising: the French presence there was still quite large, and a number of French speakers lived there, as shown even today by place-names like Sauteurs, Fontenoy, Molinière, and others.*

A slightly similar case can be found in Trinidad when Les Frères Unis (The United Brothers) Lodge was established there in 1794. This island's context is fairly unique. Originally Trinidad was colonized by Spanish adventurers—hence its name—looking for gold and silver. They quickly realized that the island—at that time essentially a swamp accompanied by a lake of tar—offered little potential, and they did not delay in crossing the twenty-mile strait that separated them from the mainland (what is now Venezuela). In order to populate the island, the Spanish government began conceiving of ways to attract people to the island. Thanks to the colonist Roume de Saint-Laurent, a native of Grenada, it sought to draw French colonists there who wanted to escape the guillotine and encouraged them to settle there with their slaves. The more slaves they brought, the more land they would be granted. This arrangement was formalized as the "cedula of population."

Attracting these colonists offered the Spanish government a dual advantage: on the one hand these were conservatives who were anti-Jacobin and loyal to the monarchy, and on the other they were Catholic

---

*Grenada remained French until 1763, the year in which it was ceded to the United Kingdom. The French, however, managed to regain possession of the island for a short period (1779–1783) before having to relinquish it once and for all.

like the Iberian colonizers. When the Scottish general Ralph Abercrombie decided to take possession of the island during the Napole-
onic Wars, the Spanish colonists, following Governor Don José María
Chacon's lead, offered only weak resistance. As a Scottish gentleman,
Abercrombie was happy to offer the island to the British crown while
respecting Spanish legislation and allowing the French colonists to keep
both their lands and their religion.

The first lodge passed through all these events unscathed. Its French
title—Les Frères Unis—had dual justification, on the one hand because
it was founded by the Grand Orient of France and, on the other, because
the majority of Trinidad's inhabitants were French planters.[5] The case
of this first lodge is quite revealing about the mobility of the colonists
of that time. The brothers had obtained a warrant dated June 27, 1788,
from the Grand Orient of France for founding a lodge at the Temple of
Micoud on Saint Lucia. It so happens that when Victor Hugues landed
on the island a year later with his infernal machine, the guillotine, the
treasurer Benoît Dert had only enough time to grab the lodge charter
before Jacobin troops burned down the temple. By chance, Benoît Dert
had a brother in Trinidad, Dominique Dert, owner of a cocoa plantation not far from Port of Spain, where the first cocoa mill was constructed on the island.[6] He then conceived the notion to go to Trinidad
and establish the lodge that was born on Saint Lucia. Once there, he
immediately initiated his brother and met French Masons from Haiti,
Martinique, and Guadeloupe, whose fear of the French revolutionaries
had driven them to seek asylum on English soil, as well as several Spanish Masons.

Les Frères Unis Lodge soon concerned itself with diplomatic matters, as it was at the whim of geopolitical events.[7] In the context of the
French Revolution, it took pains not to offend the British authorities
and was happy to renounce its French warrant for a charter from the
Grand Lodge of Pennsylvania. Then, when England was once more at
war with the United States in 1812, the lodge again shifted allegiance
in 1813, placing itself under the authority of the Grand Lodge of Scotland. It was a matter of staying on good terms with the colonial authorities under any and all circumstances.

In the French Antilles the first lodge appeared in Martinique. This was Saint Jacques de la Parfaite Union (Saint James of the Perfect Union), in the town of Saint-Pierre, which was constituted by the Grand Lodge of Clermont in 1738. This lodge assumed the distinctive title of Saint Jean de la Parfaite Union when the Saint Jean d'Écosse Lodge of Marseilles reformed it. On May 11, 1775, the Grand Orient of France granted it its constitutions, applied retroactively. From 1777 to 1789 the members of the lodge were by then a large part of the social elite, as can be seen in the list of worshipful masters of the lodge: "Bière, merchant, trade auditor; La Faye, militia captain; D'Astorg, seneschal; Dubuc, major commander"; and in the list of lodge deputies: "Schmidt, ship purser (1778–1779); Gaultier de Claubry, surgeon for the Count d'Artois (1781–1782); Bacon de la Chevalerie (1785–1789); and Colloz, former banker and forwarding agent for the Court of Rome (1787–1789)."[8]

The first lodge in Guadeloupe was created in Sainte-Anne in 1745, essentially a military lodge, and it received its constitutions from the Grand Orient of France in 1792. From 1738 to 1788 ten lodges were founded in Martinique, primarily in Saint-Pierre, and nine in Guadeloupe.[9] Three lodges even emerged in Guadeloupe during the French Revolution, but they were of short duration. As a general rule, the lodge memberships consisted of the colonial elites, the owners of the large settlements, merchants, sea captains, legal administrators, and police. These extremely insular lodges displayed a certain distrust of newcomers from the metropolis, despite the Masonic passports given them by the Grand Orient of France.[10]

The history of Freemasonry in Guyana is different because colonization took place much more slowly there. Of course, in 1763, after losing a large number of its settlements at the end of the Seven Years' War, France sought to colonize America by inspiring close to fifteen thousand men, women, and children to settle in Guyana, primarily in Kourou. An epidemic slew more than half of these immigrants. It caused such a scandal that it forced the intendant, Jean-Baptiste Thibault Chanvalon, to leave office.[11] It is claimed that the first lodge was created in Cayenne in 1763, most likely because of this sudden immigration, and that in 1774, there were even two lodges in Guyana.[12]

But the reality is more complex. According to Daniel Ligou, "Under the Ancien Régime, two lodges that we only know through allusions existed in Guyana; these are *Saint Jean de la Guyane,* mentioned in the tables from 1765 to 1778, and *La Militaire de Saint Jean,* mentioned in the tables from 1769 to 1788."[13] No lodge is listed in Guyana during the eighteenth century by Daniel Kerjan and Alain Le Bihan,[14] and André Combes dates the first one from November 17, 1888. This lodge, La Parfaite Union, obtained its constitutions from the Grand Orient of France in November 1829. According to Combes, it originally consisted of eighteen members, six of whom had been born in Cayenne. The worshipful master of this lodge was an investigating judge, Auguste Poupon, and the lodge recruited planters, magistrates, merchants, and military men. It passed into nothingness in 1840. A second lodge, the Trinosophes Guyanais, tried to establish itself in 1834 but failed due to the opposition of the former lodge's worshipful master, Poupon.[15]

A famous Freemason valiantly tried to abolish slavery on his own Guianese plantation. This was the Marquis de Lafayette, who in 1783 bought La Belle Gabrielle with the firm intention of emancipating the sixty slaves working there. He had been initiated several years earlier.*

Adrienne [his wife], deeply Christian, had a desire to teach the Negroes and forged ties with the priests of Saint Esprit who had a house in Cayenne.[16]

His plan, however, did not succeed.

In Santo Domingo the first lodge was created in Orient du Cap in 1749; the Scottish Lodge, Saint John of Jerusalem, was originally constituted by La Parfaite Loge d'Écosse de Saint Jean de Jerusalem of Bordeaux.[17] Here too the list of deputies between 1776 and 1785 is edifying: "Court de la Tonnelle, Battle Major of the Militias of Saint Francis (1777); Mazères, dragoon captain, former commander of the

---

*Lafayette is said to have been initiated in a military lodge in 1775, but doubt still persists as to the exact date and place.

Morin Quarter in Santo Domingo (1777–1778); Maydieu, merchant, and Moreau de Saint-Méry (past worshipful master, 1785)."[18] Moreau de Saint-Méry was well known as the spokesman for the colonists of Santo Domingo and a member of the Massiac Club, and he was opposed to any reforms of the slavery system, although he prided himself on being a man of the Enlightenment.[19] Around twenty lodges have been verified as existing in Santo Domingo between 1749 and independence. While all consisted of planters, merchants, and soldiers, it would seem that the relatives of Toussaint Louverture were able to gain admittance to one of these lodges in particular, La Réunion Désirée of Port Republican, the former Port-au-Prince, as explained by Jacques de Cauna.

> In fact we found there, not only his brother, Paul Louverture, commander of the Port-au-Prince arrondissement, and his nephew, Charles Bélair, commander of the Arcahaye, but also a good number of influential Whites, Blacks, and men of color, the elite of the new Louverture state, quite often of Aquitaine origin, some of whom provided the administrators of the future Haitian state, like the dark-skinned merchant Joseph-Balthazar Inginac or André Dominique Sabourin, white Creole inhabitant of the Arcahaye, in fact, who passed for a mulatto according to a spy's report that accused him of having caused "great harm" to Whites, and who became the high judge of the republic of Haiti, the second highest authority of the state—without overlooking, naturally, the Basque native Jean Baptiste Charlestéguy, "merchant," "master Mason," and "temple guard," future survivor of the massacre of whites in 1804, and responsible for reestablishing the Scottish Rite in independent Haitian Masonry. We know that, subsequently, and starting with the first president of the Republic, the Bordelais mulatto, Alexandre Pétion, the constitutions of independent Haitian Masonry automatically elected the head of state as Grand Protector of the Order, whether he was a member or not, a practice, which seems to have been initiated/inaugurated by Toussaint Louverture at least from 1800, as we shall see.[20]

It would therefore seem that, for Freemasonry as well, the island of Santo Domingo represented a distinctive case of precocious integration into the lodges of several black men, who, what's more, were the artisans of the slave revolt at the sides of the mulattos. We know that Santo Domingo was the first sugar plantation island to declare its independence, which occurred in 1804, following the slave revolt led by Toussaint Louverture in 1801.

From Abolition to Emancipation

For a long time the Caribbean lodges remained the terrain of choice for the colonial elite: planters, soldiers, merchants, and political administrators. However, as a general rule, these lodges proved capable of evolving and did not vanish following emancipation. It sometimes required local incidents to push history forward.

The case of the aptly named Albion Lodge in Barbados is quite significant in this respect. On January 8, 1832, the secretary of the lodge wrote to the adjunct grand master of the Grand Lodge of England to express his dismay at the fact that a black man named Lovelace Oviton (or Overton), a bugler in the troops of royal dragoons in Manchester, was attempting to solicit his admission into the Albion as a visitor, equipped with a Masonic certificate granted him by the Royal Clarence Lodge of Brighton, which had been affiliated with the Modern Grand Lodge of England some years before the merger of the two English grand lodges under the name of the United Grand Lodge of England in 1813. The secretary of the lodge was all the more distressed as Oviton had expressed a desire to found a lodge of black Masons in Barbados. What is more, in 1817, Oviton had intervened to try to prevent a white man from striking a black man, which earned him a short stay in prison. A month later, accused of instigating a rebellion near the Hackett Plantation, he was again incarcerated by order of the magistrate, whose name figures among the members of this same Albion Lodge.

Perhaps to find his way back into the good graces of the planters, this same Oviton had signed a declaration of loyalty to the governor in opposition to any improvement of the lot of the slaves that the British government was attempting to impose on the planters of the colony. Under the pressure of British abolitionists, the Privy Council had tried to force the colonies placed directly under its authority (like Trinidad) to adopt measures limiting the number of hours slaves could work and forbidding the use of the whip as a spur to labor.[21]

Whatever the case may be, Oviton was never admitted into Albion Lodge or given authority to create a black lodge. But the story does not end here. Paradoxically, it was this same Albion Lodge that petitioned the United Grand Lodge of England in 1840—thus some seven years after the abolition of slavery throughout the British Empire—for the right to accept blacks, precisely to allow newly emancipated slaves to join the lodges of the Empire.

This wish to integrate blacks was far from being shared by all the Caribbean lodges. For example, Amity Lodge 227 sent a missive on July 2, 1840, to the Grand Lodge of Ireland, of which it was an affiliate, asking whether the emancipation of slaves truly meant they could be admitted into the lodges.[22] The lodges of Antigua and Saint Vincent, however, followed the same track as that of the Albion Lodge. The United Grand Lodge of England gave itself time to consider a decision but ended up voting for a resolution in 1847 that altered the terms of its constitutions by replacing "free-born man" with "free man."[23] For once it was the Caribbean lodges that took the lead, and it seems that the United Grand Lodge of England waited until it was sure of their approval before deciding to make this major change.

In Trinidad, Les Frères Unis Lodge reigned long without sharing power. This was the preeminent colonialist's lodge, which steadfastly opposed every measure in favor of shortening the workdays of the slaves and was constantly sending petitions to the local administration—the *cabildo,* a remnant of the Spanish colonial system that retained its original name—advocating on behalf of the interests of the planters. Benoît Dert and his brother Dominique were owners of Tranquility Estate, a cocoa plantation. Several other plantation owners were also members of the lodge at this time: Christopher Hewitson, owner of Felicity Hall; two Corsicans, Paul Giuseppi and Cipriano Cipriani, owners of Moka

Estate; Louis Sergent, owner of Debe Estate in Maraval; Jean Boissière, owner of the sugar plantation Champs-Élysées; as well as Jean Bettancourt, Jean-Étienne Maingot, and Clément Orosco. This list is very likely incomplete. At least six members of the lodge were part of the cabildo: Jean Indave, Louis Montrichaud, De Castro, Cadet, Mendez, and Sorzano.

The lodge had closer ties to Governor Thomas Picton, who made a name for himself by his imprisonment and torture of slaves in "cachots brûlants,"* than to Commissioner William Fullerton, who had been named to his post by the British government to apply a moderating influence to Picton's behavior. It so happens that Fullerton was a Scottish Mason. On November 2, 1831, in line with several measures taken a few years earlier (in 1823), the British government promulgated an order in council that reduced working hours for slaves, provided regulations governing their food and clothes, and made arrangements that the Trinidad planters deemed prejudicial.[24] They rebelled against what they viewed as an attack on their property rights and addressed the governor as well as the Chamber of Lords with a solemn protest and petition in opposition to these new regulations.[25] Lodge member Cipriano Cipriani was one of the delegation that went to the governor to protest the Privy Council's edict and took the petition there in January 1832.[26] Another member of Les Frères Unis, Jean Besson, also joined this delegation, while their fellow lodge member José de Orosco was a member of the support committee.[27]

Les Frères Unis were long reluctant to initiate blacks. The problem appears to have been raised because the sons of some members, with their black mistresses, were refused access to the temple, but there is no solid proof. Les Frères Choisis (The Chosen Brothers) Lodge, founded in the town of San Fernando in 1823, was the first to initiate black members after it received a charter—but not without some difficulty—from the provincial English Grand Lodge following the refusal of the Trinidad Masons, who worked under the authority of the Scottish and Irish Grand Lodges, to grant one.[28] Subsequently, all the founders of the Philanthropic

---

*Prison cells where torture was practiced.

Lodge in 1830 were free blacks, generally of French origin. Ironically enough, Vincent Patrice, a member of Les Frères Unis, established this lodge.[29] Jean-Jacques Rousseau, a former worshipful master of the Grand Orient of France, invested much energy into this lodge after fighting for the integration of black officers into the Trinidad militia.[30]

There were several planters' lodges active in Jamaica, such as the Saint James and Union Lodges in Montego Bay and the Harmony Lodge on Green Island, under the banners of both the Ancient and Modern Lodges. However, Freemasons, contrary to the Baptists who had supported the great slave revolt in 1831 known as the Christmas Rebellion, very clearly took the side of the plantation owners.

After Haiti declared its independence, French Freemasons broke with the Grand Orient of France and turned to the Grand Lodge of Pennsylvania, which founded a provincial Grand Lodge of Santa Domingo in 1802. Under Jean-Jacques Dessalines, the first ruler of an independent Haiti, Masonry vanished in that country. The Grand Orient of Haiti was not founded until 1823.

The Antilles's lodges were late to initiate blacks. On July 4, 1828, however, two inhabitants of Martinique, Louis Fabien and Charles Cyrille Bissette, the famous abolitionist, were initiated into the Trinosophes Lodge of the Grand Orient of France in Paris, and the orator of the lodge gave a renowned speech.

> All eyes have turned with interest to these two last candidates, victims of a barbarous prejudice and martyrs of the most odious iniquity. Each is feeling the keenest emotion and plans to cooperate in forgetting the iniquities of an arbitrary colonial tyranny that forced them to empty the cup of bitterness to the dregs.[31]

No doubt alarmed by the evolution of Freemasonry, in 1846 the governor dissolved the four Martinique lodges: La Trigonométrie, Sainte Trinité, La Concorde, and La Réunion des Arts, which were suspect of encouraging progressive ideas. At least two lodges espoused the abolitionist cause: La Trigonométrie in Fort Royal and La Réunion des Arts, for which Bissette was a deputy when it was reformed under the

Second Republic.[32] The two major abolitionist figures, Bissette and Victor Schoelcher, were Freemasons. Schoelcher had been initiated into the Parisian lodge Les Amis de la Vérité (The Friends of Truth) in 1822.

On May 23, 1848, Mayor Hervé de Saint Pierre, with the support of his Masonic colleague, councilor Thomas Jean Baptiste Cochinat, brought the motion against slavery to a vote.

> Considering that no French land can have slaves, the municipal council of Saint Pierre unanimously requests that His Lordship the Governor decree the complete abolition of slavery in Martinique.[33]

The lodge Les Emules d'Hiram (Hiram's Disciples), founded in 1835 by the Orient de Saint-Rose in Guadeloupe, was the first to respond to the initiative of five free black men who were initiated in France, and three white men, who had the specific goal of permitting the initiation of blacks.[34] This measure was immediately condemned by La Paix Lodge in Pointe-à-Pitre, which described Les Emules d'Hiram as "savage,"[35] and wrote of it in the following terms to the Grand Orient of France.

> The time has not yet come for the class of colored men to have the right to create a Masonic Temple on their own, not because we think that they should not enjoy the benefits of this splendid Institution . . . but they should complete their apprenticeship among those who preceded them in the quarry. . . . Once they have acquired the necessary education, we would hasten to assist their first efforts and to be the first to applaud their noble endeavor.[36]

The reader can fully appreciate the Jesuitical nature of this letter to the Grand Orient.

A Diversified Masonic Landscape in the Caribbean Today

Before the emancipation of the slaves the primary function of Freemasonry was to maintain the most close-knit contact possible between the colonial elites and the homeland and thereby strengthen the Empire—British or French. Ironically, though, it also encouraged the transition between colonial and local elites when each country gained its independence and the former French colonies took on the status of overseas departments.

Several members of the local legislative assemblies, several governors, and, in the postcolonial period, several general governors were Masons. Two important Barbados politicians were members of local lodges: Grantley Adams (1898–1971) and Errol Walton Barrow (1920–1987). Although it never took any official political position, Freemasonry seems to have accompanied the islands' independence.

The first general governor appointed by the British after Barbados gained its independence in 1966 was a black Freemason, Sir Winston Scott, a member of Thistle Lodge. Still today, with the exception of the Prince Hall Grand Lodges, the majority of Caribbean lodges are affiliated with the Grand Lodge of Scotland or the United Grand Lodge of England, through the intermediary of a provincial grand lodge.

I must express serious reservations if the social integration capacity of the lodges is brought up: Caribbean Freemasonry, as elsewhere, has rarely attracted the most underprivileged classes. Traditionally it was the elites who joined the lodges. Workers and small craftsmen have often preferred joining the friendly societies like the Foresters and the Mechanics, which are sometimes labeled Poor Man's Freemasonry. This phenomenon is only present in the English-speaking lands. However, the Mechanics have four clubs for men as well as a women's chapter in French Guyane today.[37]

The majority of lodges in the English-speaking Caribbean are under the banner of the British Grand Lodges—English or Scottish. Some Masons chose, though, to create lodges that were entirely independent of the British Grand Lodges and to gather together in the Prince Hall Grand Lodge of the Caribbean. This grand lodge includes lodges in Barbados, Trinidad, Saint Lucia, and even Martinique. While its organization is independent, it is obvious that the eyes of the Prince Hall Caribbean brothers are all turned toward black American Freemasonry.

The Guyanese lodges of the twentieth century boasted several major political figures. First and foremost was Félix Éboué (1884–1944), governor of Martinique, Guadeloupe, and then Chad. He rallied the Congo to support the Free French forces and became governor of French Equatorial Africa. He was initiated in 1922 to La France Equinoxiale (Grand Lodge of France, Cayenne). His wife, Eugénie Éboué-Tell, who gave him considerable support in his struggle, joined Le Droit Humain (Human Rights).[38] His daughter Ginette was a member of La Grand Lodge Féminine de France, and a lodge in Martinique still bears her name today.*

The lawyer Gaston Monnerville (1897–1991) was elected as a radical socialist deputy of French Guyane in 1932, mayor of Cayenne (1935–1940), senator of French Guyane (1946–1948), then radical socialist president of the Council of the Republic and Senate for twenty years (1947–1968). He was initiated at a young age—eighteen—into Verité Lodge n° 280 of the Grand Lodge of France. He was also a member of the Prévoyance Lodge n° 88 and the Supreme Council of France. On May 5, 1981, at the age of eighty-four, he gave a speech on Abbé Grégoire on the premises of the Grand Lodge of France.[39]

Though less well known than his predecessors, Justin Catayé (1916–1962) played an important role in the political history of French Guyane. This mathematics teacher at the Félix Éboué High School, a native of Martinique, finished his studies in Bordeaux, enlisted in the Free French forces in 1943, and founded the Guyanese Socialist Party (PSG) in 1956, the same year that he started the newspaper *Debout Guyane.* As a deputy and supported by the Guyanese Democratic Front (FDG), which consisted of all the left-wing groups in French Guyane, he demanded in the National Assembly that French Guyane's administration be given full autonomy. It so happens that during this parliamentary session he learned that the Foreign Legion outpost in French Guyane had provoked a strike and demonstrations that had been harshly put down by the Prefect Érignac. He cut short his attendance at the assembly to return to Cayenne, but his airplane crashed on June 22 when flying over Guadeloupe. Catayé was a member of La France Equinoxiale, like Éboué.

---

*This is La Loge Ginette Éboué, affiliated with the Grand Loge Féminine de France.

The lodges of Martinique, Guadeloupe, and French Guyane are divided up between the large French obediences: Grand Orient of France, Grand Lodge of France, Droit Humain, Grand Loge Féminine de France, Grand Lodge of Memphis Misraïm, and the French National Grand Lodge. Also to be noted is the presence of the International Initiatory and Traditional Order of the Royal Art (OITAR). The debate on allowing women members has yet to reach the overseas lodges of the Grand Orient, with the exception of Saint Martin, where the Concorde-Perrinon Lodge has already initiated two women. The differences between obediences have been put on a back burner in Martinique, where the brothers routinely make visits beyond recognition protocols. However, we do not see the Prince Hall brothers visiting the other lodges of the island.

At the roots of the Prince Hall Grand Lodge of the Caribbean we find the Masonic Club, launched in 1960 in Barbados by "brother G. Halley Marville," who was initiated a Mason "on sight" on January 21, 1960, by the Grand Lodge of California during a visit to the United States. On July 18, 1961, seventeen members officially launched the Masonic Club. In 1965 the Prince Hall Grand Lodge of New York gave a warrant to the Prince Hall Memorial Lodge n° 100 (today it is n° 1) presided over by Marville and consisting of thirty-six members.

Gradually other lodges obtained charters.

The lodge of Mount Ayangana n° 3 of Guyana, on April 15, 1968
The lodge of Adrian C. Richardson n° 104 in Saint Martin, Dutch Antilles, August 2, 1971
The Hermon Lodge n° 105 in Saint Lucia, August 4, 1971
The King David Lodge n° 106 in Barbados on August 6, 1971
The Tamrin Lodge n° 113 in Guyana on November 8, 1979
The Perseverance Lodge n° 116 in Dominica
The Daniel O. Braithwaite Memorial Lodge n° 118 in Barbados, April 28, 1984
The Celestial Lodge n° 119 in Guyana, April 24, 1985[40]

The Prince Hall Grand Lodge of the Caribbean was founded on

August 24, 1993. Its headquarters is in Barbados, and it is the only grand lodge to unite both French- and English-speaking lodges. Today it includes eleven lodges and around 350 members. The most recent lodges are Fraternity of the Caribbean n° 10 in Martinique; King Court n° 13 in Antigua and Barbuda; Destiny Lodge in Puerto Rico; Cornerstone Lodge n° 14 in Barbados; and Acacia Lodge in Saint Martin. There are thus two lodges in Saint Martin and six in Barbados.

In Barbados the Prince Hall Grand Lodge of the Caribbean has established a system of education scholarships, the Austin Belle Junior Memorial Scholarship, for children of Masons wishing to obtain a higher education. The Lodge n° 1 of Barbados awards these grants, which cover a three-year period. In addition, once a year the Masons of The Prince Hall Masons in Barbados take part in a series of conferences dedicated to the history of Freemasonry and more broadly to black history and to the African cultural legacy. These take place in February— Black History Month. Both Masonic and profane speakers are invited to give lectures, but the speakers are by and large black.

On the other hand, contrary to the Caribbean lodges affiliated with England and Scotland, which have no Eastern Star branches, the Prince Hall Grand Lodge of the Caribbean has female chapters, as does the Prince Hall Grand Lodge of the United States. Just like this latter, the Caribbean lodges obviously do not recognize the members of these chapters as Freemasons but only as benevolent companions responsible for implementing charitable activities on behalf of their Masonic husbands and relatives.

The Grand Chapter Rita-G has five chapters in Barbados and one on the island of Saint Lucia.[41] The first chapter was created in Barbados in 1974: the Sarah Memorial Chapter n° 78, federated by the Grand Chapter Eureka of the Eastern Star of the State of New York. An independent grand chapter came into existence on Barbados in April 1996, numbering some eighty-five "ladies" and thirty-nine "brothers." The grand chapter was named Rita-G in honor of Rita Gibbs-Goddard, a Barbados native who lived in New York and was a past matron of Fidelity Chapter n° 54; she was presented as a licensed lay reader and Eucharistic lay minister, meaning a secular member of the Eucharistic Church. Of course, the Prince Hall Grand Lodge of the Caribbean always mirrored the American Landmarks and imposed a belief in God on all its members. The same was true in the women's chapters.

Freemasonry is flourishing in both the French and English areas of the Caribbean. Quite often membership is a sign of social recognition. Its members take great pride in being Masons, though the brothers in the French Caribbean are more discreet in broadcasting their affiliation than their English counterparts. The same gap separates the lodges in the homeland that are liberal, secular, and republican Masons, with a deep reverence for freedom of conscience, from those that boast the ancient English and American Landmarks and belief in God. A certain discretion characterizes all the Masons of the islands, however, whatever their convictions, as the area of circulation is much more restricted than in the homeland, and, because of this, anonymity is nonexistent.

To Each His Own Path

Why would someone become a Freemason in Boston or any other British colony during the eighteenth century? What did they do in the lodges? What do they do there today? These questions, which in appearance are most simple, most often inspire evasive responses. It would be a mistake to view this as a simple obsession for secrecy. Ironically, most Masons, whether black or white, would find it hard to come up with an answer.

Looking at it closer, however, the important thing is not what one does in the lodge. In fact, while Latin Freemasonry encourages works on social subjects that inspire debates, which in principle are calm and courteous, the lodges of English origin behave quite differently. Their members meet only to recite various catechisms, those of the apprentice and fellowcraft, depending on their grades. No personal work and thus no discussion have grounds to take place. The brothers gather at banquets after the meetings, where they are at complete ease to discuss whatever they like. Under these conditions it is easy to see that the Masonic meetings will have a tendency to gradually become shorter and the banquets longer.

When someone is a Freemason he will have an opportunity to meet people whose paths he is unlikely to cross somewhere else. As James Anderson puts it so well, "Whereby Masons become the Centre of the Union, and the Means of conciliating true Friendship among Persons that must have remained at a perpetual distance."[1] Freemasonry is first and foremost a context, a space that allows individuals to communicate.

The ritual practiced in a lodge cements bonds without constituting an objective in itself. The majority of Masons would most likely agree.

Mimicry

A black American is much closer to a white American in his Masonic practice than to a black member of the Grand Orient of France, for example. Indeed, black Freemasons have displayed a certain mimicry of their white counterparts. They have adopted the same organizational style, the same rituals, and the same jurisprudence in the event of litigation. As a general rule, the lodges of English origin are spots for ideal conviviality because, despite the impressive sermons made during initiations, they demand a basically minimal commitment from their members. The brothers are perfectly free with their opinions, provided they are not too loud when airing them, and therefore can mingle with each other in a fairly harmonious way. They are not asked to perform any specific actions, because the only requirement is fraternal behavior, so the sole risks for conflict are of a personal nature.

American Freemasons, whatever their skin color, carefully avoid any debates of a political or religious nature. Such conduct is, of course, recommended by Anderson's *Constitutions*. Nevertheless, the so-called Latin Freemasonry, which is often considered irregular by Anglo-Saxon Freemasons, tends to believe all subjects are worthy of discussion, provided the discussion is democratic and without animosity. To the extent that American Freemasons do not perform any personal tasks, not even symbolically, it is obvious that they would forbid all discussion inside the lodge. On the other hand, once the meeting is over no subject is taboo.

Black Freemasons fully share this notion. This explains why the Prince Hall Grand Lodges, despite their affinities with the Grand Orient of France, never managed to forge official ties with an obedience that accepts works on religious or political subjects. The Prince Hall Grand Lodges' refusal to form closer relations with the Grand Orient is based on the fact that it is not recognized by the white American grand lodges on the pretext that it does not require its members to believe in God, that it maintains official relationships with a women's grand lodge and co-ed lodges, and, as of recently, that it has accepted women as members.

Freemasons and Proud of It

The Prince Hall Freemasons conform strictly to the American model. They exhibit the same ostracism displayed by their white brothers to lay obediences and the same outdated and condescending attitude toward women. Women are relegated into subaltern associations, where they can run receptions, charity bazaars, and other good works.

Also, like American white Masons, they proudly sport their Masonic insignia and have no hesitation about parading through the streets in them. Secrecy concerns the ritual more than the individual. Contrary to what happens in France, for example, Masonic rituals rarely take place in bookstores. In contrast, everyone or almost everyone knows who is a Mason in the United States. This ostentatious side is revealing of the pride felt by Americans who bear the title of Freemason. In the United States membership in a lodge is evidence of a certain social status.

Does this all mean that American Freemasonry is a pretty envelope but an empty one? How is it different from the service clubs? In the lodge—as in the Rotary Club—men make each other's acquaintance and forge bonds, and a social network is gradually woven together. Ironically enough, although it rejects all deep political or cultural discussion, Anglo-Saxon Freemasonry has this somewhat magical power of inspiring its members to take an interest in public life: to play a role in society that is more than just charitable. This was the case during the American Revolution. Many individuals practiced democratic virtues in the lodge before pursuing them in the outside world. It is well known that the number of lodges doubled during the War for Independence. It would seem that, quite simply, the lodges of that time attracted individuals anxious to play a role in the changing political landscape, and their motives were encouraged by meeting others of a similar bent.

This hypothesis is valid for black Masons. More than others, black Americans had limited social structures for providing assistance; like their churches but minus the dogma, Masonic lodges formed a valuable context for meeting one another and pooling resources.

It was precisely because there was no power of a philosophical, political, or unionized nature at stake that Masons had a desire to express their personal feelings after the meetings, while benefiting from a relatively innocent audience. By giving members self-confidence and inspiring them to take action, the lodge encouraged its members to seek advancement, both for themselves and for American blacks in general.

Exclusion and Its Opposite

Imitation of their white counterparts utterly failed to provide black Masons with any protection against exclusion. They were victimized by the most elementary racism on the part of their white "brothers," despite all the principles of equality and fraternity these latter officially proclaimed. Of course there were some white brothers who showed the exception that proves the rule. This brings to mind the efforts of grand masters like William Silas Whitehead of New Jersey and William H. Upton of Washington state, and of those Masons who wrote in support of equality and labored to obtain recognition of black Freemasonry, like Harold Van Buren Voorhis. Isolated Masons did not hesitate to break the rules in order to force received opinion to evolve. This was the case of the Colorado Masons who, at the urging of the Masonic youth organization DeMolay, accepted the youths' recruitment of a young black man in 1945, before any white grand lodge had granted official recognition to the Prince Hall Grand Lodge.*

There were more than likely other individual initiatives that were discreet and therefore remain in obscurity. However, for more than a century the white grand lodges refused to grant those of Prince Hall the slightest consideration. Alongside extreme cases like that of Nathan Bedford Forrest, first grand wizard of the Ku Klux Klan, white Freemasons had no fear of displaying racist positions that defied the most elementary principles of Masonic universalism. In the sugar isles of the

---

*See Harry W. Bundy's letter of April 3, 1946, to Harry A. Williamson in appendix 3.

Caribbean, Freemasonry was long a prerogative of the plantation owners, and it took some time for the freed slaves to be accepted or to create their own lodges.

Trying to find rational explanations for this rejection is no easy task. By definition, racism defies all logic. It can be asked if the exclusion of which black Freemasons were victims might have origins that were more social in nature than racial. Racism and social distinction are extremely deep-rooted in the United States. Ultimately, whether white Masons were racist because they were elitists or elitists because they were racist amounts to the same thing. It goes without saying that white Masons of the South spontaneously displayed their racism toward their black brothers because they were permeated by the ambient segregationist attitudes that governed that region before, during, and after the Civil War.

A Simple Barber

Racism was displayed in much less overt fashion in the Northern states. Even in these states, white Masons long held strong reservations concerning blacks, thereby revealing a certain backwardness in comparison to society overall. Black Masons, however, were not members of the working class. The vast majority of them was—and still is—members of the middle class. However, white Masons prefer to keep their distance from black Masons for reasons having to do with social status. The acerbic remark of a New York grand master about his counterpart at Prince Hall, "a simple barber," is quite revealing (see chapter 11). While not admitting it, the white Mason had the impression that the acceptance of a black into his lodge would have lowered its social standing and thus reduced its prestige. Certainly all black Masons were middle class, but *black* middle class, which means they were necessarily a rung lower on the ladder than their white counterparts in American society.

For this reason it can be said that white Masons were always in unison with the surrounding society. While the motives for exclusion in the South were primarily racist of a most elementary kind, in the North they were essentially of a social nature, even though they naturally took on a racist spin. White Freemasons were compelled to evolve, because discrimination became less starkly visible in American society as a whole. However, attitudes still reflect a North/South division. Racism still rages in the Southern states and has not vanished from the grand lodges of this region. Those in Louisiana and Florida, to cite only two cases, still ignore the principles of universal fraternity.

In the majority of the United States, but essentially in the North, relations between black and white Masons have become normalized or at least are subject to the laws of reason. Varying degrees of fraternal exchanges have been established. After suffering from exclusion for such a long time, despite its efforts to imitate white Freemasonry, today black Freemasonry is more prone to exhibiting its distinguishing attributes. It can take consolation in the fact that it was never the target of anti-Freemason efforts as relentlessly as its white counterpart. It remained unaffected by the storm, and the Morgan affair barely touched it. White lodges were harshly criticized on this occasion. During the 1830s they had been accused—without proof, naturally—of having murdered a brother named Morgan out of revenge for his unseemly revelation of secrets. The affair took on immense proportions and became fodder for electoral campaigns, inspiring the creation of the Anti-Masonic Party and giving birth to 140 anti-Masonic local newspapers, according to William R. Denslow.[2] It was during this period that black Freemasonry was just beginning to develop, and it remained unknown to the public at large. It did not have to suffer from this regrettable affair.

Recruiting Crisis

The Prince Hall Lodges are suffering today from a recruiting crisis, as is all American Freemasonry, but in lesser proportions. Their membership rolls have not been cut in half over the past forty years, as is the case for white Masonry.* Still, today, the highest number of members is found in Alabama, which cannot be coincidental. It should come as no surprise that the bastion of black Freemasonry also played the same role during

*See chapter 14. White American grand lodges had four million members in 1964 and fewer than two million in 1999, according to Paul Bessel, who cites data from the Masonic Service Association of North America on his website, www.bessel.org.

the battle for civil rights. Masonic principles are in perfect keeping with the theme of human dignity. Many Freemasons were also active in the NAACP, an organization that has always advocated for the equality of American citizens and is still active today, in contrast with many seemingly more radical organizations that were much more short-lived. W. E. B. Du Bois, founder of the NAACP, was invited to become a Freemason. That he was chosen by his brothers clearly shows the importance these latter gave to the fight against racism. Conversely, the fact Du Bois accepted their invitation is evidence of the esteem enjoyed at that time by Prince Hall Masonry among black intellectuals. Like Booker T. Washington, Du Bois encouraged Masons to educate themselves.

This feature is not, of course, specific to black Freemasonry. However, education has played a major role for black Americans from the abolition of slavery to the present. Black Americans have been skilled at taking advantage of certain characteristics of universal Freemasonry. This is how belief in the perfectibility of the individual, combined with the Protestant work ethic, found a concrete application: the black American could raise his social status thanks to his work, like all other Americans, but at the price of greater effort. Among the fundamental Masonic principles, blacks embraced those concerning human dignity and the desire for the betterment of the individual and society. The notion of work, depreciated among many blacks because of the heavy weight of slavery in the past, was rehabilitated by Freemasonry. Man can free himself through his labor. This value, which is given particular honor in Europe by Protestants and Marxists, was not naturally accepted by American blacks. Freemasonry allowed them to take this step and adopt it without giving the impression of making a concession to white society at the expense of their honor.

Overall, black Americans are comfortable asserting their African origins, even while claiming their own distinctive identity. Freemasonry allows them to reconcile their marvelous oral tradition with a written one. On the one hand, blacks grant great importance to the written word, such as the constitutive charters of the lodges, in the quest for legitimacy as American brothers. On the other hand, they give greater value to the oral tradition as it is found in both Masonic tradition and

African culture. Freemasonry affords them greater maneuvering room by adhering to an oral tradition that is passed on from one generation to the next, at the risk of being subjected to constant revision. The rituals are certainly learned by heart and resistant to caprice, but every Mason has an impression that he can take from the source whatever he finds good. It is this viewpoint that allowed Martin Robison Delany in his time to proclaim that Freemasonry had black origins. Because oral tradition was in no way discredited by Freemasonry, American blacks were able to spontaneously align with it. In fact, by highlighting this tradition Freemasonry conferred on black Americans the dignity they were seeking.

Social Progress

In many countries Freemasonry has helped individuals advance in society, not, as too often claimed, by giving its members an illegitimate advantage to the detriment of the profane (a fairly marginal phenomenon when all is said and done), but by inspiring them to educate themselves and acquire a skill. Freemasonry fully achieved its role on both the educational and professional levels. Many mutual-aid societies, savings and loan institutions, and scholarships awarded to students have undeniably helped black Americans improve their social status. The notion of solidarity is preferred to that of the charity that is preached in the more aristocratic Masonic settings in both England and the United States. Black Freemasonry's role is not limited to individual assistance, as shown by its privileged ties with the NAACP in the fight for civil rights and still today against discrimination.

However, despite this militant past, black Freemasonry has sometimes been accused by black separatists of being soft and a group of Uncle Toms. It is true that Masons like Delany, who advocated for the emigration of American blacks to Liberia, are rare. However, a larger number of black Masons did display admiration for Haiti and its president, Jean-Pierre Boyer, in particular. They even encouraged emigration to Haiti and gave one of their grand lodges Boyer's name. However, as a general rule, black Freemasons were more inclined to preach integration than separation. The essentially universal message of Masonry makes a poor fit with narrow nationalism. It is also true that the election of President Barack Obama has rendered the separatism hypothesis obsolete.

Good Conscience on Both Sides

Nevertheless, it seems that the heads of Prince Hall are now weary of soliciting favors from white Masons. The attitude of the United Grand Lodge of England, which long consisted of only recognizing those grand lodges that put in a request, has raised sharp criticism. Black Freemasons see no reason why they should go begging for recognition. So while they now have the possibility to form solid ties with a certain number of white grand lodges, they are keeping their distance and proclaiming total independence. In Caribbean societies, at the crossroads of several colonial cultures but in the context of independence, Freemasonry permits its members to forge a new identity that does not imply a complete rupture from the grand lodges of the homeland. We find both provincial grand lodges that are affiliates of the homeland lodges and autonomous Prince Hall Grand Lodges. In the United States, on the other hand, out of fear of being absorbed by white Freemasonry and thereby losing their identity, blacks have preferred to keep independent grand lodges.

Black Freemasonry, which is strongly elitist, maintains a bourgeois prerogative, and its members feel no need to fraternize with men they tend to look down on. Though white Freemasons—as they have done elsewhere—seek to soothe their guilty conscience by erecting some footbridges to their black counterparts, the latter are not particularly anxious to strengthen such painfully forged bonds and are more than content with the current situation.

Freemasonry is universal, of course, but the American Freemason is first and foremost a white or a black man. Contemporary Freemasonry is no longer racist, at least in most states, but it is perfectly adapted to the current communitarian tradition at a time when, ironically, a black president is representing the country. Just as American society respects the diversity of its many communities, American Freemasonry, like a fine kaleidoscope, prefers the juxtaposition to the merger of colors. Little inbreeding can be found between the square and the compass.

A Question of Democracy

By René Le Moal

Outside of historians, researchers, or initiates in quest of the roots of Freemasonry, James Anderson's *Constitutions* has a scarcity of readers today. This is probably a shame.

We know that the book appeared in London in 1723, after being worked on for a long time by two clergymen. Although Anderson, a Presbyterian pastor of Scottish origin, signed this book with his name, at least a part of it was written by another pastor, the Anglican Jean-Théophile Desaugliers, who was of French descent. The book was intended to instruct Freemasons in their duties and obligations while providing an immemorial history and even songs of their movement. To grasp some of the phrases in this work, whose resonance remains strong, it is good to keep in mind that both were ministers of denominations that had once been violently opposed to each other. Essentially, Anderson's *Constitutions* is conveying a message of peace during a murderous period in English history, and for this reason the book is still deserving of attention. Its publication date should be compared with that of the European discovery of America in 1492 as well as the beginning of the Atlantic slave trade and its consequential effects on the way people of color were viewed.

Constitutions attracted little notice in France at that time and had little influence. The most widespread translation, by Louis François de la Tierce, would not appear until 1842 (in Germany), hardly convenient for the translator but faithful to its authors in its philosophy. After that an almost complete silence fell over this document, with no sign of any particularly deferential citations from either historians or officials during the entire nineteenth century. It would not be rediscovered until the twentieth century and the period following the Second World War, when the Grand Orient of France extracted a completely consensual phrase whose generous, universal tone was not of a nature to shock anyone, either in the lay obediences or the others: French or foreign. Henceforth read at the beginning of every lodge meeting, this phrase, extracted from article 1 of the *Constitutions,* could—isolated in this way—give meaning to the life of each individual.

> Whereby Masons become the Center of the Union, and the Means of conciliating true Friendship among Persons that must have remained at a perpetual distance.

The *Constitutions* is not really regarded in France as a foundational work, as is generally the case for the philosophical movements, but it does retain historical value.

However, there are other phrases in the *Constitutions* that are not so inclusive and soothing as the one ritually cited in French lodges, even though they cannot and should not be read with yesterday's mind-set, as history has had its way with both mentalities and institutions. The most contentious expression—for the subject at hand here—is found in article 3, devoted to the candidates for membership in Freemasonry. They must be "good and true Men, free-born, and of mature and discreet Age, no Bondmen, no Women." Nothing could be clearer, but this is the phrase that causes the greatest vexation.

"Free-born" clearly and almost exclusively targets the blacks whose position was that of a slave or a freed slave, which obviously makes them ineligible to either receive the Masonic illumination or carry it thenceforth into society. It is obvious, though not stated, that the door is not closed to those of even African or Indian descent who were born free, even if their parents were not. But how many people like that could one expect to find as candidates for acceptance into a lodge in Great Britain of 1723?

Today the expression is deemed unfortunate, even if some like to believe that Anderson was looking at it from a philosophical angle, as did the philosopher John Locke. Even so, it has left a stain on the history of Freemasonry. A more flattering phrase would have been preferable, especially when cited with the words that also excluded women, whom Anderson, off the cuff, referred to as "serfs." It can be interpreted, but it cannot be erased; moreover it would be long retained, albeit under increasingly softened terms.

What is racism? In his *Dictionary of the French Language* (1863–1873) the Freemason Emile Littré,* a positivist philosopher and member of the Académie Française, devoted a long passage, studded with fine citations from authors of the classics, to race, but nothing to racism. So would that mean it did not exist? It would not be until the period between the two World Wars, followed by the anti-Semitic horrors of the second, that philosophers began giving it serious attention.

Racism is an attitude that an individual or group can adopt as a way of seeing and receiving the Other. But this is the worst possible thing. None can improve themselves without others, whether or not they are part of one's immediate surroundings or are as yet unknown men or women who will nurture a person's integration into the world and subsequent progress in it. "Responsibility is something imposed upon me by the sight of another person's face," writes Emmanuel Levinas, who adds, "The meeting of the Other commits me." Racism and the republic are incompatible, even antinomic. Remember: "Men are born free and equal in rights" (as stated in France's 1789 Declaration of the Rights of Man and Citizen). This is the foundation of the building.

Racism has become the gangrene of European societies. It imperils the values that have been laboriously established in their hearts and laws. "Communities" are born and organized that then openly express their hostility to others based on such problematic concepts as religion, ancestral roots, or, more frankly, skin color, if it is not simple hostility

---

*Littré was received in a Grand Orient of France Lodge on July 8, 1875, in the same meeting as Jules Ferry, the same Jules Ferry whose writings are now being revisited because of texts targeting "the inferior races."

to other "communities" on principle. This is a form of social suicide. This should be well known enough not to require extensive discussion. This attitude has been the subject of many learned and useful dissertations today. Terms like *racialization* and *racialism* are now common enough to warrant entries in the dictionary. We should not overlook the fact that France's National Assembly proposed legislation during its May 17, 2013, session that would require the deletion of the word *race* from French legislation—which would not, of course, eliminate racism.

Was Anderson racist? Cécile Révauger's book, which can be described without hesitation as unique as it is truly without precedent in the French language, is the fruit of painstaking research of American archives, which are often difficult to gain access to, and a long series of interviews of American historians and officials—both black and white. It is not a convocation before the tribunal of history to be followed by an inevitable verdict of guilty. If it were, then Anderson would not be alone among the accused. And it is likely this case would be dismissed.

It is not only article 3 in Anderson's book that was cited by American whites, though, to deny the young black American Prince Hall's request (Anderson's *Constitutions* were published in 1734 in the American colonies by Benjamin Franklin). They also used other pretexts that ill-concealed their true motive: racism, the innate evil of the young American society that grew out of slavery and had shaped white minds and made them view blacks as inferior beings who were necessarily of low morals and intellect and not to be associated with under any circumstances, even if they had become free and prosperous. The emancipated slave, filled with memories of the horrors he had seen and experienced, conscious of his status but wishing to integrate into a society whose benefits he could see from the distance he was held from it, just like Freemasonry, about which he had been told much that was good, had no other option but to turn to London. It was thus from London he obtained, after several mishaps that the author recounts in detail, a charter in good and due form, which can still be consulted today. An opportunity to take delight in the "pragmatic spirit of the English" that the French and other Europeans find so fascinating? It is not only that, but in this instance, London was not racist.

It may come as a surprise that this rebuff came at the hands of white Americans in Boston, the capital of a state in the northeastern United States, where there were never plantations of the kind that could be found so plentifully in slave centers like Alabama and Louisiana. The multiform roots of the paradox have long been identified. In 1996, Dominique Schnapper wrote "Racism" in Monique Canto-Sperber's *Dictionnaire de philosophie morale:* "In the slave states, the system of authority and hierarchy through which the system of white domination was asserted was imposed thanks to strict rules of etiquette."[1] However, the North, which consisted of industrialized states, offered employment to emancipated blacks, who soon began competing with whites for jobs. In 1832, in *Journey to America,* the French author and political theorist Alexis de Tocqueville wrote, "The White no longer distinctly perceives the barrier that separates him from the degraded race, and he shuns the Negro with the more pertinacity since he fears lest they should some-day be confounded together." A spatial segregation in the North corresponded to the racial lynching in the South: separate neighborhoods, separate schools, and so forth.

And separate Freemasonries. Legitimized by the certificate from the mother lodge of all the world's Freemasons at this time, the construction on which Prince Hall had laid the first stone and which today bears his name was built gradually over time in the face of white hostility, scorn, or indifference. As Cécile Révauger painstakingly demonstrates, in document after document, blacks quickly realized that they would draw much greater advantage for themselves and for their community by following a Masonic path separate from whites, who, with few exceptions, wanted nothing to do with them. There was no need to continue spreading and wasting their strength on countless attempts to gain admittance or recognition, which most often were only sources of humiliation and always of uncertain results.

Better, much better even, they gave their Freemasonry a social dimension that was ethical as well as effective, intended to permit their people to survive, to give them the potential to create their own businesses and to obtain retirement and medical benefits. Aligning with whites in their way of viewing Freemasonry by saying no to women in lodges, but yes to women in distinct affiliated organizations dedicated to charity, black Freemasonry also does not differ from its white counterpart on other fundamental questions: belief in God, patriotism, and so forth. The way the organizations mirror one another is striking—and all the more so when we know that many whites still deny their counterparts' validity.

This is how over the years blacks created a grand lodge in most American states that inevitably and proudly bears the name of the founder of black Freemasonry in the United States: Prince Hall. Each state's grand lodge represents all the black lodges in that state. Just as each state also includes, and has for a long time, a white grand lodge, a foreign visitor can be dumbstruck at the sight of the more than fifty examples of this duplication—a duplication that could easily be described as basically racial if this word was not so painful for a Freemason to write. Painful and scandalous. But as this book says, American blacks have found it satisfying. Even better, it has helped them advance internally as well as integrate into American society. It has allowed them to establish a Freemasonry in which they found what they could not find elsewhere, in any case not from white society in the United States. They are proud to be Freemasons. The foreign visitor accepts it, albeit with a certain indignation and shame. However, in its natural context, a country in which communities of all kinds can multiply ad infinitum and loudly take the floor and exert political pressure, this is not viewed in any way as a subject of indignation.

If this visitor to the United States is a Freemason of the Grand Orient of France and identifies himself as such, he will find all the doors of American Masonic temples closed, especially if he is a she, whether or not the lodge at which he or she wishes to attend a meeting is black or white. The reason: his or her obedience does not meet the required criteria. Just think: an obedience that does not oblige the individual to believe in God and grants initiation to women under the same conditions demanded of men . . . This speaks volumes of the feat accomplished by Cécile Révauger in putting together this chronological and sociological investigation, but it should also be pointed out that as the beneficiary of a Fulbright Award she was able to meet with officials and scholars of both Freemasonries in complete liberty and frankness, far from the temple.

I have already said that her book is unique. It should be read by all Freemasons of both sexes, for whom this is a fundamental principle: racial discrimination cannot be established in Freemasonry. But we know full well that nothing can ever be taken for granted. Also of great interest is the value that Prince Hall carries for part of Caribbean Free-masonry in an essentially communitarian approach.

RENÉ LE MOAL is the editorial director of *La Chaîne de l'Union* [The Chain of Union], a philosophical magazine published by the Grand Orient of France, and the author of *La Franc-Maçonnerie: une quête philosophique et spirituelle de la connaissance* [Freemasonry: A Philosophical and Spiritual Quest for Knowledge] (Paris: Armand Colin, 2005).

Appendices

Contents

Commentary of William H. Upton's Letter

Letter from Harry W. Bundy, Grand Secretary of the
Masonic Temple of Denver, Colorado, to
Harry A. Williamson, April 3, 1946

APPENDIX IV Prince Hall Grand Lodges   256

Prince Hall Grand Lodges in the United
States by Alphabetical Order

Prince Hall Grand Lodges in the United
States in Decreasing Order

Appendix I

Original Prince Hall Charter,
General Regulations, and Petition

Original Prince Hall Charter

Issued to Prince Hall, Etc.,
on September 20, 1874
By Thomas Hall, Earl of Effingham,
Acting Grand Master, The Grand Lodge of England

Know all men by these presents: Thus were we greeted by the Grand Lodge of England, on the 20th day of September A.L. 5784, A.D. 1784; the following said Greeting and warranted 459, granted by the Grand Lodge of England on petition of Prince Hall, Boston Smith, Thomas Sanderson, and several other Masons, of Boston, constituting them into a regular Lodge for Free and Accepted Masons. To all and ever our Right Worshipful and loving Brethren, we, Thomas Hall, Earl of Effingham, Lord Howard, etc., etc., etc.; acting grand master under the authority of His Royal Highness, Henry Frédéric, Duke of Cumberland, etc., etc., etc., Grand Master of the Most Ancient and Honorable Society of Free and Accepted Masons, send Greetings: Know ye, that we, at the humble petition of our right trust and well beloved Brethren Prince Hall, Boston Smith, Thomas Sanderson, and several other Brethren residing in Boston, New England, in North America, do hereby constitute the said Brethren into regular Lodge of Free and Accepted Masons, under the title or denomination of the African Lodge, to be opened in Boston aforesaid, and do further at their petition hereby appoint the said Prince Hall to be Master, Boston Smith, Senior Warden, and Thomas Sanderson, Junior Warden, for the opening of the said Lodge, and for such further time only as shall be thought proper by the Brethren thereof, it being our will that this our appointment of the above officers shall in no wise affect any future election of officers of the Lodge, but that such election shall be regulated agreeably by such by-laws of said Lodge as shall be consistent with the general laws of the Society, contained in the Book of Constitution and we hereby will require you, the said Prince Hall, to take especial care that all and everyone of said Brethren are, or have been regularly made Masons, and that they do observe, perform and keep all the rules and orders contained in the Book of Constitutions; and further, that you do, from time to time, cause to be entered in a book kept for the purpose, an account of your proceedings in the Lodge, together with such rules, orders, and regulations as shall be made for the good government of the same; that in no wise you will omit once in every year to send to us, or our successors, grand master, or to Roland Holt, Esq., our Deputy Grand Master, for the time being, an account in writing of your said proceedings and copies of all such rules, orders and regulations as shall be made as aforesaid, together with a list of the members of the Lodge, and such sum of money as may suit the circumstances of the Lodge, and reasonably be expected toward the Grand Charity. Moreover, we hereby will and require you the said Prince Hall, as soon as conveniently may be, to send an account in writing, of what may be done by virtue of these presents.

Given at London under the hand and seal of Masonry, this 29th day of September A.L. 5784, A.D. 1784. By the Grand Master's Command Witness: Wm. White, G.S. R. Holt, D.G.M.

The General Regulations of the African Lodge
(Transcripts of Prince Hall Letters)

1. As all Masons are obliged to obey the moral law we therefore Exclude from this Lodge all stupid Atheists and Irreligious libertines; yet at the same time we allow every man to Enjoy his own Religion so that they be men of Honesty and Honor & free-born.

2. We admit none but those who are of a Peaceable subject to the civil Powers where they live free from all plots and conspiracies against the peace of the same.

3. No member of this Lodge is suffered to be absent therefrom when warned to appear without giving some good reason for his doing or Pay the sum of three shillings as a fine to the Lodge.

4. We admit none into this Lodge under the Age of twenty-one and having a tongue of Good Report for this Reason no man can be admitted a member of the same till he hath propounded at least one month that the Brethren may inquire into his character.

5. All preferment among us is by real worth and personal merit only for fear of Slander being brought upon the Noble order and a Disgrace to our Lodge.

6. No man can be admitted a member of this Lodge for less money than three pounds and two good Bondsmen for his Good behavior within and without the Lodge.

7. When meeting in the Lodge we forbid all profane language all indecent behavior in the Lodge under penalty of paying to the Lodge the sum of ten shillings and be liable to being expelled for six months. There and all other Laws that the Lodge shall think Proper to make you are to observe as true and Sincere men from God that the Noble Craft may Not Be Disgraced by your bad conduct by those that are without; a man so let be Prince Hall M^r In the Lodge Room.

Boston January 15, 5779
and in the year of our Lord 1779

Petition against Slavery Addressed by Prince Hall to the Counsel
and House of Representatives of Massachusetts Bay
January 13, 1777

𝔓etition

To the Honorable Counsel & House of Representatives for the State
of Massachusetts Bay in General Court assembled, January 13, 1777.

The Petition of A Great Number of Blacks, who are detained in a
state of Slavery in the Bowels of a free & Christian Country Humbly showing: "That your Petitioners apprehend that they have, in
Common with all other Men, a Natural and Unalienable Right to
that freedom which the great Parent of the Universe hath bestowed
equally on all mankind and which they have never forfeited by any
compact or agreement whatever. But they were unjustly dragged by
the hand of cruel Power from their dearest friends and some of them
even torn from the embraces of their tender parents—From a popu-
lous pleasant and plentiful Country—and in violation of the Laws
of nature and of nations and in defiance of all the tender feelings of
humanity, brought together to be sold like beasts of burden & like
them condemned to Slavery for Life, among a People professing the
mild Religion of Jesus.

A people not insensible of the sweets of rational freedom nor
without Spirit to resent the unjust endeavors of others to reduce
them to a state of Bondage and Subjugation. Your Honors need not
to be informed that A Life of Slavery—like that of your petitioners,
deprived of every social privilege, of everything requisite to render
Life tolerable is far worse than Non-existence. In imitation of the
laudable example of the Good People of these States, your petitioners have long and patiently waited the event of petition after petition, by them presented to the Legislative Body of this State and
cannot but with grief reflect that their success hath been but too
similar. They cannot but express their astonishment that it has never
been considered that every Principle from which America has acted

in the course of her unhappy Difficulties with Great Britain pleads Stronger than a thousand arguments in favor of your petitioners. They therefore humbly beseech your Honors to give this petition its due weight and consideration & cause an act of the Legislature to be passed whereby they may be restored to the enjoyment of that freedom which is the Natural right of all men—and their Children (who were born in this land of Liberty) may not be held as Slaves after they arrive at the age of twenty-one years. So may the inhabitants of this State (no longer chargeable with the inconstancy of acting, themselves, the part which they condemn and oppose in others) be prospered in their present glorious struggle for Liberty, and have those Blessings secured to them by Heaven of which benevolent minds cannot wish to deprive their countrymen.

And your Petitioners as in Duty bound shall ever pray.

Prince Hall, Job Lock
Peter Bess, Jack X Peippont (his mark)
Lancaster Hill, Nero X Funilo (his mark)
Brister Slenfen, Newport X Summer (his mark)

What Regular Grand Lodges Have Said about Negro Masonry

Prepared by Masonic Research Associates
(Anchorage, Alaska, printed after 1960, 8 pages)

These are extracts from the complete text, which contains forty-nine numbered statements without any chronological or geographical order. The numbers below correspond to the numbers in the original text.

1. The Grand Lodge of New York holds the same opinion now as in the past, that all persons claiming to be Masons, tracing back to African Lodge, Prince Hall Grand Lodge, or any Negro Grand Lodge, or Lodges descending therefrom, are clandestine.

    (The Grand Lodge of New York, 1899.)

4. But no Grand Lodge, lawfully existing and having jurisdiction, ever "regularized" the lodges, which Prince Hall attempted to create, and they were and have remained clandestine lodges, whether in making Masons, chartering lodges, organizing Grand Lodges, or forming a National Grand Lodge, are Masonically absolutely void, and will remain so until they shall be legalized by a Grand Lodge of the jurisdiction, save that the Grand Lodges and the National Grand Lodge never can be made regular.

    (The Grand Lodge of Maine, 1899.)

5. African Lodge, even in the days of its legitimacy, was never anything but a subordinate lodge. Its actions in issuing charters to other Negro lodges were a plain defiance of Masonic law and a usurpation of powers inherent in Grand Lodges alone. As for those lodges deriving illegal charters from the African Lodge, they never have, for a single moment, had anything but a clandestine existence, and neither have the colored Grand Lodges formed by these illegal bodies.

    (The Grand Lodge of Maine, 1948.)

7. Resolved. That this Grand Lodge does not recognize the so-called African or colored Masonic organization, or membership, as existing in this state, or the United States of America.

    (The Grand Lodge of Colorado, 1885.)

9. So-called Colored Lodges are held as irregular, and therefore persons belonging to them are not recognizable as Masons.

(The Grand Lodge of Colorado, 1885.)

10. Resolved. That we are unequivocally opposed to, and protest— recognizing persons as Masons who claim to have been made Masons in Lodges working under Charters issued by Prince Hall, African Grand Lodge of Boston, or Prince Hall Grand Lodge of Massachusetts, as we hold all such to be spurious Masons and un-Masonic bodies.

(The Grand Lodge of Nevada, 1899.)

11. It therefore follows that all Negroes claiming to have been made Masons in such lodges (Prince Hall) have been and are irregular and clandestine, having been so declared by legal and legitimate Grand Lodges of competent authority.

(The Grand Lodge of Wyoming, 1900.)

15. 3–15 Sec. 2. Any and all organizations, associations or persons within the State of Michigan, professing to have any authority, power or privileges in Ancient Craft Masonry, not derived from the Grand Lodges, are declared to be clandestine and illegal, and all Masonic intercourse with or recognition of them or any of them is prohibited.

(The Grand Lodge of Michigan, 1953.)

[The Grand Lodge of Michigan has never granted any authority to "any Negro grand lodge in Michigan," consequently all Negro grand lodges in Michigan are clandestine.]

22. The whole course of "Negro Masonry" in the United States is affected by taints which cannot be effaced.

(The Grand Lodge of Massachusetts, 1898.)

25. We assume upon the facts, which have been so many times set forth and established beyond all question, and with which the fraternity must be familiar, that these so-called Lodges and Grand Lodges (colored) are not only not regular or lawful, but are utterly without law or right in a Masonic point of view—and tested by rules that the fraternity established for its government more than a hundred years ago, and which have been observed and upheld ever since, all of these organizations of

so-called Negro Masonry are not only clandestine and spurious, but with few exceptions seem entirely satisfied with their own independent existence and the practice of their system.

(The Grand Lodge of New Hampshire, 1899.)

44. The Grand Lodge does not recognize as legal or Masonic any body of Negroes working under their charters in the United States, without respect to the body granting such charters, and they regard all such Negro lodges as clandestine, illegal, and un-Masonic; and, moreover, they regard as highly censurable the course of any Grand Lodge in the United States which shall recognize such bodies as Masonic Lodges.

(The Grand Lodge of Texas, 1898.)

45. There are, so we are reliably informed, Prince Hall Negro Lodges throughout Texas. These are clandestine lodges in our jurisdiction.

(The Grand Lodge of Texas, 1948.)

48. Under date of April 12, 1960, the Grand Secretary of the United Grand Lodge of England wrote: "Prince Hall was never appointed provincial grand master of any territory, and the Warrant of Constitution of 1784 conferred no power on any member of African Lodge to constitute other Lodges or to create a Grand Lodge."

N.B: Neither the Grand Lodge of England nor the Grand Lodge of Scotland nor the Grand Lodge of Ireland nor any of the 58 regular Grand Lodges in the United States and Canada have ever recognized any of the Prince Hall Grand Lodges. This is *prima facie* evidence that these 61 Grand Lodges, whose membership composes the overwhelming majority of the regular Masons of the world, consider the Prince Hall Grand Lodgers to be CLANDESTINE.*

---

*This *nota bene* is the concluding paragraph of this document written by the Masonic Research Association. It follows the survey of the forty-nine statements from grand lodges. Given the fact that number 48 is the statement of the grand secretary of the United Grand Lodge of England, dated April 12, 1960, we can conclude that this text was written a short time later.

Appendix II

"Heroines of Jericho"

(I)

We are the Heroines of Jericho,
The female relatives of Masons, you know;
We are the Heroines of Jericho,
We shall not be moved.

Chorus:

We shall, we shall, we shall not be moved,
We shall, we shall, we shall not be moved,
Like the rock of Gibraltar
We shall not be moved.

(II)

As we travel through this land,
We are forming loyal bands;
We are the Heroines of Jericho,
We shall not be moved.

(III)

More than fourteen thousand on Texas soil,
The banner for right we will unfurl,
We are the Heroines of Jericho,
We shall not be moved.

(IV)

If your ideals and morals are right,
Come and help us make this fight;
We are the Heroines of Jericho,
We shall not be moved.

(V)

New York, Ohio, and Washington DC,
Utah, Oklahoma, and Pennsylvania,
Florida, Alabama, and California,
Are all in this band.

(VI)

Missouri, Kansas, and New Jersey,
Illinois, Indiana, and Mississippi;
Big-hearted Texas is in the lead,
And she will carry on.

(VII)

Kansas, Idaho, and West Virginia,
Nebraska, Tennessee, and Iowa;
Baltimore, Maryland wears the cord,
And helps to carry on.

(VIII)

Dennis of Waco is doing all she can
To have the Carolinas join the band;
Chicago and St. Louis are really doing fine,
And Texas leads the gang.

M. H. C. Brown
Harry A. Williamson Collection, 1831–1965, reel 16.
Undated, but it is probably from the 1920s.
Schomburg Center.

Appendix III

Letters

Extracts from the Letter Sent by William H. Upton, Grand Master of the Grand Lodge of Washington, to William Sutherland, Grand Master of the Grand Lodge of New York, on the Subject of "Recognition of Negro Lodges"

(The Recognition of Negro Grand Lodges by the Grand Lodge of Washington, June 15, 1898, in *Proceedings of the Grand Lodge of New York,* 1899, 36–39.)

William H. Upton, Grand Master, The Most Worshipful Grand Lodge
of Free and Accepted Masons of Washington
Office of the Grand Master,
Walla Walla, Washington,
December 8, 1898

To Most Worshipful William A. Sutherland,
Grand Master of Masons, Rochester, N.Y.

We did several distinct things, for most of which we have been criticized; but we have been most severely denounced for things which we did not do at all, for example, for "recognizing Negro Grand Lodges."

May I be pardoned for calling attention to what the Grand Lodge did do, and pointing out some things which she did not do?

She received a respectful petition from two men who claimed to be brother Masons, and referred it to a committee, two members of which were two Past Grand Masters well-known, wherever Masonry is known, for exceptional ability and Masonic knowledge—and both, it so happened, natives of slave states. In that did she transcend her right?

After a year, she received a report from that committee which has been praised in the highest terms by Masonic scholars of international reputation, in American and foreign lands—and not one statement of fact in it has been refuted or rendered even doubtful by those who have denounced it.

On the recommendation of that committee, she adopted certain resolutions. What were they?

In the first, the Grand Lodge expressed, as its OPINION, an opinion which, I supposed, has ever been accepted as an axiom, throughout the Masonic world, except in a few Southern States of America where even Landmarks are made to bend before race prejudice. The second resolution is divisible into two parts: In the first part of it the Grand Lodge merely expressed her adherence to what has been her practice throughout the whole of her existence, viz.: to refrain from undertaking to bind the consciences of our members upon a question which is essentially one of history. If this be a crime, this Grand Lodge has been guilty for forty years, and others have been guilty for a century and a half.

The second part of that resolution was an answer to the query, How far back must a Man's Masonic pedigree be traced before we can know that he traces to Prince Hall? The answer was obvious; it is universally admitted that the first Negro body claiming to be a Grand Lodge traced to Prince Hall, and that is consequently affiliated with two other similar bodies claiming the same descent. Hence the Grand Lodge, for the guidance of its OWN MEMBERS, and dealing with a matter of its private concerns, with which it would be gross impudence for any other Grand Lodge to interfere, again had the hardihood to express AN OPINION, viz.: the "opinion" that "FOR THE PURPOSE OF TRACING SUCH ORIGIN," id est, origin from Prince Hall, the three Negro bodies above referred to might be treated as though they had been Grand Lodges; that is to say, that in her "opinion," to trace to either of these three is—What? To prove legitimacy? Not at all:—IS TO TRACE TO PRINCE HALL. Now whether this opinion is correct or erroneous, the largest question now before the Masonic world is, Has an American Grand Lodge a right to have and express an opinion without the consent of the Grand Lodge of Kentucky and her confederates? I have no doubt as to how posterity will answer that question, and very little as to how freemen will answer it.

And when you remember, most Worshipful Grand Master, that it is upon this resolution that our enemies have based their absurd and silly

statement that we have "recognized Negro Grand Lodges"—ignoring the
fact that the Grand Lodge adopted the report of the committee, which
expressly declared that "No proposal to enter into relations with the
Negro Grand Lodge is involved."—I think you will hardly wonder that I
am reminded of the line, "fools rush in where angels fear to tread."

The third resolution, also related solely to our internal affairs. We
do not admire the spectacle, exhibited in some States, of two bodies
of men each calling itself a Grand Lodge of Masons and each applying
opprobrious epithets to the other. If there are to be two Grand Lodges in
this State, we desire that they should at least cultivate the Masonic virtue,
harmony. We are quite aware that a single Grand Lodge is the ideal; and
we might charter lodges of Negroes, healing any that we find irregular,
had we desired to do so. Personally, I do not doubt that it will come to
that, fifty or a hundred years from now, as it is in foreign countries; but
we know what an outcry this would have been in the ex-slave States—to
say nothing of the fact that most of us are not without some degree of
race prejudice in our own breasts. And so we adopted a modus vivendi
that seemed to us, at the time, not wholly without merit. Inasmuch as
we declared our purpose to tolerate no colored Lodges except as shall
be "established strictly in accordance with the landmarks of Masonry,"
I do not see how the legality of our action can be questioned—except
by denying that, subject to the Landmarks, the Grand Lodge of
Washington "has supreme jurisdiction over all matters of Ancient Craft
Masonry" in this State, and has the sole right to decide as to what Lodges
in this State she will regard as regular. Upon the very different question,
as to whether her action was wise, the Grand Lodge would, of course,
gladly receive suggestions from any friendly source, but she will expect
those suggestions to be made in language not heretofore unknown
among Masons and gentlemen—not in the dialect recently adopted by
the Grand Lodge of Kentucky—whose committee sought to conceal
naked ignorance and misrepresentation beneath a garment of vulgar
obscenity.

I have written thus fully, Most Worshipful Grand Master, because
the Grand Lodge of Washington values the good opinion of the Grand
Master and the Grand Lodge of New York; and I have ventured to

trespass so extensively upon your time, because I am convinced a grand master will not begrudge time expended if it enables him to view the action of a brother in a truer light, or saves him from being a party to a great injustice.

Fraternally Yours,
William H. Upton,
Grand Master of Masons

Commentary on William H. Upton's Letter

Grand Master Upton's great prudence here cannot escape notice. The Grand Lodge of Washington did not give absolute recognition to the black lodges; it was solely concerned with the lodges of its state and conferred recognition on them individually after having verified each lodge's origins. By doing this, the grand master was simply invoking the principle of "territorial exclusivity." If only one grand lodge is sovereign in each state, it is its decision to determine whether it will grant recognition to the lodges in that state. It would seem that the other grand lodges forgot this principle in these particular circumstances and began meddling in the internal matters of the Washington Grand Lodge. Upton's indignation seems perfectly justified. It will be noted that he dealt with the Grand Lodge of New York, to whom he furnished detailed, courteous explanations about the position of his own grand lodge, in an entirely different manner than did the grand lodges of the South, which had not hesitated to insult the Grand Lodge of Washington in a way that was hardly Masonic and allowed their racist prejudices to be seen clearly. Upton was mistaken when he predicted blacks and whites would mingle in the same grand lodges in the twentieth century. Nevertheless, he was a pioneer in bringing together the most enlightened Masons.

Letter from Harry W. Bundy, Grand Secretary of the
Masonic Temple of Denver, Colorado, to Harry A. Williamson,
April 3, 1946

On the Subject of a Young Black Becoming a Member of the Masonic Youth
Organization DeMolay (Harry A. Williamson Collection, Schomburg Center).

Harry W. Bundy
Grand Secretary,
Of the Most Worshipful Grand Lodge of Ancient Free and Accepted
    Masons of Colorado
Masonic Temple
Denver 2, Colorado

Mr. Harry A. Williamson
1914 Prospect Avenue,
Bronx 59, New York

April 3, 1946
Dear Brother Williamson,
I have come home from a visit to the Western section of Colorado
where the York Rite bodies were holding their annual festival. This was
terminated Friday and I then left for Gunnison, another city in that
area, where the DeMolay chapters of the State were holding their annual
basketball tournament. I had quite a surprise on that occasion and will
relate it to you.

I arrived in Gunnison while the tournament was in progress, going
immediately to the gymnasium where a large crowd was in attendance.
In the crowd I noticed a young Negro boy, the only colored person
in the entire gymnasium of the Western State College, which was
sponsoring our De Molay tournament. I casually asked if the boy
were a student at Western State. The DeMolay official said "No, he
is a member of Valley Chapter, Order of DeMolay, at Rocky Ford,
Colorado." I asked him if he was sure of that and he said yes, that they
wondered what to do when he presented himself for registration as
a player in the team yesterday but since he has a card issued by the
Chapter and the boys assured us that he was entirely acceptable to

them and four of them offered to room with him so they let him go ahead, pending my decision. As you may imagine I was quite pleased at the democratic attitude of the youngsters and also somewhat surprised that the only instance in the United States should have occurred in one of the chapters in my jurisdiction and without any record of the instance coming to my attention until it was an accomplished fact and a year's time had elapsed.

I found no objection on the part of any of the 150 DeMolay boys from 15 different chapters to his presence. I certainly had none except from the standpoint of the boy himself in thinking of the hurt that is bound to come to him when in later years, he may expect men of the Masonic Order to be as democratic in their attitude. I called him aside later and had a heart-to-heart talk about the matter. His father is a cobbler in Rocky Ford, Colorado, a sort of roadside philosopher, much respected and liked by the whites of that community. Claude, the boy in question, told me that when he informed his father he had petitioned for membership in the DeMolay chapter, his father told him that if by any chance he was elected, he would probably be the only Negro boy in the United States belonging to that Order and that the responsibility of his would be in proportion to the whites, as 1 to 100,000, and the subsequent attitude of the whites toward the Negroes in connection with fraternal matters might rest on his shoulders. With that in mind he allowed his son to go ahead.

He was regularly elected and received the Degrees in Valley Chapter. He makes no attempt to mix socially with the whites when there is a social event where girls are present although he would be welcome. His delicacy is probably unappreciated to the extent that it should be. The advisor of the Chapter when questioned, said that having been Master of the Lodge two years had learned a lecture in which he was told that Masonry regarded no man in his race, creed, or opinion and that it was the internal and not the external qualifications of a man, which should be considered, and when the petition was presented to him, that for the life of him, he could not see any reason why it should not take its course with petitions from any other boy.

I asked him if there was any objection from the Masons. He said that all approved of the action taken and that the only trouble he had was with one of the Mothers Circle who, to use his expression, "just raised Hell about letting a nigger into the DeMolay organization." Knowing that there would be some repercussions from her associates in the city of Rocky Ford, he looked at the data in connection with the boy's petition and called her on the phone asking if she knew that it was her son who brought the petition in! Since that time she has been extremely cooperative, and there has been no friction whatever.

Harry W. Bundy

Appendix IV

Prince Hall Grand Lodges

PRINCE HALL GRAND LODGES IN THE UNITED STATES BY ALPHABETICAL ORDER*

Prince Hall Grand Lodges	Number of Members	Number of Lodges
Alabama	30,822	593
Alaska	170	5
Arizona	313	11
Arkansas	3,200	118
California	5,650	87
Colorado	833	17
Connecticut	1,500	15
Delaware	800	17
District of Columbia	5,100	25
Florida	6,500	199
Georgia	10,107	194
Illinois	NA	75
Indiana	2,100	37
Iowa	NA	7
Kansas	1,392	42
Kentucky	2,400	67
Louisiana	7,823	169
Maryland	4,762	98
Massachusetts	1,287	27
Michigan	2,900	47
Minnesota	400	14
Mississippi	17,910	357
Missouri	2,549	64
Nebraska	286	8

---

*From Paul Bessel's website with his permission.

Prince Hall Grand Lodges	Number of Members	Number of Lodges
Nevada	165	6
New Jersey	3,145	52
New Mexico	NA	NA
New York	6,500	77
North Carolina	18,000	325
Ohio	4,904	62
Oklahoma	6,000	129
Oregon	143	8
Pennsylvania	7,600	107
Rhode Island	280	5
South Carolina	16,000	306
Tennessee	6,500	172
Texas	10,201	424
Virginia	10,865	208
Washington	2,958	60
West Virginia	592	25
Wisconsin	NA	650

PRINCE HALL GRAND LODGES IN THE UNITED STATES IN DECREASING ORDER

List of Prince Hall Grand Lodges in the United States in decreasing order, based on the list on Paul Bessel's website, "PHA Statistics," updated October 17, 2012. Figures based on the list established by the Prince Hall Directory in 1997 and data from the U.S. Census Bureau.*

Prince Hall Grand Lodges	Number of Members
Alabama	30,822
North Carolina	18,000
Mississippi	17,910
South Carolina	16,000
Virginia	10,865
Texas	10,201

*Reproduced with the kind permission of Paul M. Bessel.

Prince Hall Grand Lodges	Number of Members
Georgia	10,107
Louisiana	7,823
Pennsylvania	7,600
Florida	6,500
New York	6,500
Tennessee	6,500
Oklahoma	6,000
California	5,650
District of Columbia	5,100
Ohio	4,904
Maryland	4,762
Arkansas	3,200
New Jersey	3,145
Washington	2,958
Michigan	2,900
Missouri	2,549
Kentucky	2,400
Indiana	2,100
Connecticut	1,500
Kansas	1,392
Massachusetts	1,287
Colorado	833
Delaware	800
Wisconsin	650
West Virginia	592
Minnesota	400
Arizona	313
Nebraska	286
Rhode Island	280
Alaska	170
Nevada	165
Oregon	143

Notes

Introduction. Interpreting the Black Experience

1. Walkes, *Black Square and Compass,* foreword, xv.
2. Interview granted the author when she began her research during her visit to the headquarters of the Prince Hall Grand Lodge in Harlem, March 1999.
3. Walkes, "Our History."
4. Upton, *Critical Examination of Objections;* Voorhis, *Negro Masonry in the United States.*
5. Muraskin, *Middle Class Blacks in a White Society;* Williams, *Black Freemasonry and Middle-Class Realities.*
6. Harland-Jacobs, *Builders of Empire.*
7. Roundtree and Bessel, *Out of the Shadows.*
8. Tabbert, *American Freemasons.*
9. See mainly the articles by Paul Rich: Rich and de los Reyes, "Recovering a Rite"; and Sesay, "Dialectic of Representation." On the other hand, the Caribbean remains the poor relative of Masonic historiography.
10. Papers relating to early Freemasonry in the Caribbean, 515 documents compiled by Susan Snell, archivist at the Library and Museum of Freemasonry (London ref code: GBR 1991 HC22).
11. Sadler, *Masonic Facts and Figures.*
12. Cherry, "Dear Sir and Brother," 12–21.

Chapter One. Prince Hall Legend and History

1. Diamond, *Prince Hall, Social Reformer,* 99.
2. Ibid, 32.

3. See Walkes, *Prince Hall Masonic Quiz Book,* 1–2; and Walkes, *Black Square and Compass,* 1–15.

4. Sherman, "Negro National or Compact Grand Lodge," 148.

5. Williamson, *Prince Hall Primer,* 5.

6. See Landmark n° 18; Mackey, *Revised Encyclopedia of Freemasonry,* vol. I, 561.

7. Walkes, *Black Square and Compass,* 20–21.

8. Ibid., 21.

9. Ibid., 5.

10. Ibid., 9.

11. *Proceedings of the 100th Anniversary,* 35–38.

12. Harkins, *Masonic Research Associates of Alaska,* 28.

13. Sherman, "Review of Prince Hall," 308.

14. Report reprinted in its entirety in Cass, *Negro Freemasonry and Segregation.*

15. Walkes, *Prince Hall Masonic Quiz Book,* 4. Walkes cites Harry E. Davis but cannot prove the historical validity of his remarks.

16. Cass, *Negro Freemasonry and Segregation.*

17. For more on this, see Walkes, *Black Square and Compass.*

Chapter Two. The Birth of Black Freemasonry

1. Williamson, *Prince Hall Primer,* 5.

2. Cited in Cass, *Negro Freemasonry and Segregation,* 21.

3. Letter of Prince Hall to "Mr. Willis," dated December 31, 1782, reproduced from *Prince Hall's Letter Book,* in Woodson, "Documents Relating to Negro Masonry," *Journal of Negro History,* vol. XXI, n° 4, October 1936, 413.

4. See Delany, *Origins and Objects of Ancient Freemasonry,* 19.

5. I would like to thank Susan Snell, archivist of the Library and Museum of Freemasonry, for recently bringing my attention to this correspondence of Prince Hall with the United Grand Lodge of England. These letters can be consulted easily. They are filed under the heading "Prince Hall Letters: HC28/A/1–8" and "HC28/A/10–12."

6. See Woodson, *Journal of Negro History,* 420–25, for a detailed account of the granting of the charter from this correspondence.

7. Prince Hall Letters, HC28/A/10–12, Library and Museum of Freemasonry.

8. Ibid., 14.

9. Sherman, "Negro National or Compact Grand Lodge," 149.

10. Prince Hall Grand Lodge of Massachusetts, August 25, 1870.

11. Sherman refers to this in "Negro National or Compact Grand Lodge," 34, footnote 1.
12. Walkes, *Black Square and Compass,* 29.
13. Williamson, *Prince Hall Primer,* 13.
14. Upton, "The True Text of the Book of Constitutions, " *Ars Quatuor Coronatorum,* no. 13 (1900): 54–65.
15. Sherman, "Negro National or Compact Grand Lodge," 149.
16. Williamson, *Prince Hall Primer,* 5.
17. Walkes, *Prince Hall Masonic Quiz Book,* 33.
18. Woodson, "Documents Relating to Negro Masonry," 426.
19. Ibid.
20. According to Walkes, *Prince Hall Masonic Quiz Book,* 33–55.
21. Williamson, Schomburg Center Papers, 1831–1965, reel 5, 1954, 13.
22. Mentioned in Delany, *Origins and Objects of Ancient Freemasonry,* 20. This dissident Grand Lodge is also mentioned in Jones, "Argument in Relation to Free Masonry," 32.
23. Delany, *Origins and Objects of Ancient Freemasonry,* 21.
24. Walkes, *Prince Hall Masonic Quiz Book,* 60.
25. Ibid., 70–72.
26. *Proceedings of the Sixth Triennial Session,* 8, cited in Walkes, *Prince Hall Masonic Quiz Book,* 65.

Chapter Three. The Major Principles

1. Hinks, *To Awaken My Afflicted Brethren,* 182–83.
2. Ibid., 1–22.
3. Delany, *The Origins and Objects of Ancient Freemasonry,* 28.
4. Ibid., 32.
5. Ibid.
6. Bruce, "Mission and the Opportunity of the Negro Mason," 3.
7. Washington, *Up from Slavery.*
8. Ibid., 17.

Chapter Four. Abolitionism

1. Figures from Fohlen, *Histoire de l'esclavage aux États-Unis,* 124.
2. Ibid., table, 125.
3. Ibid.
4. Franklin and Moss, *From Slavery to Freedom,* 65.

5. *Proceedings of the 100th Anniversary,* 11.

6. Ibid., 16.

7. Ibid., 12–13.

8. Woodson, "Documents Relating to Negro Masonry," 428.

9. Cass, *Negro Freemasonry and Segregation,* 99–100.

10. Petition cited by Cass.

11. Cox, *Great Black Men of Freemasonry,* 50–52.

12. See Poirier, "De la terre promoise au cauchemar."

13. Proceedings, J. Drummond's letter, 17.

14. *The New York Morning Post and Daily Advertiser,* Printed and Published by William Morton, April 8, 1788, no. 1268; Woodson, "Documents Relating to Negro Masonry," 426–29.

15. Prince Hall to the grand master adjunct of the England Grand Lodge, letter, May 23, 1788, Prince Hall Letters HC 28/A/1–8 and HC 28/A/10–12. "Thomas Saunderson, Secretary, letter signed, Prince Hall." I would like to thank Susan Snell, archivist of the Library and Museum of Freemasonry in London, for bringing my attention to these letters.

16. Woodson, *Journal of Negro History* XXI, no. 4 (October 1936): 430.

17. Hall, "Charge Delivered to the African Lodge, 4–5" (report, Arthur A. Schomburg, grand secretary).

18. Ibid.

19. See Walkes, *Black Square and Compass,* 24–30.

20. See Hinks, *To Awaken My Afflicted Brethren,* 72.

21. Letter from Prince Hall to Lady Huntingdon, cited in Walkes, *Black Square and Compass,* 24.

22. Walkes, *Black Square and Compass,* 29.

23. Letter from Prince Hall to Absalom Jones, September 16, 1789, cited in Hinks, *To Awaken My Afflicted Brethren,* 71.

24. Ibid., 71 (referring to incident discussed previously).

25. Franklin and Moss, *From Slavery to Freedom,* 145–47.

26. Hinks, *To Awaken My Afflicted Brethren,* 73.

27. Ibid., 265.

28. The expression "Grand African Lodge 459" appeared on June 15, 1827, according to Walkes, *Prince Hall Masonic Quiz Book,* 33–34.

29. Hinks, *To Awaken My Afflicted Brethren,* 71–72. Grand Master Sullavou confirms that John Hilton was grand master of the Prince Hall Grand Lodge of Massachusetts from 1836 to 1847 in *Proceedings of the 100th Anniversary,* 21.

30. Cox, *Great Black Men of Freemasonry,* 17.

31. Walkes, *Black Square and Compass,* 35.

32. Walkes, *Black Square and Compass,* 4. See the footnote on Sierra Leone.

33. Cox, *Great Black Men of Freemasonry,* 50–52.

34. Williamson, *Story of the Carthaginian Lodge n° 47,* 5.

35. Hinks, *To Awaken My Afflicted Brethren,* 103.

36. "Report of the Committee on Foreign Correspondence," 57.

37. "Extracts from the Grand Master's Address, December 5, 1870," *Proceedings of the Grand Lodge of Pennsylvania.*

38. "Address of Past Grand Master Sullavou, September 29, 1884," *Proceedings of the 100th Anniversary,* 21.

39. Delany, *Origins and Objects of Ancient Freemasonry,* 32.

40. Delany, "Political Destiny of the Colored Race," in Hinks, *To Awaken My Afflicted Brethren,* 250.

41. Cox, *Great Black Men of Freemasonry,* 63–64.

42. Delany speech cited in Walkes, *Prince Hall Masonic Quiz Book,* 43.

43. See Paul Bessel's website, "Masonic Recognition Issues," http://bessel.org/masrec/phachart.htm (accessed May 21, 2015).

44. Walkes, *Black Square and Compass,* 39.

45. Williamson, *Prince Hall Primer,* 34.

46. Walkes *Black Square and Compass,* 52.

47. Williams, *Black Freemasonry and Middle-Class Realities,* 45.

48. Roberts, *House Reunited.*

49. Voorhis, *Our Colored Brethren,* 77.

50. Mackey, *Revised Encyclopedia of Freemasonry,* s.v. "Landmark," 561.

51. "Speech of the Grand Master, December 3, 1879," in *Proceedings of the Most Ancient and Honorable Fraternity of Free and Accepted Masons of the State of New York from December 1877 to June 1879,* 16.

52. Jones, "Argument in Relation to Free Masonry," 15.

53. Ibid, 10–11.

54. See "Narrative of the Life of Frederick Douglass," in Gates, *Classic Slave Narratives;* and Williamson, *Celestial Lodge n° 3,* 29.

Chapter Five. Education

1. Hall, "Charge Delivered to the African Lodge."

2. Hall, "Charge Delivered to the Brethren," 10.

3. Letter cited in Upton, *Prince Hall's Letter Book,* 61.

4. Cox, *Great Black Men of Freemasonry,* 17, 52, 166.

5. Ibid., 160.

6. "Opening Address of the Grand Master Thomas Thomas, at the Annual Communication of the Most Worshipful Prince Hall Grand Lodge of Boston, December 20, 1883," in *Proceedings of the 100th Anniversary,* 32.

7. Ibid., 32–33.

8. Washington, *Up from Slavery,* 85.

9. Ibid., 155. See the comment to "learn some industry."

10. Booker T. Washington, quoted by Du Bois in "The Souls of Black Folk," from *Selected Writings,* 30.

11. Ibid., 51.

12. Ibid. See also chap. 6 in this book, "The Fight for Civil Rights."

13. Cherry, "Dear Sir and Brother." I am grateful to Martin Cherry, archivist of the Library and Museum of Freemasonry in London, for bringing this point to my attention.

14. Du Bois, "Crisis, November 1910," 107.

15. Du Bois, "Philadelphia Negro," 26.

16. Du Bois, "Crisis, November 1910," 106.

17. Williamson, *Celestial Lodge n° 3,* 13.

18. Bruce, "Mission and the Opportunity of the Negro Mason," 5.

19. Williamson, "Masons Aid in Education."

20. "Proceedings, Grand Lodge of Texas, 1947. Report of the Committee on Education," cited in Muraskin, *Middle-Class Blacks in a White Society,* 227.

21. Walkes, *Prince Hall Masonic Quiz Book,* 98.

Chapter Six. The Fight for Civil Rights

1. Franklin and Moss, *From Slavery to Freedom,* 255–59.

2. See Denslow, *10,000 Famous Freemasons,* vol. I, 63; and Walkes, *Black Square and Compass,* 85.

3. The short list would include Grant, *Way It Was in the South,* 101; Purvis, *Dictionary of American History,* 218; and Roberts, *House Reunited,* a book on American Freemasonry during the Civil War, which mentions Forrest's membership as a Freemason on page 72, or was one of the first members.

4. Jones, "Argument in Relation to Free Masonry," 12.

5. Muraskin, *Middle-Class Blacks in a White Society,* 219.

6. Bruce, "Mission and the Opportunity of the Negro Mason."

7. Voorhis, *Our Colored Brethren,* 46.

8. Muraskin, *Middle-Class Blacks in a White Society.*

9. Ibid., 220.

10. Ibid., 221–22.

11. Ibid., chap. 3, note 8.

12. Franklin and Moss, *From Slavery to Freedom,* 289.

13. Du Bois, "Socialism and the American Negro," 307.

14. See the *Pittsburgh Courier* article from April 21, 1947, in the Williamson Fund, reel 16, Schomburg Center.

15. Muraskin, *Middle-Class Blacks in a White Society,* 228.

16. Ibid., 231.

17. Ibid., 233–34.

18. Ibid., 230.

19. Walkes, *Prince Hall Masonic Quiz Book,* 95.

20. Muraskin, *Middle-Class Blacks in a White Society,* 247.

Chapter Seven. The Cooperative Ideal

1. Hall, "Charge Delivered to the Brethren," 7.

2. Williams, *Black Freemasonry and Middle-Class Reality.*

3. See Franklin and Moss, *From Slavery to Freedom,* 286–87.

4. *Minutes of Carthaginian Lodge n° 47,* in Harry A. Williamson Fund, Schomburg Center, reel 16.

5. Brooks, *Official History and Manual of the Grand United Order of Odd Fellows in America,* 90.

6. Ibid., 222, "The Principles and Purposes of Odd Fellowship."

7. Ibid., 227, "The Objects and Benefits of the Order."

8. Ibid., 218.

9. Ibid., 103.

10. Muraskin, *Middle-Class Blacks in a White Society,* 165.

11. Brooks, *Official History and Manual of the Grand United Order of Odd Fellows in America,* 6.

12. Williamson, *Celestial Lodge n° 3,* 16.

13. Muraskin, *Middle-Class Blacks in a White Society,* 136.

14. *Proceedings of the Prince Hall Grand Lodge, Massachusetts, 1873.*

15. Williamson, *Celestial Lodge n° 3,* 6.

16. Muraskin also mentions this association. See Muraskin, *Middle-Class Blacks in a White Society,* 140.

17. Williamson, *Celestial Lodge n° 3,* 22.

18. Ibid., 28.

19. Crawford, *Prince Hall Counselor,* 90.

20. Walkes, *Prince Hall Masonic Quiz Book,* 95.

21. Muraskin, *Middle-Class Blacks in a White Society,* 156.

22. Walkes, *Prince Hall Masonic Quiz Book,* 95.

23. Statement by the grand master from *Proceedings of the Grand Lodge of Alabama, 1909;* quoted in Muraskin, *Middle-Class Blacks in a White Society,* 141.

24. Muraskin, *Middle-Class Blacks in a White Society,* 141–49.

25. Ibid., 170.

26. "Story of Peter Ogden," cited in Brooks, *Official History and Manual of the Grand United Order of Odd Fellows in America,* 45.

27. Williamson, *The Genuineness and Historic Legality of Prince Hall Affiliated Masonry.*

Chapter Eight.
Women and Black Freemasonry

1. "By-Laws," in "Origin and History of the Adoptive Rite in the District of Columbia," in Davis, *History of Freemasonry among Negroes,* 205. Several minutes of meetings of the grand chapters are available online. All mention both a grand patron and a grand matron. See, for example, Amaranth Grand Chapter, Order of the Eastern Star, Prince Hall Affiliation, State of Ohio, www.phaohio.org/amaranth/histoesfile.html (accessed May 22, 2015). On this same site we can read that the Grand Chapter of the Amaranth of Ohio elected its worthy grand matron and grand patron every two years. The same is probably true for the other chapters.

2. "Revised Constitution and By-Laws of the International Conference of Grand Chapters, OES," in Davis, *Story of the Illinois Federation of Colored Women's Clubs,* 203.

3. See Buisine, *La Franc-Maçonnerie anglo-saxonne et les femmes,* 190–201.

4. Williamson, *Masonic Digest,* 105.

5. Ayers, "Origin and History for the Adoptive Rite among Black Women."

6. Voorhis, *Negro Masonry in the United States,* 66ff. Also see Sommers, "Caché, mais bien en vue," 82–83, 365–85.

7. Ayers, "Origin and History for the Adoptive Rite among Black Women."

8. Williamson, *Prince Hall Masonic Digest;* Ayers, "Origin and History for the Adoptive Rite among Black Women."

9. Williamson, *Prince Hall Masonic Digest,* 106.

10. *Proceedings of the 5th Annual Communication, Arkansas,* June 1890, 16.

11. Williamson, *Story of the Carthaginian Lodge n° 47,* 26.

12. M. H. C. Brown, "Song of the Heroines of Jericho," undated, probably from the 1920s.

13. Williamson, *Prince Hall Masonic Digest,* 105.

14. Address Delivered by Mrs. S. Joe Brown before 9th Biennial Conference. "Earliest Records of the Eastern Star," from 1857, cited in E. L. Davis, *The Story of the Illinois Federation of Colored Women's Clubs,* 23.

15. Voorhis, *Eastern Star,* 66–67.

16. Albert Pike, quoted in Mackey, *Revised Encyclopedia of Freemasonry,* 303.

17. Williamson, *Prince Hall Masonic Digest,* 101.

18. "Revised Constitutions and By-Laws of the International Conference of Grand Chapters, OES," Article III, cited in Davis, *History of Freemasonry among Negroes,* 203.

19. "Origin and History of the Adoptive Rite in the District of Columbia," in Davis, *History of Freemasonry among Negroes,* 15–16.

20. Rich and de los Reyes, "Recovering a Rite," 219–34.

21. Williamson, *Prince Hall Masonic Digest,* 134.

22. Ibid., 135.

23. Ibid., 104.

24. See in particular Williamson's February 4, 1941, letter to Voorhis in *Correspondence between Harry Williamson and H. V. B. Voorhis,* in the New York Grand Lodge, Livingston Library.

25. *Official Proceedings of the 141st Annual Communication, Pennsylvania,* 19.

26. Williamson, *Story of the Carthaginian Lodge n° 47,* 26.

27. Ibid., 27.

28. Williamson, *Celestial Lodge n° 3,* 7.

29. Davis, *Story of the Illinois Federation of Colored Women's Clubs,* 55. Elizabeth Lindsay Davis, the author of this history of the Eastern Star, was herself a member of this Boston grand chapter.

30. Ibid., 174.

31. Ibid., 177.

32. "Eastern Star Leader to Visit Bronx District," 1944, Harry A. Williamson's personal archives.

33. *Proceedings of the Annual Sessions of the Grand Chapter, Indiana, 1891–1900,* 15.

34. Cossandra Wheeler, personal correspondence with the author, May 15, 2013.

35. Rich and de los Reyes, "Recovering a Rite." See also Gray, "Listing of Past

Grand Matrons and Patrons." I am grateful to Paul Rich for giving me access to this article as well as for his correspondence with the Eastern Star chapters.

Chapter Nine. Jazzmen and Black Artists

1. American National Biography Online, www.anb.org (accessed May 22, 2015).

2. Imbert, "Jazz en vies"; Imbert, *Jazz suprême.*

3. Tirro, *Jazz, A History,* 91.

4. Imbert, "Jazz en vies," 145–46; Imbert, *Jazz suprême,* 72.

5. Ibid.

6. Armstrong, *Satchmo,* 29.

7. Ibid., 225.

8. Ibid., 163.

9. Quoted in Imbert, *Jazz suprême,* 138.

10. Nat King Cole, quoted in Haskins and Benson, *Nat King Cole,* 18.

11. Haskins and Benson, *Nat King Cole,* 82.

12. Ibid., 138–39.

13. Imbert, *Jazz suprême,* 215.

14. I will simply mention Tresner, *Craft's Noyse,* 25.

15. Hinton, *Playing the Changes,* cited in Imbert, "Jazz en vies."

16. See Walkes, *Prince Hall Masonic Quiz Book,* 33–44.

17. Armstrong, *Satchmo,* 84.

18. Ibid., 142–43.

19. This entire letter to the editor is quoted in Haskins and Benson, *Nat King Cole,* 140–41.

20. Ibid., 162–63.

21. See Gerlach, "Robeson, Paul."

22. Robeson, *Here I Stand,* cited by Cox in *Great Black Men of Freemasonry,* 286.

23. Cox, *Great Black Men of Freemasonry,* 170.

24. Tirro, "Armstrong, Louis (August 4, 1901–July 6, 1971)."

25. This statement can be found on these two websites: www.angelfire.com/tx/masonicmusic/home/html and Oak Forest Lodge #1398, "An Organization Is Judged" http://mastermason.com/oakforest1398/fams.htm (accessed June 22, 2015).

26. See www.freemsonry.bcy.ca/biography/armstrong_l/armstrong_l.html (accessed June 22, 2015).

27. Ibid.

28. Peretti, "Basie, Count."

29. Cox, *Great Black Men of Freemasonry,* 45. Unfortunately Cox indicates no initiation dates and neglects to supply the locations of the lodges.

30. Elliott, "Blake, Eubie."

31. Cox, *Great Black Men of Freemasonry,* 51.

32. Ibid., 52. The news account of this opera can be found at Campbell, "Old and New Versions of Opera Reviewed."

33. Kernfeld, "Calloway, Cab."

34. Hinton's autobiography, *Playing the Changes,* cited in Imbert, "Jazz en vies," 157. Cox does not mention this book.

35. Dufour, "Cole, Nat King."

36. Cox, *Great Black Men of Freemasonry,* 97. Cox does not mention the grand lodge; however it is definitely the Prince Hall Grand Lodge, and it appears at Masonic Lodge Information, "USA–Prince Hall–California."

37. Collier, "Ellington, Duke."

38. Detail noted in Imbert, *Jazz suprême,* 138.

39. Cox, *Great Black Men of Freemasonry,* 138–39. Cox speaks of the "Acacia Grand Lodge." I found a website for the Prince Hall Acacia Lodge of Washington D.C., which I presume is the same lodge: www.mwphgldc.com/?page_id=1100 (accessed May 23, 2015).

40. Kernfeld, "Hampton, Lionel."

41. This information is provided by Cox and not by Barry Kernfeld on the American National Biography Online website. It therefore needs to be verified as I have come across a number of factual errors in Cox's book; generally they do not concern the Masonic references but other biographical details. American National Biography Online is more reliable.

42. Cox, *Great Black Men of Freemasonry,* 177.

43. Ibid., 208. This was not the subject of a specific article, but it is cited in several others found on the American National Biography Online website.

44. Ibid.

45. I am citing the description of Nicolas Vallone, to whom I give my thanks, who also found the proof of McDowell's Masonic affiliation at Documenting Reality, "Mississippi Fred McDowell," www.documentingreality.com/forum/f226/mississippi-fred-mcdowell-94533 (accessed June 16, 2015). Photos of McDowell in his coffin and of his grave can be seen on this site. They are also available on Flickr at www.flickr.com/photos/josepha/2173391978 (accessed June 16, 2015).

46. Imbert, *Jazz suprême,* 74, 177.

47. Cox, *Great Black Men of Freemasonry,* 285–86; Gerlach, "Robeson, Paul."

48. Cox, *Great Black Men of Freemasonry,* 296.

49. Ibid.

Chapter Ten. The Brothers Who Were
Excluded in the Name of the Great Principles

1. Anderson, *Constitutions,* article 3.

2. Letters exchanged by William White, grand secretary of the Grand Lodge of England, and Prince Hall, worshipful master of the African Lodge n° 459 of Boston, in 1792; see Woodson, "Documents Relating to Negro Masonry," 423–25.

3. Mackey, *Revised Encyclopedia of Freemasonry,* vol. I, 561.

4. Delany, *Origins and Objects of Ancient Freemasonry,* 19.

5. Communication of Prince Hall to the *Columbian Sentinel,* May 2, 1787; see Woodson, *Journal of Negro History,* 420.

6. See Révauger, *Le fait Maçonnique au XVIIIᵉ siècle en Grande Bretagne et aux Etats-Unis,* 74–75, 123–26.

7. Sherman, "Negro National or Compact Grand Lodge," 149.

8. Ibid., 150.

9. Letter of William A. Sutherland, grand master of the New York Grand Lodge, to William H. Upton, grand master of the Washington Grand Lodge, December 20, 1898, in *Negro Masonry Proceedings,* New York, 1899, app., 47.

10. *What Regular Grand Lodges Have Said about Negro Masonry,* prepared by Masonic Research Associates (Anchorage, Alaska, n.d.). This undated document was published after 1960. Excerpts can be read in appendix 1.

11. Ibid.

12. Cass, *Negro Freemasonry and Segregation,* 138. The committee mentioned here was set up by the Massachusetts Grand Lodge in 1946.

13. Ibid., 130.

14. Williams, *Black Freemasonry and Middle-Class Realities,* 17.

15. Davis, *History of Freemasonry among Negroes,* 235.

16. Mackey, *Revised Encyclopedia of Freemasonry,* vol. I, 344.

17. Upton, *Prince Hall's Letter Book,* 62–63.

18. Denslow, *10,000 Famous Freemasons,* vol. III, 49. Denslow adds that the Prince Hall Grand Lodge of Massachusetts offered Findel a jewel and various Masonic adornments, which were housed in the Bayreuth Museum until the advent of Nazism.

19. Findel, "Treatise on Masonry," 20–24.

20. "Report of the Committee on Foreign Correspondence," 40–57.

21. Ibid., 47.

22. Ibid., see the section on the Prince Hall Grand Lodges.

23. *Proceedings of the 5th Annual Communication of the Grand Lodge of the State of Alaska*, 57.

24. Williamson, *Freemasonry among Men of Color*, 24.

25. Ibid., 25.

26. Williamson, *Prince Hall Primer*, 49–50.

27. *American Masonic Review* 1, no. 3 (Summer 1992): 7.

28. Declaration of the Committee on Information for Recognition of the Conference of Grand Masters of Masons in North America, cited in Bessel, "U.S. Recognition of French Grand Lodges," 7.

Chapter Eleven. The Racism of White Freemasons

1. Hall, "Charge Delivered to the Brethren," 11.

2. See Kaplan and Kaplan, *Black Presence in the Era of the American Revolution*.

3. Walkes, *Prince Hall Masonic Quiz Book*, 87.

4. Denslow, *10,000 Famous Freemasons*, vol. III, 340.

5. Mackey, *Revised Encyclopedia of Freemasonry*, vol. III, 1410.

6. Ibid., 1411.

7. Walkes, *Prince Hall Masonic Quiz Book*, 88, footnote 6.

8. Albert Pike, cited in Walkes, *Prince Hall Masonic Quiz Book*, 84.

9. I would like to thank Brent Morris for drawing my attention to this point. See also de Hoyo, "On the Origins of the Prince Hall Scottish Rite Rituals," 51–67; and Ayers, "Origin and History for the Adoptive Rite among Black Women."

10. Delany, *Origins and Objects of Ancient Freemasonry*, 22, footnote.

11. *Proceedings of the Most Worshipful Fraternity of Free and Accepted Masons of the State of New York*, New York, 1897–1902, 37.

12. Letter of William Sutherland to William H. Upton, December 8, 1898, in *Negro Masonry Proceedings*, 45.

13. Ibid.

14. Letter of William Sutherland to William H. Upton, January 19, 1899.

15. Harkins, *Symbolic Freemasonry among the Negroes of America*, 29.

16. Ibid., 17.

17. Ibid., 20.

18. Ibid., 25.

19. Ibid., 22.

20. Ibid., 29.

21. By Luther A. Smith, 33rd degree, in Harkins, *Symbolic Freemasonry among the Negroes of America*.

22. *Address of the Grand Master, Kentucky, 1898*, 6.

23. *Proceedings of the Grand Lodge of Alabama, 1866*, cited by Williamson, 47, n° 216.

24. From the letter of Mississippi Grand Master Edwin J. Martin to William D. Wolfskiel, grand master of New Jersey, August 25, 1908; see Voohis, *Our Colored Brethren*, 34. William J. Whalen, an American author hostile to Freemasonry in general, naturally took pleasure in citing this extract from the statement by the Mississippi grand master; see Whalen, *Christianity and American Freemasonry*, 24.

25. Declaration of Frederic Speed, grand secretary of the Grand Lodge of Mississippi, in the *Southland* (Vicksburg, Miss.), April 24, 1909, cited in Williamson, *Prince Hall Primer*, 46.

26. Virginia correspondent responding to the Grand Lodge of West Australia, *Proceedings of Grand Lodge of Virginia*, 1913, app., 59, cited in Williamson, *Prince Hall Primer*, 47–48.

27. "Declarations of the Grand Lodges of Illinois and Kentucky," cited in Walkes, *Prince Hall Masonic Quiz Book*, 80.

28. Walkes, *A Prince Hall Masonic Quiz Book*, 81.

29. Ibid.

30. For more on Indians in Freemasonry, see Denslow, *Freemasonry and the American Indian;* or Latham, "American Indian in Freemasonry."

31. Walkes, *Prince Hall Masonic Quiz Book*, 83. The soldier's name was Reed.

32. "What Regular Grand Lodges Have Said about Negro Masonry," last page.

33. Williamson, *Prince Hall Primer*, 21.

Chapter Twelve. Some Attempts to Come Together

1. Voohis, *Negro Masonry in the United States*, 76–77.

2. Walkes, *Prince Hall Masonic Quiz Book*, 101.

3. Lodge of St Andrew's, *An Ancient Tale Told New;* see Révauger, *Le fait Maçonnique*, 179–82.

4. Articles from December 1, 1867 and 1870, "The Lodge of Saint Andrew's and the Massachusetts Grand Lodge," cited in Voorhis, *Negro Masonry in the*

United States, 107.

5. Voorhis, *Negro Masonry in the United States,* 77.

6. Cass, *Negro Freemasonry and Segregation,* 70–90.

7. Ibid., 90.

8. Voorhis, *Negro Masonry in the United States,* 76.

9. Cass, *Negro Freemasonry and Segregation,* 70.

10. Ibid.

11. Williamson, letter of June 12, 1953, to the French Lodge of the Grand Orient of France, L'Atlantide, of New York, Williamson Collection, reel 5, Schomburg Center. For more concerning the relations between Prince Hall and the Grand Orient of France, see chap. 13.

12. Williamson, *Prince Hall Primer,* 35, n° 163.

13. Letter of Conant Voter, grand master of Vermont, to Harold B. Voorhis, grand master of New Jersey, March 20, 1946, in *Correspondence between H. Williamson and Voorhis on Negro Masonry, 1941–1951,* Schomburg Center.

14. Ibid.

15. Williamson, *Negroes and Freemasonry,* 24.

16. See also the correspondence between Henry Sadler and Frederic Monroe, recently studied by Martin Cherry, which makes numerous allusions to the battle waged by William H. Upton for the recognition of black Freemasons, in Cherry, "Dear Sir and Brother." Cherry also gave a speech on this theme: "Grand Lodges and Official History?"

17. Declaration of the grand master during the meeting of the grand lodge, November 25, 1946, cited in full by Cass, *Negro Freemasonry and Segregation,* 132–42; Hilton, cited by Cass, *Negro Freemasonry and Segregation,* 141–42.

18. This is what Joseph Cox told me in the interview he granted me in March 1999.

19. Findel, "Treatise on Masonry," 20–24.

20. Concerning these international congresses, people will find it to their advantage to consult Mollès' recent thesis, "Triangle atlantique et triangle latin."

21. Diamond, *European Masonic Congress.*

22. Mollès, "Triangle atlantique et triangle latin."

23. Delany, *Origins and Objects of Ancient Freemasonry,* 6. This was the era of the National or Compact Grand Lodge. See chap. 2.

24. Walkes, *Prince Hall Masonic Quiz,* 100.

25. Ibid., 101.

26. See Bessel, "PHA Chart."

27. Bessel, "Historical Maps."

Chapter Thirteen. Prince Hall and the
French Masonic Obediences

1. *The New England Craftsman of Boston,* October 1917, 424–26, cited by Williamson, the Williamson Fund, Schomburg Center, reel 4, 1952, 19.

2. "Report of the Committee on Foreign Correspondence," 55.

3. For fuller detail, see Hazareesingh and Wright, *Francs-Maçons sous le second empire,* 156–57.

4. This is a translation of the original French text from Williamson, *Data Concerning the Holy Bible.*

5. Ibid., 20.

6. Ibid. Statement issued by Prince Hall Grand Lodge of New York.

7. Letter from the Grand Lodge of France to the Grand Lodge of New York, July 20, 1917, cited in Williamson, *Data Concerning the Holy Bible,* 21. This is Williamson's translation.

8. Williamson speaks of "the bogus Grand Body," without naming it, in *Prince Hall Masons and the Grand Orient de France,* 77.

9. Williamson, *Data Concerning the Holy Bible,* 2.

10. Correspondence between Greene and Williamson, in Walkes, *French Masonic Incident,* www.thephylaxis.org.

11. Denslow, *10,000 Famous Freemasons,* vol. IV, 333; Cox, *Great Black Men of Freemasonry,* 201.

12. Williamson, *Data Concerning the Holy Bible,* 12.

13. Ibid., 113. Williamson gives a detailed account of this visit. I personally had the pleasure of meeting Maurice Shire, of the Lodge L'Atlantide, who was this lodge's worshipful master in 1953. The account he gave me of the visit of members of the Prince Hall Lodge corresponds perfectly with Williamson's account.

14. Ibid.

15. Ibid., 114–15.

16. Davis, *History of Freemasonry among Negroes,* 235. For more on these international congresses of the supreme councils, see Mollès' thesis, "Triangle atlantique et triangle latin." This thesis was written under the direction of Denis Rolland and submitted in Paris on December 12, 2012.

17. Williamson, *Questions and Answers Concerning the GODF,* 117.

18. Roberts, "Qui sont ces maçons de Prince Hall?" 25–33.

19. *Proceedings of the 11th Annual Communication, Missouri, 1877,* 12–13. The April 28, 1877, issue, "Decret du Grand Orient de France," is quoted in full.

20. Williamson, *Data Concerning the Holy Bible,* 70.

21. Ibid., 1–2.
22. Ibid., 12.
23. Letter addressed to William O. Greene from Paul Chevalier, 1951, in Walkes, *French Masonic Incident,* 3.
24. Letter from Paul Chevalier to Harry Williamson, November 27, 1951.
25. Letter from Harry Williamson to Paul Chevalier, January 1, 1952.
26. Letter from Harry Williamson to G. Lewis, grand master of Louisiana (Prince Hall), July 16, 1952.
27. Williamson, "Recherches sur les loges militaires 'Prince Hall.'" See also Williamson, "Les hommes de couleur dans la Maçonnerie américaine."
28. H. N. Brown, *Freemasonry among Negroes and Whites in America.*
29. Harkins, *Symbolic Freemasonry,* 29, and chapter 8.
30. H. N. Brown, *Freemasonry among Negroes and Whites in America,* 2 (dedication).
31. This rank is according to Walkes, *Black Square and Compass,* 150.
32. H. N. Brown, "La prétendue clandestinité de la Maçonnerie noire de Prince Hall aux Etats-Unis," 284–92. *Clandestinité* is an Anglicism. The proper translation would have been "*irrégularité.*" I am grateful to Pierre Mollier, librarian for the Grand Orient of France Library in Paris for bringing the role of Harvey Newton Brown to my attention.
33. Harvey Newton Brown, letter from El Paso, Texas, in *Renaissance traditionnelle,* nos. 21–22 (January–April, 1975): 166.

Chapter Fourteen. The Perspective of Prince Hall Freemasons: The Separatist Temptation

1. Révauger, "Shays, Daniel (1747? –1825)."
2. Prince Hall letter, in *Proceedings of the 100th Anniversary,* 16.
3. Jones, "Argument in Relation to Free Masonry," 5.
4. William A. Sutherland, letter of January 20, 1898, in *Correspondence between Harry Williamson and H. V. B. Voorhis,* 57.
5. Davis, *History of Freemasonry among Negroes,* 248.
6. Williamson, *Prince Hall Primer,* 31.
7. Crawford, *Prince Hall Counselor,* ix.
8. *National Association for the Advancement of Colored People* statistics cited in Walkes, *Prince Hall Masonic Quiz Book,* 95.
9. Maine Grand Lodge Proceedings, May 8, 1996; file put together by Paul Bessier on the recognition of the Prince Hall Grand Lodges, George Washington Masonic National Memorial, Alexandria, Virginia.

10. Number advanced by the Phylaxis Society and given in Walkes, *Prince Hall Masonic Quiz Book,* 95.

11. See Bessel, "PHA Chart."

12. Bessel, "Masonic Statistics: Graphs, Maps, Charts."

13. Crawford, *Prince Hall Counselor,* 94. For more on the Alpha Lodge, see chap. 9 in part 3.

14. "Grand Master's Address," August 21, 1877, in *Proceedings of the 11th Annual Communication, Missouri, 1877,* 14.

15. Ibid., 5–17.

16. See chap. 5.

17. *The Order of Saint Joseph, Preamble,* in Williamson Fund, reel 16, Schomburg Center.

18. *Pittsburgh Courier,* "Two Summer Camps for Colored Children," Saturday, 30, 1945, in Williamson Fund, reel 16, Schomburg Center.

19. Nye and Morpurgo, *History of the United States,* vol. 2, 594.

20. "Temple Group to Meet April 8, at the YMCA," *Past Master Topics* 7, no. 3 (March 24, 1945) (available from Williamson Fund).

21. Williamson, *Celestial Lodge n° 3,* 14.

22. This information was given me personally by Joseph Cox when I interviewed him at his home in the Bronx in March 1999.

23. The incident was recorded in Voorhis, *Our Colored Brethren,* 31.

24. "Prince Hall Masons of the State of New York Honor the Grand Lodge of Liberia," 3.

25. Crawford, *Prince Hall and His Followers,* 12.

26. Ibid., 88–89.

27. Davis, *History of Freemasonry among Negroes,* 248.

28. Williams, *Black Freemasonry and Middle-Class Realities,* 7.

29. Williamson, *Prince Hall Primer,* 58.

30. Statement by Joseph Cox, author of *Great Black Men of Freemasonry,* during an interview he granted me in March 1999.

Chapter Fifteen. The Caribbean Masonic Space: Between Prince Hall and Europe

1. Gould, *History of Freemasonry,* v. 99. However, Jessica Harland-Jacobs only mentions two lodges on Antigua in 1743, erected by the provincial grand master of the Windward Isles, as well as two more on Saint Kitts; Harland-Jacobs, *Builders of Empire,* 39.

2. Atwell, *Albion Lodge 196 E.R.*

3. Jacobs, *Fédon's Rebellion in Grenada.*

4. Gould, *History of Freemasonry,* v. 101.

5. Révauger, "A quels saints se vouer?" 33–47.

6. Pocock, *Out of the Shadows of the Past,* 8, 534, footnote.

7. Révauger, "Franc-Maçonnerie et émacipation dans la Caraïbe anglophone," 155–69.

8. Kerjan and Le Bihan, *Dictionnaire du Grand Orient de France,* s.v. "Loges des colonies." 204. See also Ursulet, *Franc-Maçonnerie aux Antilles françaises,* 32–34.

9. Ibid., 33.

10. Ibid., 35.

11. See Godfroy's thesis, *Kourou—1763.*

12. See http://emsomipy.free.fr/Colonies/Odo/02.Louis%20XV.htm (accessed June 23, 2015).

13. Ligou, *Dictionnaire de la Franc-Maçonnerie,* 557.

14. Kerjan and Le Bihan, *Dictionnaire du Grand Orient de France.*

15. André Combes, "La Franc-Maçonnerie aux Antilles et en Guyane françaises," 174.

16. Bardoux, 1892, cited in Elisabeth Liris in "Lafayette, Joseph-Paul-Yves-Roch-Gilbert du Motier," 166.

17. Kerjan and Le Bihan, *Dictionnaire du Grand Orient de France,* 205.

18. Ibid.

19. See Cauna, "Moreau de Saint-Méry, Médéric Louis Elie (1750–1819)," 2027–29.

20. Cauna, "Toussaint-Louverture, François-Dominique (1743–1803)," 2675–79.

21. Downes, "Freemasonry in Barbados, 1740–1900," 62.

22. Clarke, "Irish Freemasonry in Barbados."

23. *Proceedings of the Grand Lodge of England,* 1847 (Library and Museum of Freemasonry, London).

24. Seemungal, "Notes on Members of LUB," private archives.

25. Révauger, *Abolition of Slavery.*

26. Frazer, *History of Trinidad,* 250–73.

27. Seemungal, "Notes on members of LUB," private archives, see his entry, "Cipriani."

28. Révauger, "A quels saints se vouer?" 33–47.

29. Charles, "200 Years of Freemasonry in Trinidad and Tobago, an Overview."

30. Verteuil, *Temples of Trinidad,* 179.

31. Cited in Ursulet, *La Franc-Maçonnerie aux Antilles françaises.*

32. Combes, "La Franc-Maçonnerie aux Antilles et en Guyane françaises," 172.

33. Ursulet, *La Franc-Maçonnerie aux Antilles françaises,* 78–79.

34. Combes, "La Franc-Maçonnerie aux Antilles et en Guyane françaises," 170.

35. Ursulet, *La Franc-Maçonnerie aux Antilles françaises,* 53.

36. Ibid.

37. I received this information courtesy of a Guyanese member of the Mechanics.

38. Renauld, *Félix Éboué et Eugénie Éboué-Tell.*

39. See Jean-Laurent Turbet's site: www.jlturbet.net (accessed June 23, 2015).

40. Prince Hall Grand Lodge of Caribbean website, http://mwphglc.zoomshare .com/2.html. (accessed June 23, 2015).

41. For more on the Eastern Star, see this website: http://ritagcar.zoomshare.com (accessed June 23, 2015).

Conclusion. To Each His Own Path

1. Anderson, *Constitutions.*

2. Denslow, *10,000 Famous Freemasons,* vol. III, 230.

Afterword. A Question of Democracy

1. Schnapper, "Racism," 1247–52.

Bibliography of Masonic Speeches and Annals

Prince Hall Speeches

Hall, Prince. "A Charge Delivered to the Brethren of African Lodge on the 25th of June 1792." Delivered at the Hall of Brother William Smith in Charlestown, by the Right Worshipful Master Prince Hall. (Printed at the request of the Lodge and sold at the Bible and Heart, Cornhill, Boston, 1792.)

Hall, Prince. "A Charge Delivered to the African Lodge, June 24, 1797, at Menotomy, Mass." Delivered by the Right Worshipful Prince Hall. Published by the desire of the members of said lodge, 1797 (reprinted, Arthur A. Schomburg, grand secretary).

Annals of the Lodges and Grand Lodges of Prince Hall

Alabama

Proceedings of the Grand Lodge of Alabama, 1866.

Arkansas

Proceedings of the 5th Annual Communication of the Grand Lodge of the State of Arkansas. Pine Bluff: Newman, 1890; Little Rock: Blocher and Mitchell, 1890, 64 pages.

California

Proceedings of the 6th and 7th Annual Communication of the M. W. Sovereign Grand Lodge for the State of California, 1881. Oakland: Tribune Steam Book, 1882.

Georgia

Proceedings of the Grand Lodge of Georgia. Alexandria, Va.: George Washington Masonic National Memorial, 1990.

Idaho

Idaho Grand Lodge Proceedings. Alexandria, Va.: George Washington Masonic National Memorial, 1991.

Kentucky

Address of the Grand Master and Report of a Special Committee to Whom Was Referred the Action of the Grand Lodge of Washington on the Subject of Recognizing Negro Masonry. Louisville: Grand Lodge of Kentucky, 1898.

Louisiana

Louisiana Grand Lodge Proceedings, 1993. Alexandria, Va.: George Washington Masonic National Memorial, February 8, 1993.

Maine

Maine Grand Lodge Proceedings. Alexandria, Va.: George Washington Masonic National Memorial, 1996.

Massachusetts

St. Andrew's Lodge. *An Ancient Tale Told New, Bicentennial Memorial, 1756–1956.* Boston: Lodge Publication, 1958.

Proceedings of the Prince Hall Grand Lodge of the Most Ancient and Honourable Fraternity of Free and Accepted Masons, Boston, Massachusetts, for the Year 1873. Boston: Prince Hall Grand Lodge, 1874.

Proceedings of the 100th Anniversary of the Granting of Warrant 459 to African Lodge at Boston, Sept. 29, 1884. Boston: Franklin Press, 1885.

Missouri

Proceedings of the 11th Annual Communication of the Grand Lodge of the State of Missouri and Its Jurisdiction, Commencing August 21, 1877. St. Louis: C. R. Barns, 1877, 187 pages.

New York

Constitution and Statutes of the Most Worshipful United Grand Lodge of Free and Accepted Masons of the State of New York. New York: Tobitt and Bunce, 1876.

The Craftsman's Club Constitutions and By-Laws. New York: League Press, 1905, 9 pages.

Correspondence between Harry Williamson and H. V. B. Voorhis and Others on Negro Masonry, 1941–1951. Archives of the New York Grand Lodge, Livingston Library.

Negro Masonry Proceedings. New York: 1899, Appendix, 56 pages.

The Recognition of Negro Grand Lodges by the Grand Lodge of Washington, June 15, 1898.

Proceedings of the Most Ancient and Honorable Fraternity of Free and Accepted Masons of the State of New York from December 1877 to June 1879. New York: George O'Hare, 1880.

Proceedings of the Most Worshipful Fraternity of Free and Accepted Masons of the State of New York. New York: George E. O'Hara, 1897–1902.

Roster of the Most Worshipful Grand Lodge of the State of New York, 1913–1914.

Ohio

History, Constitution and By-Laws of Excelsior Lodge n° 11, Prince Hall, Warranted 1865. Prince Hall Temple, Cleveland, Ohio, 1926, 26 pages.

Pennsylvania

Abstract of the Proceedings of the Grand Lodge of the State of Pennsylvania from December 27, 1869 to December 17, 1874. Philadelphia: 1875, 112 pages.

Official Proceedings of the 141st Annual Communication, Most Worshipful Prince Hall Grand Lodge of the State of Pennsylvania, A. L. 595. Archives of the New York Grand Lodge, Livingston Library, 19.

Proceedings of the Grand Lodge of Pennsylvania for the Year 1873. Prince Hall Grand Lodge, 1874.

Annals of the Lodges or
Grand Lodges of the Eastern Star

Arkansas, Grand Chapter, Order of the Eastern Star, Colored, Proceedings of the 5th Annual Communication of the Grand Chapter, State of Arkansas, June 10. 1890. Little Rock: Mitchell and Bettis, 1890.

By-Laws of the Alpha Chapter n° 1. Order of the Eastern Star. New York: League Press, 1903, 9 pages.

Constitution and By-Laws of the Grand Chapter of the Order of the Eastern Star. Terre Haute: C. W. Brown, 1901, 38 pages.

Proceedings of the Annual Sessions of the Grand Chapter, Order of the Eastern Star of the State of Indiana 1890–1892. Terre Haute: C. W. Brown, Moore and Langen; Louisville, Ky.: A. J. Domeck, 1891–1900.

"Report of the Committee on Foreign Correspondence." In *Proceedings of the 5th Annual Communication of the Grand Lodge of the State of Arkansas.* Pine Bluff: Newman, 1877, 40–57.

Bibliography

American Masonic Review 1, no. 3 (Summer 1992): 7.

Anderson, James. *Constitutions.* Abingdon, Va.: Quatuor Coronati Lodge, 1976.

Armstrong, Louis. *Satchmo: My Life in New Orleans.* New York: Prentice Hall, 1954.

Atwell, N. G. D. *Albion Lodge 196 E.R., A History 1790 to 1976.* Barbados: Cot Printery, 1976.

Ayers, Jessie Mae, past grand worthy matron. "Origin and History for the Adoptive Rite among Black Women." *Prince Hall Masonic Digest* (1992). www.jabron.net/amaranth/oeshist.html (accessed June 25, 2015).

Bessel, Paul M. "U.S. Recognition of French Grand Lodges in the 1900s." *Heredom, the Transactions of the Scottish Rite Society* 5 (1996): 7.

———. "Historical Maps." Paul M. Bessel's Homepage. http://bessel.org/masrec/phamapshistorical.htm (accessed May 24, 2015).

———. "Masonic Statistics—Graphs, Maps, Charts." Paul M. Bessel's Homepage. http://bessel.org/masstats.htm (accessed May 24, 2015).

———. "PHA Chart." Paul M. Bessel's Homepage. http://bessel.org/masrec/phachart.htm (accessed May 24, 2015).

Brooks, Charles H. *The Official History and Manual of the Grand United Order of Odd Fellows in America, a Chronological Treatise.* Philadelphia: 1902. Reprint, Freeport, N.Y.: Books for Libraries Press, 1971.

Brown, Harvey Newton. *Freemasonry among Negroes and Whites in America, A Study in Masonic Legitimacy and Regularity.* Nottingham: Mireles Print Company, July 1965.

———. "Letter from El Paso, Texas." *Renaissance traditionnelle,* nos. 21–22 (January–April, 1975): 166.

———. "La prétendue clandestinité de la Maçonnerie noire de Prince Hall aux Etats-Unis." *Renaissance traditionnelle,* no. 7 (July 1971): 284–92.

Brown, M. H. C. "Song of the Heroines of Jericho." New York: The Williamson Fund, reel 16, Schomburg Center, 1920s(?).

Bruce, John Edward. "The Mission and the Opportunity of the Negro Mason." Address delivered before the Craftsmen's Club, New York City, March 6, 1910. New York, Livingston Library.

Buisine, Andrée. *La Franc-Maçonnerie anglo-saxonne et les femmes.* Paris: Guy Tredaniel, 1995.

Campbell, Mary. "Old and New Versions of Opera Reviewed." *Telegraph* (Nashua, N.H.), July 26, 1967. http://news.Google.com/newspapers?nid=2209&dat=19670726&id=C64rAAAAIBAJ&sjid=kf0FAAAAIBAJ&pg=7170,2596513 (accessed May 23, 2015).

Cass, Donn A. *Negro Freemasonry and Segregation.* Harwood Heights, Ill.: Ezra Cook, 1957.

Cauna, Jacques de. "Moreau de Saint-Méry, Médéric Louis Elie (1750–1819)." In *Le Monde maçonnique des Lumières. Dictionnaire prosopographique,* III, by Charles Porset and Cécile Révauger, 2027–29. Paris: Champion, 2013.

———. "Toussaint-Louverture, François-Dominique (1743–1803)." In *Le Monde maçonnique des Lumières. Dictionnaire prosopographique,* III, by Charles Porset and Cécile Révauger, 2675–79. Paris: Champion, 2013.

Cauna, Jacques de, and Cécile Révauger. *La société de plantation, regards croisés. Caraïbe francophone, anglophone et hispanophone.* Paris: Indes Savants, 2013.

Charles, Emile. "200 Years of Freemasonry in Trinidad and Tobago, an Overview." *Masonic Seminar on Masonry in Trinidad and Tobago, Continuing Masonic Education* (1995).

Cherry, Martin. "Dear Sir and Brother. A Prince Hall Mason's Letters to an English Masonic Librarian at the Beginning of the Twentieth Century." *Phylaxis* 39, no. 3 (2012): 12–21.

———. "Grand Lodges and Official History? An Early Twentieth-Century Tale." Speech delivered at the International Conference on the History of Freemasonry symposium, Edinburgh, May 2013.

Clarke, David. "Irish Freemasonry in Barbados." Unpublished article written in 2001, in the private collection of Gilmore Rocherford.

Cole, Maria, and Louie Robinson. *Nat King Cole: An Intimate Biography.* New York: Morrow, 1971.

Collier, James Lincoln. "Ellington, Duke (April 29, 1899–May, 24, 1974)." American National Biography Online. www.anb.org.

Combes, André. "La Franc-Maçonnerie aux Antilles et en Guyane françaises de 1789 à 1848." In *La période révolutionnaire aux Antilles*. Edited by Roger Toumson and Charles Porset. Paris: Centre National de la Recherche Scientifique, 1986.

Cox, Joseph Mason Andrew. *Great Black Men of Freemasonry, 1723–1982*. New York: Blue Diamond Press, 1982.

Crawford, George W. *Prince Hall and His Followers, Being a Monograph on the Legitimacy of Negro Masons*, 1877; reprint, New York: AMS Press, 1971.

————. *The Prince Hall Counselor, A Manual of Guidance Designed to Aid Those Combatting Clandestine Freemasonry*, 1965; reprint, Michigan: Harlo Press, 1979.

Davis, Elizabeth Lindsay. *The Story of the Illinois Federation of Colored Women's Clubs*. Des Moines: Bystander Press, 1925.

Davis, Harry. *A History of Freemasonry among Negroes in America*. United Supreme Council, Northern Jurisdiction, 1946.

de Hoyo, Art. "On the Origins of the Prince Hall Scottish Rite Rituals." *Heredom: The Transactions of the Scottish Rite Society* 5 (1996): 51–67.

De Keghel, Alain. *La Franc-Maçonnerie en Amérique du Nord*. Paris: EDIMAF, 2002.

————. *Le Défi maçonnique américain*. Paris: Dervy, 2015. English translation forthcoming.

Delany, Martin Robison. *The Origins and Objects of Ancient Freemasonry and Its Introduction into the United States and Its Legitimacy among Colored Men. Treatise Delivered before St. Cyprian Lodge n° 13, June 24th, 1853*. Pittsburgh: W. H. Haven, 1853.

Denslow, William R. *Freemasonry and the American Indian*. Missouri Lodge of Research, 1956.

————. *10,000 Famous Freemasons*, 4 vols. Richmond, Va.: Macoy, 1958.

Diamond, Arthur. *European Masonic Congress Says Distinctions between Races in Masonry Is Wrong*. New York: Livingston Library, 1912.

————. *Prince Hall, Social Reformer*. Introductory essay by Coretta Scott King. New York: Chelsea House, 1992.

Documenting Reality. "Mississippi Fred McDowell." www.documentingreality .com/forum/f226/mississippi-fred-mcdowell-94533 (accessed May 23, 2015).

Downes, Aviston D. "Freemasonry in Barbados, 1740–1900. Issues of Ethnicity and Class in a Colonial Polity." *Journal of the Barbados Museum and Historical Society* 53 (2007): 62.

Du Bois, William Edward Burghardt. "The Crisis, November 1910." In *Selected Writings*. New York: Signet, 1970.

———. "The Philadelphia Negro." In *Selected Writings*. New York: Signet, 1970.

———. "Socialism and the American Negro." *Against Racism: Unpublished Essays, Papers, and Addresses, 1887–1961*. Amherst: University of Massachusetts Press, 1988. (The essay was written in May 1960.)

———. "The Souls of Black Folk." In *Selected Writings*. New York: Signet, 1970.

Dufour, Ronald P. "Cole, Nat King (March 17, 1919–February 15, 1965)." American National Biography Online. www.anb.org.

Elliott, William G. "Blake, Eubie." American National Biography Online. www.anb.org.

Findel, Gottfried Joseph. "Treatise on Masonry." In *Proceedings of the Prince Hall Grand Lodge of the Most Ancient and Honourable Fraternity of Free and Accepted Masons, Boston, Massachusetts, for the Year 1873*. Boston: Prince Hall Grand Lodge, 1874, 20–24.

Fohlen, Claude. *Histoire de l'esclavage aux États-Unis*. Paris: Perrin, 1998.

Franklin, John Hope, and Alfred Moss Jr. *From Slavery to Freedom*. New York: McGraw Hill, 1947. 7th ed., 1994.

Frazer, Lionel Mordaunt. *History of Trinidad*. Vol. II. London: Frank Cass and Co, Ltd., 1971.

Gates, Henry Louis Jr. *The Classic Slave Narratives*. New York: Mentor, 1987.

———. *The Signifying Monkey, A Theory of African-American Literary Criticism*. Oxford, England: Oxford University Press, 1988.

Gerlach, Larry R. "Robeson, Paul." American National Biography Online. www.anb.org.

Godfroy, Marion. *Kourou—1763, le dernier rêve de l'Amérique française*. Paris: Vendémiaire, 2011.

Gould, Robert Freke. *History of Freemasonry*. Revised by Dudley Wright. London: Caxton & Co., 1884.

Grant, Donald L. *The Way It Was in the South: The Black Experience in Georgia*. New York: Birch Lane Press, 1993.

Gray, David L. "Listing of Past Grand Matrons and Patrons." Amaranth Grand Chapter, Order of the Eastern Star, Prince Hall Affiliation, State of Ohio. www.phaohio.org/amaranth/histoesfile.html (accessed May 22, 2015).

Grimshaw, William Henry. *Official History of Free Masonry among the Colored People in North America*. New York: Macoy, 1848.

Harkins, Thomas. *Symbolic Freemasonry among the Negroes of America. An Answer to their Claims of Legitimacy and Regularity.* Asheville: privately published, 1963.

Harland-Jacobs, Jessica. *Builders of Empire. Freemasonry and British Imperialism, 1777–1927.* Chapel Hill: University of North Carolina Press, 2007.

Haskins, James, and Kathleen Benson. *Nat King Cole: The Man and His Music.* London: Robson Books, 1986.

Haywood, H. L. *Freemasonry and Roman Catholicism.* Chicago: Masonic History Company, 1960.

Hazareesingh, Sudhir, and Vincent Wright. *Francs-Maçons sous le second empire.* Rennes, France: Presses Universitaires de Rennes, 2001.

Henderson, Kent. *Masonic World Guide. A Guide to the Grand Lodges of the World for the Travelling Freemason.* London: Lewis Masonic, 1984.

Hinks, Peter P. *To Awaken My Afflicted Brethren. David Walker and the Problem of Antebellum Slave Resistance.* State College: Pennsylvania State University Press, 1997.

Hinks, Peter P., and Stephen Kantrowitz, eds. *All Men Free and Brethren: Essays on the History of African American Freemasonry.* Foreword by Leslie A. Lewis. Ithaca: Cornell University Press, 2013.

Hinton, Milt. *Playing the Changes.* Nashville: Vanderbilt University Press, 2008.

Imbert, Raphaël. *Jazz suprême.* Paris: François Bourin, 2013.

———. "Jazz en vies. De l'exemplairité du fait spiritual et maçonnique chez les musiciens du jazz." *L'Homme,* no. 200 (2011): 141–74.

Jacob, Margaret C. *Living the Enlightenment: Freemasonry and Politics in Eighteenth-Century Europe.* Oxford, England: Oxford University Press, 1991.

———. *The Origins of Freemasonry: Facts and Fictions.* Philadelphia: University of Pennsylvania Press, 2005.

———. *The Radical Enlightenment: Pantheists, Freemasons, and Republicans.* London: G. Allen & Unwin, 1985.

Jacobs, Curtis. *Fédon's Rebellion in Grenada, 1795–1796.* Paris: Harmattan, 2009.

Jones, John. "An Argument in Relation to Free Masonry among Colored Men." Chicago, 1866. New York: Masonic Documentation, 2002.

Kaplan, Sidney, and Emma Nogrady Kaplan. *The Black Presence in the Era of the American Revolution.* Amherst: University of Massachusetts Press, 1989.

Kerjan, Daniel, and Alain Le Bihan. *Dictionnaire du Grand Orient de France au XVIIIᵉ siècle.* Rennes, France: Presses Universitaires de Rennes, 2012.

Kernfeld, Barry. "Calloway, Cab (December 25, 1907–November 18, 1994)." American National Biography Online. www.anb.org.

————. "Hampton, Lionel (April 20, 1908–August 31, 2002)." American National Biography Online. www.anb.org.

Labarthe, Elyette Benjamin, and Eric Dubesset, eds. *Emancipations caribéennes.* Paris: Harmattan, 2010.

Latham, J. Fred. "The American Indian in Freemasonry." The American Indian and Freemasonry, Research Lodge no. 2. Des Moines, Iowa, 1974.

Ligou, Daniel. *Dictionnaire de la franc-Maçonnerie.* 6th rev. ed. by Charles Porset and Dominique Morillon. Paris: PUF, 1987.

Liris, Elisabeth. "Lafayette, Joseph-Paul-Yves-Roch-Gilbert du Motier, Marquis de [La Fayette] (1757–1834)." In *Le Monde maçonnique des Lumières. Dictionnaire prosopographique,* by Charles Porset and Cécile Révauger, 166. Paris: Champion, 2013.

Mackey, Albert. *Revised Encyclopedia of Freemasonry.* The Masonic History Company, 1909. Reprint, Richmond, Va.: Macoy, 1946.

Masonic Lodge Information. "USA–Prince Hall–California." www.masonic-lodge .Info/MLI/mli2305.htm (accessed May 23, 2015).

Mollès, Dévrig. "Triangle atlantique et triangle latin: L'Amerique latine et le systemme-monde maçonnique (1717–1921)." Thesis, University of Strasbourg, December 2012.

Muraskin, William. *Middle-Class Blacks in a White Society: Prince Hall Freemasonry.* Berkeley: University of California Press, 1975.

Nye, R. B., and J. E. Morpurgo. *A History of the United States.* Vol. 2. London: Pelican, 1972.

Oak Forest Lodge #1398. "An Organization Is Judged by the Company It Keeps." http://mastermason.com/oakforest1398/fams.htm (accessed May 23, 2015).

Peretti, Burton W. "Basie, Count (August 21, 1904–April 26, 1984)." American National Biography Online. www.anb.org.

Pocock, Michael Roger. *Out of the Shadows of the Past, the Great House of Champs-Elysées, Trinidad and the Families Who Lived There, 1780–1932.* Port of Spain, Trinidad and Tobago: Paria Publishing House, 1993.

Poirier, François. "De la terre promise au cauchemar: les plantations de la Sierra Leone (1787–1810)." In *La Société de plantation, regards croisés. Caraïbe francophone, anglophone et hispanophone.* Edited by Jacques de Cauna and Cécile Révauger. Paris: Indes Savants, 2013.

Porset, Charles. *Hiram Sans-Culotte? Franc-Maçonnerie, lumières et revolution.* Paris: Honoré Champion, 1998.

Porset, Charles, and Cécile Révauger. *Le Monde maçonnique des Lumières. Dictionnaire prosopographique.* Paris: Champion, 2013.

"Prince Hall Masons of the State of New York Honor the Grand Lodge of Liberia. Impressions of Robert T. Browne." *Masonic Quarterly Review* 1, no. 3 (June 1920).

Purvis, Thomas L. *A Dictionary of American History.* Oxford, England: Blackwell, 1995.

Renauld, George. *Félix Éboué et Eugénie Éboué-Tell. Defenseurs des peuples noirs.* Paris: Detrad aVs, 2007.

Révauger, Cécile. *The Abolition of Slavery: The British Debate, 1787–1840.* Paris: PUF, 2008.

———. *Le Fait maçonnique au XVIIIe siècle en Grande-Bretagne et aux États-Unis.* Paris: EDIMAF, 1990.

———. "Les Frères Unis: The United Brothers' Lodge: The French Touch in Trinidad." *Journal of Caribbean History,* vol. 42: 2, 2008, pp. 187–204.

———. "Freemasonry in Barbados, Trinidad and Grenada: British or Homemade?" *Journal for Research into Freemasonry and Fraternalism,* no. 1, Equinox, First Semester, 2010, pp. 79–93.

———. *La querelle des "anciens" et des "modernes." Le premier siècle de la franc-Maçonnerie anglaise.* Paris: EDIMAF, 1999.

———. "Shays, Daniel (1747?–1825)." In *Le Monde maçonnique des Lumières. Dictionnaire prosopographique,* by Charles Porset, and Cécile Révauger. Paris: Champion, 2013.

Révauger, Cécile, and Jacques C. Lemaire. *Les Femmes et la franc-maçonnerie des lumières à nos jours. La Pensée et les Hommes.* Brussels: La Pensée et les Hommes, 2011.

Rich, Paul, and Guillermo de los Reyes. "Recovering a Rite: The Amaranth, Queen of the South, and Eastern Star." *Heredom: The Transaction of the Scottish Rite Research Society* 6 (1997): 219–34.

Roberts, Allen E. *House Reunited: Civil War, Aftermath, Brotherhood.* Highland Springs, Va.: Anchor Communications, 1996.

———. *House Undivided. The Story of Freemasonry and the Civil War.* Richmond, Va.: Macoy, 1960.

———. "Qui sont ces maçons de Prince Hall?" *Points de vue initiatiques. Cahiers de la Grande Loge de France,* no. 107 (1997). Translated by Michaël Segal.

Roundtree, Alton G., and Paul M. Bessel. *Out of the Shadows: The Emergence of Prince Hall Freemasonry.* Camp Springs, Md.: KLR Publishing, 2006.

Sadler, Henry. *Masonic Facts and Figures.* Wellingborough, Northhampshire, England: Aquarian Press, 1985.

Schnapper, Dominique. "Racism." In Canto-Sperber, Monique. *Dictionnaire de philosophie morale.* Paris: PUF, 1996.

Sesay, Chernoh M. Jr. "The Dialectic of Representation: Black Freemasonry, the Black Public, and Black Historiography." *Journal of African and American Studies* (2013). Springer.com (accessed June 25, 2015).

Sherman, John M. "Les hommes de couleur dans la Maçonnerie américaine." *Le Symbolisme* (November–December 1954): 113–28.

———. "The Negro National or Compact Grand Lodge." *Ars Quatuor Coronatorum,* no. 92 (November 1980): 148–49.

———. "Review of Prince Hall, Life and Legacy by Charles H. Wesley." *Ars Quatuor Coronatorum,* no. 90 (November 1978): 308.

Sommers, Susan Mitchell. "Caché, mais bien en vue: l'Ordre de l'Eastern Star dans l'historiographie des societies féminines américaines." In *Les Femmes et la franc-maçonnerie des lumières à nos jours* by Cécile Révauger and Jacques C. Lemaire, 82–83, 365–85. Brussels: La Pensée et les Hommes, 2011.

Tabbert, Mark A. *American Freemasons, Three Centuries of Building Communities.* Lexington, N.Y., and London: National Heritage Museum and New York University Press, 2006.

Tirro, Frank. "Armstrong, Louis (August 4, 1901–July 6, 1971)." American National Biography Online. www.anb.org.

———. *Jazz, A History.* New York: Norton, 1993.

Toumson, Roger, and Charles Porset. *La Période révolutionnaire aux Antilles.* Paris: Centre National de la Recherche Scientifique, 1986.

Tresner, Jim, 33rd degree Grand Cross. *The Craft's Noyse: Composers Who Were Freemasons.* Silver Spring, Md.: The Masonic Service Association, 2000.

Upton, William H. *A Critical Examination of Objections to the Legitimacy of the Masonry Existing among the Negroes of America.* Philadelphia: J.B. Lippincott, 1899.

———. *The Prince Hall's Letter Book.* Margats, UK: H. Keble, 1900.

———. "The True Text of the Book of Constitutions." *Ars Quatuor Coronatorum,* no. 13 (1900): 54–65.

Ursulet, Léo. *La Franc-Maçonnerie aux Antilles françaises aux XVIIIe et XIXe siècles, les cent ans de la loge droit et justice.* Le Lamentin, Martinique: Centre Philosophique et Culturel Droit et Justice, 2009.

Verteuil, Anthony de. *Temples of Trinidad.* Port of Spain, Trinidad and Tobago: Litho Press, 2004.

Voorhis, Harold Van Buren. *The Eastern Star: The Evolution from a Rite to an Order.* Richmond: Macoy, 1938; reprint, 1976.

———. *Negro Masonry in the United States.* New York: Henry Emerson, 1945.

———. *Our Colored Brethren, The Story of the Alpha Lodge of New Jersey.* New York: Henry Emerson, 1971.

Walker, David. *An Appeal to the Colored Citizens of the World.* Cited with commentary in *To Awaken My Afflicted Brethren. David Walker and the Problem of Antebellum Slave Resistance* by Peter Hinks. State College: Pennsylvania State University Press, 1997.

Walkes, Joseph A. *Black Square and Compass.* Richmond, Va.: Macoy, 1994.

———. *A Prince Hall Masonic Quiz Book.* Richmond, Va.: Macoy, 1989.

———. "Our History." The Phylaxis Society. www.thephylaxis.org/phylaxis/history .php (accessed December 6, 2013).

Washington, Booker T. *Up from Slavery.* London: Penguin Classics, 1986.

Whalen, William J. *Christianity and American Freemasonry.* Milwaukee: Bruce Publishing, 1987.

"What Regular Grand Lodges Have Said about Negro Masonry." Anchorage, Alaska: Masonic Research Associates, printed after 1960.

Williams, Loretta J. *Black Freemasonry and Middle-Class Realities.* Columbia: University of Mississippi Press, 1980.

Williamson, Harry A. *Celestial Lodge n° 3, 1826 to 1951.* New York: Schomburg Center, 1908.

———. *Data Concerning the Holy Bible . . . and the Grand Orient de France.* New York: The Williamson Fund, reel 4, Schomburg Center, 1952, 19.

———. *Freemasonry among Men of Color in New York State.* New York: Compiled by the Committee on Masonic Information, Prince Hall Grand Lodge, 1954.

———. *The Genuineness and Historic Legality of Prince Hall Affiliated Masonry Affirmed and Decreed to the Supreme Court of the United States of America.* New York: Harry A. Williamson Fund, Schomburg Center, 1928.

———. Harry A. Williamson Collection. New York: Schomburg Center Papers, 1831–1965, reel 5, 1954, 13.

———. "Les hommes de couleur dans la Maçonnerie américaine." *Le Symbolisme* (November–December 1954): 113–28.

———. *A Masonic Digest for Freemasonry in the Prince Hall Fraternity*, 1951. New York: Williamson Collection, reel 14, Schomburg Center.

———. "Masons Aid in Education." *Chronicle*, March 22, 1947. Article on microfiche. New York: Harry A. Williamson Papers, Schomburg Center.

———. *Negroes and Freemasonry*. New York: Schomburg Center for Research, 1920.

———. *The New England Craftsman of Boston*. October 1917, 424–26. New York: The Williamson Fund, reel 4, Schomburg Center, 1952.

———. *Prince Hall Masonic Digest*. Harry A. Williamson Collection. New York: Schomburg Center.

———. *Prince Hall Masons and the Grand Orient de France*. 1953. www.thephylaxis .org/walkes/france.

———. *The Prince Hall Primer*, Richmond, Va.: Macoy. Rev. ed., 1956.

———. *Questions and Answers Concerning the GODF*. New York: Schomburg Center for Research, 1952.

———. "Recherches sur les loges militaires 'Prince Hall.'" *Le Symbolisme* (November–December 1955): 113–20.

———. *The Story of the Carthaginian Lodge n° 47*. New York: Schomburg Center for Research, 1949.

Woodson, Carter G. "Documents Relating to Negro Masonry." *Journal of Negro History* XXI, no. 4 (October, 1936): 426–29.

———. *Journal of African-American History*. www.jaah.org.

Index

Books of Related Interest

The Secrets of Masonic Washington
A Guidebook to Signs, Symbols, and Ceremonies at
the Origin of America's Capital
by James Wasserman

The Templars and the Assassins
The Militia of Heaven
by James Wasserman

An Illustrated History of the Knights Templar
by James Wasserman

The Lost Treasure of the Knights Templar
Solving the Oak Island Mystery
by Steven Sora

The Lost Colony of the Templars
Verrazano's Secret Mission to America
by Steven Sora

Founding Fathers, Secret Societies
Freemasons, Illuminati, Rosicrucians, and the Decoding of the Great Seal
by Robert Hieronimus, Ph.D., with Laura Cortner

Secret Practices of the Sufi Freemasons
The Islamic Teachings at the Heart of Alchemy
by Baron Rudolf von Sebottendorff
Translated by Stephen E. Flowers, Ph.D.
Introduction by Stephen E. Flowers, Ph.D.

The Suppressed History of America
The Murder of Meriwether Lewis and
the Mysterious Discoveries of the Lewis and Clark Expedition
by Paul Schrag and Xaviant Haze
Foreword by Michael Tsarion

INNER TRADITIONS • BEAR & COMPANY
P.O. Box 388 • Rochester, VT 05767
1-800-246-8648 • www.InnerTraditions.com

Or contact your local bookseller